An Ecological Approach to Perceptual Learning and Development

An Ecological Approach to Perceptual Learning and Development

ELEANOR J. GIBSON AND
ANNE D. PICK

OXFORD
UNIVERSITY PRESS

OXFORD
UNIVERSITY PRESS

Oxford   New York
Auckland   Bangkok   Buenos Aires   Cape Town   Chennai
Dar es Salaam   Delhi   Hong Kong   Istanbul   Karachi   Kolkata
Kuala Lumpur   Madrid   Melbourne   Mexico City   Mumbai   Nairobi
São Paulo   Shanghai   Taipei   Tokyo   Toronto

First published in 2000 by Oxford University Press, Inc.
198 Madison Avenue, New York, New York 10016

www.oup.com

First issued as an Oxford University Press paperback, 2003

Oxford is a registered trademark of Oxford University Press

Library of Congress Cataloging-in-Publication Data
Gibson, Eleanor Jack.
    An ecological approach to perceptual learning and development /
Eleanor J. Gibson, Anne D. Pick.
        p.   cm.
    Includes bibliographical references and index.
    ISBN 0-19-511825-1; 0-19-516549-7 (pbk.)
    1. Perception in infants.   2. Perceptual learning.
3. Infant psychology.   I. Pick, Anne D.   II. Title.
BF720.P47G53   2000
155.4'137—dc21   99-28267

9 8 7 6 5 4 3 2 1

Printed in the United States of America
on acid-free paper

Preface

This book aims to present a point of view consistent with biological evolutionary principles and at the same time with meaningful, humanistic ones. More specifically, it aims to make sense of a wealth of evidence now available on the way perception develops in early life; to present a way of thinking about how learning occurs in the process of perceiving; to show how perceptual development underlies knowledge about the world; and to relate these ideas to the ecological approach to perception as conceived by James J. Gibson and carried on by many able psychologists.

The human species enjoys by all counts the longest period of development of any we know of, including the other primates. What is going on during that long period? What are infants, for many months incapable of locomotion or even of handling objects, learning during this period? Plenty, as we will show. Many people have been amazed and impressed by the intellectual achievements of Helen Keller, both blind and deaf. How could she have a concept of "water," for example, when her tutor first spelled it in her hand? Her achievements are amazing, indeed, but we understand them better when we remember that she suffered the illness that robbed her of sight and hearing at 19 months. Now we know that those first 19 months provide developing infants with a wealth of experience that they do indeed use to advantage. They are acquiring an education by their own efforts, from the start.

Anyone who takes the time to think about it will recognize that perceptual learning has to play a large and important role in development. It is, we suggest, the only way of learning about the world, about oneself, and about the relation between these two interdependent entities before a child can benefit from verbal instruction. Prelinguistic infants may be able to think, but they must have matter for thought. They are indeed interested in language, and they listen to speech attentively. Even here, perceptual learning plays a principal role. We learn the basics about what people are trying to communicate to us, where things are, what things are useful for, how to control objects and people, and many other things long before we can understand a compound sentence. Prelinguistic infants of 10 to 12 months already know a great deal about the world around them. They have accomplished this for the most part on their own, spontaneously motivated and independent of applied "reinforcers." A good theory of perceptual learning helps us understand how this accomplishment is possible.

Many factors interact in this early acquisition of major knowledge, including ones within the young organism. They make their contributions interactively, at different points in development. The view we take in this book stresses the contributions of physical growth, motor development, and other organismic factors. Information flows from them as well as from the world. But at the very core lies the interaction of animal and environment. The notion of animal-environment reciprocity and its importance for perceptual learning is the underlying theme of this book.

Many friends and colleagues have helped us immeasurably by contributing to our thinking about perceptual learning and development, critically reading all or parts of the manuscript, and generously giving advice and encouragement. We are especially grateful to Karen Adolph, Lorraine Bahrick, Rachel Clifton, Marion Eppler, Ross Flom, Douglas Gentile, Marjorie Grene, Marian Heinrichs, Carolyn Palmer, Herbert L. Pick, Jr., Ad Smitsman, Nelson Soken, and Arlene Walker-Andrews.

This book would never have happened at all, of course, were it not for the ideas of James J. Gibson, who inspired us to contemplate how his ecological approach would apply to perceptual development. It turns out to be a wonderful fit, we think, and we wish he could have seen how it works.

June 1999   E.J.G.
                                                                                                                             A.D.P.

Contents

An Ecological Approach to Perceptual Learning and Development

1

✦ ✧ ✦ ✧ ✦

Historical Perspectives
and Present-Day Confrontations

A book on perception should begin with what perception is about. The answer is at once easy and hard. It is easy because perceiving is something we all engage in, hardly stopping even in sleep. Perceiving is our means of keeping in touch with the world, of obtaining information about the world and where we are in it. The process of obtaining this information is so natural that it can be hard to explain that there are problems in understanding it. There are, and they have persisted over centuries. Are you and the world separate entities? If so, how is it that you can know about what goes on outside you? This question of how we come by knowledge of the world is as old as humanity. We have learned a good deal about the activity of perceiving. It is an ongoing activity, a search for information specifying the events and layout around us. It is a continuous process, and it provides us with fundamental knowledge that we take for granted.

Persistent Issues in the Study of Perceptual Development

Psychological approaches to understanding how we acquire knowledge of our world and ourselves by perceiving have roots in early philosophical positions on fundamental issues about human knowledge. These epistemological positions persist as assumptions underlying contemporary views of perceiving. Three such issues are: the origins of knowledge, dualism or the mind-body problem, and the nature of development. We begin with these and trace their influence on present-day contemporary approaches to the study of perceptual development.

3

Perhaps the oldest issue is the question of where knowledge originates. Does it come from the world? Of course, we have knowledge of ourselves, too. Could it be that ideas about the world and ourselves are somehow implanted in our minds, along with a faculty of reason that allows us to construct logically a kind of representation of the world and ourselves in it? Two opposed views, rationalism—nativism on the one hand and empiricism on the other, have flourished for centuries. Rationalism is a view usually associated with Immanuel Kant, a German philosopher, who thought that ideas about major concepts such as space, time, and causality were innate, implanted in our minds a priori, without learning, and that we used these ideas to construct our views of the world. Perceiving took its meaning from concepts; according to Kant, "percepts without concepts are blind." Descartes was another well-known rationalist, scientist as well as philosopher, who held that we were endowed with a soul and a mind that could direct our behavior and inform our views about the world and ourselves.

The British empiricists, notably John Locke and David Hume, took firm issue with the rationalist doctrines of innate ideas. The empiricists had a strong influence on early views of perception that held that mental content was derived from experience. These extreme empiricists thought infants were born without knowledge of any kind and had to learn for themselves as the world impinged on their senses. Empiricists have always made learning a central part of their theories, generally emphasizing association as the process that cements ideas together. Learning as an associative process of accretion dominated American perceptual theory for decades.

René Descartes was largely responsible for a second major epistemological position eventually carried into psychology. Animals respond to stimuli, and their responses can be observed and analyzed, he thought, in purely mechanistic terms. Humans, however, have minds that contain mental representations, images, thoughts, and concepts, inner structures that are not observable to the outsider and that direct and intervene in behavior. This mind-body dualism, central to major arguments of other philosophers, was inherited by early psychologists in the form of positions as to what the content of psychology should be.

Titchener, for example, thought that psychology should deal only with mental content. He defined psychology as "the source of existential experience regarded as dependent on the nervous system" (1929, p. 142). Psychology was to study "sensations," whereas biology was to study "behavior." Many psychologists define psychology in terms of mental representations and seek to objectify their positions by identifying mind with the nervous system. Hebb (1974), speaking for a later generation, said that "psychology is about the mind" (p. 74) but went on to say that "mind is the capacity for thought, and thought is the integrative activity of the brain" (p. 75). This is a popular idea today among cognitive psychologists, who stress mental representations and hope to link them to neural architecture.

A third issue continuing to influence contemporary research concerns development—the nature of the changes that occur and the causes for them. Are there qualitative changes in the course of development? Or is the course of development one of linear, incremental quantitative change? Positions on this issue motivate inquiry about so-called discontinuities as opposed to continuities in development. This issue is less firmly rooted in early philosophical positions than the other two; however, it is an issue that has pervaded the study of development for many decades.

Piaget's is the best-known theory representing the view that development is characterized by discontinuities. It was his view that development occurs in stages, in a regular progression of preordained steps. There is orderly, regular development within a stage, but eventually there is a reorganization of cognitive structures leading to a qualitatively different new phase of development. The alternative view that development is incremental and continuous is represented by psychologists who performed early experiments on learning with infants and children (e.g., Razran, 1933; Jones & Yoshioka, 1938) and who emphasized similarity in learning skills and outcomes for children and adults (Munn, 1946).

Theorists of perception have taken various positions on these persisting issues. Approaches to perceptual development can be distinguished by their apparent empiricist or rationalist assumptions about the origins of knowledge. They can also be distinguished by their emphasis on the role of responses and action in perceptual development or on the role of mental processes and internal representations of knowledge—vestiges of dualism and its influence on what is the proper domain for psychology. This distinction is related to another opposition, a structural approach concerned with content, in contrast to a functional approach concerned with change and adaptation to environmental conditions. There are also two views of perceptual development as continuous or stagelike, varying in their relative emphases on the importance of learning in perceptual development. We present an overview of major approaches to perceptual development, alluding to important distinctions between those approaches and the ecological approach, before proceeding, in the next chapter, to present the ecological approach.

Early Theories of Perceptual Development

Although psychologists did not talk explicitly about perceptual learning as important in development until 40 or so years ago, implicit theories of perceptual learning have existed far longer than that, for example in the writings of the British philosophers Berkeley and the two Mills, James and his son, John Stuart. They taught that laws of association between sensations and other mental elements such as images accounted for perceptual development. Berkeley was responsible for the notion that because the retina is flat, excitations from it must result in depthless sensations, thus making associations with other sensations, such as those involved in touching things, responsible for perceived depth. A quite different principle was introduced by Helmholtz (1821–1894), the great physicist and physiologist. He believed that perception develops by inference from previous experience. He thought that the inferences were unconscious, but they nevertheless were like conclusions drawn from premises and already existing knowledge.

The two principles, association on the one hand and inference on the other, underlay nearly all the early theoretical accounts of perceptual development. An important variation was introduced by William James, the great American psychologist (James, 1890), who brought a functional view to psychology. He relied on association as an explanatory principle, but he introduced a new conception of what was to be explained. Specifically, explanations of perception must take account not only of the mental content, but also of its *function* as a process. James supposed that the function of perception was discrimination, and that discrimination was improved by practice. His examples included wine tasting, skilled performances such as tightrope walking, and refined sensitivity of all kinds. Consistent with his empiricist stance, he believed all perception to be the outcome of experience. He wrote that "infants must go through a long education of the eye and the ear before they can perceive. *Every perception is an acquired perception*" (1890, Vol. 2, p. 78).

Even William James did not succeed in bringing learning into a prominent emphasis in developmental psychology. The best-known developmental psychologist in America in the first half of this century was Arnold Gesell, a physician and an ardent believer in maturation. He was chiefly interested in motor development and saw it as differentiating through orderly stages from the head down and the center outward, all as a result of maturational determinants, especially neural ones. Work with his colleagues (A.I. Gesell, Ilg, & Bullis, 1949) emphasized maturational trends in vision as well. In Europe the influential developmental psychologist Piaget was writing about stages in cognitive development, but his work did not have an impact on American psychology until the 1950s. Meanwhile, learning had become the popular topic in American psychology.

Learning theory, originating as a theory of associations of elementary mental content, began in experimental psychology as the study of memory. But as behaviorism took over in American psychology, there was a shift to another version of association: the association of stimulus and response, elaborated as the theory of conditioning. Discrimination learning was interpretable in this context, and there resulted a vast body of literature on discrimination learning. Perhaps it was inevitable that the concept of perceptual learning should be introduced at the height of this trend, in an attempt to identify the problem of perceptual learning, give it a name, and establish it theoretically.

Theories of Perceptual Learning

In 1955 J.J. Gibson and E.J. Gibson published a paper titled "Perceptual Learning: Differentiation or Enrichment," in which they defined perceptual learning and contrasted two ways of viewing it. Perceptual learning was defined as a change in what was perceived. One view was that initial sensory reception was *enriched* and supplemented by the addition of something, be it associated ideas, learned responses, or some form of inference. The other view was that perception begins as unrefined, vague impressions and is progressively *differentiated* into more specific percepts, becoming more finely tuned to variations in what is presented in stimulation. The first view had many precedents, as we have seen, but the second view was relatively novel in psychology, although the notion of differentiation as a process of development was a familiar one in biology.

We have constructed a diagram of theories of perceptual learning in order to highlight relations, and to identify important contrasts (see fig. 1.1). It includes the theories of the 1950s, and then the theories influencing developmental psychology today. The diagram is a sort of family tree, as it depicts the lines of descent of major conceptual issues.

Enrichment Theories

Consider first the enrichment theories. These theories have in common the notion that originally barren reception of stimuli is supplemented by some form

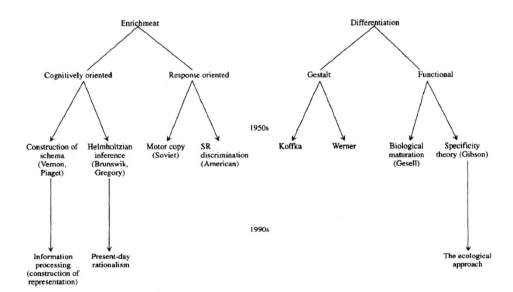

FIGURE 1.1. Chart showing historical lines of descent of theories of perception.

of accrual or interpretation. What was thought to be added varied, but the eventual perception was inevitably in decreased correspondence with stimulation.

In the 1950s two types of enrichment theory flourished, one response oriented and the other cognitively oriented. One version of response-oriented theory was derived from behaviorism in American psychology. This theory defined perceptual learning as "changes in stimulus-response relationships under controlled conditions of practice," and as a "part of the broader problem of associative learning" (Postman, 1955). Stimulus-response theories could be translated into discrimination learning in paradigms for research, and a theory evolved that mediating learned responses removed the ambiguity from originally confusing stimuli, a process known as "acquired distinctiveness of cues" (N.E. Miller & Dollard, 1941). Two at first confusable stimuli could be made distinct by conditioning different responses to them. The theory led to a number of experiments (see E.J. Gibson, 1969, pp. 63 ff.).

A different version of response-oriented theory was promoted by Russian psychologists, referred to by them as "reflection theory." External objects, according to this theory, come to be perceived as having corresponding properties in perception by formation of a motor copy that reproduces features of the object so as to yield a likeness. Orienting movements of the hands and the eyes are thought to be of special importance (Zaporozhets, 1960) in forming the perception. This theory gave rise to research too, often with children, and it might involve tracing objects with the hand and recording eye movements (see E.J. Gibson, 1969, pp. 54 ff.).

Even before the influence of behaviorism diminished in America, another kind of enrichment theory was evolving in Europe and England, again with several versions but all of them cognitive rather than response oriented. Perception was thought of as being a way of knowing, not merely a discriminating response or a construction by responses. One such theory was a cognitive construction theory. Representations of objects were thought to be constructed in the "mind's eye," so to speak, resulting in a "schema." The term "schema" played a part in the memory theorizing of Bartlett, a well-known British psychologist, and it was carried into perception theory by his student M.D. Vernon. As she explained its significance,

> Thus we may postulate that every act of perception consists of the extremely exact registration, in the receptor areas of the cortex, of even the minutest qualities and variations in the sensory patterns conveyed to them: followed by a combination and integration of certain of these qualities resulting in a new construction—a percept which is not isolated but exists as a part of a systematic categorization of experience in concepts and schemata. (Vernon, 1954, pp. 14 ff.)

Constructing the schema and fitting new percepts into schemata was the essence of perceptual learning for Vernon. Perception involved a kind of classification into schemata, she thought. Identifying and assigning to a category depended on constructing the categories, somehow, through experience.

Another version of a schema theory is more familiar to American developmental psychologists. Piaget began publishing detailed developmental observations of his own children in the 1930s. His first English translations became available in the 1950s, when he began to exert a powerful influence on the cognitive psychology just beginning to replace behaviorism.

As we noted earlier, Piaget thought that cognitive development occurred in stages. The first stage, during the first two years of life, he called the sensorimotor stage. Schemata were constructed at first as a result of reflex action but eventually as exploratory activity that represented the world and formed the early cognitive content of the mind. The two processes responsible for this construction were assimilation and adaptation to the surrounding environment of the child. Piaget did not call this a perceptual learning theory, because he thought of perception as a "figurative" process, static, momentary, and never reaching true cognitive status. He belongs with the enrichment theorists, nevertheless, because for him perception was indeed bare, impoverished, and momentary; it needed to be supplemented with schemata, which supplied the important cognitive content. It is never entirely clear in Piaget's writing how perception relates to a schema, but it "nourished" the schema in some way and was assimilated into it. Piaget's was the only truly developmental theory of those we consider.

The key process in cognitively oriented theories of perceptual learning was not necessarily construction of a schema or representation. Inference from experience or other premises was thought by some theorists to be the basis for meaningful perception, carrying on the legacy of Helmholtz's notion of unconscious inference from sensory data. Egon Brunswik, an Austrian psychologist who fled to the United States at the time of World War II, was an avid exponent of perceptual learning who wrote very explicitly about it (see E.J. Gibson, 1969; Postman & Tolman, 1959). For him, the important question about perception was how a stimulus exciting a receptor surface (a "proximal" stimulus) becomes a cue to an object (a "distal" stimulus) that corresponds to the perception. He thought that the perceiver must weigh the evidence from knowledge of previous occurrences and make the most probable inference about the true identity and properties of the object. He called his theory a "probabilistic cue theory" to explain how a stimulus, itself proximal to the receptor surface, became an index to the distal thing.

The necessity of making inferences from impoverished sensory data has been emphasized by others, including R. Gregory, who called his theory an "active" one to underline the role of inference in supplementing sensory data:

Active theories, taking a very different view, suppose that perceptions are constructed, by complex brain processes, from fleeting fragmentary scraps of data signaled by the senses and drawn from the brain's memory banks—themselves constructed from snippets from the past. On this view, normal everyday perceptions are not selections of reality but are rather imaginative constructions— fictions based (as indeed is science fiction also) more on the stored past than on the present. (Gregory, 1991)

Gregory's view of perception as beginning with poor, inadequate hints of what exists around us is thus similar to other enrichment theories, which had to assume some supplementing process to account for our perception by learning from past experience.

Differentiation Theories

Must we assume that perception can only develop by adding something to a sensory core? In organic growth, development progresses toward greater specificity. A fertilized egg develops by division, gradually becoming an organism with organs or parts fulfilling specific functions to adapt an animal for the requirements of living. A psychological analogy with organic growth and individuating functions is obviously more related to biology and to Darwinian perspectives on development than to physics and chemistry, which inspired early psychologists in the empirical tradition to search for mental elements.

The early differentiation theories of perceptual learning and development were sketchy, perhaps because biology was a latecomer in science. There were the Gestalt psychologists, who eschewed analysis into elements and denied association as a process. Their contribution to developmental theory was small, however. Koffka's *Growth of the Mind* (1931) did introduce differentiation, as did Werner's developmental psychology (Werner, 1961), a kind of distant cousin of Gestalt psychology. In the biological tradition and more in the functional tradition brought to U.S. psychology by William James was Gesell's maturational stage theory of development, which emphasized differentiation but was not concerned with perception.

So what had a differentiation theory to offer in 1955? The theory proposed by J.J. Gibson and E.J. Gibson (1955) was called a *specificity* theory and began with an assumption radically different from all enrichment theories. Rather than assuming that the information available from the environment was punctate, bare, and fleeting, they suggested that information available from the environment was rich, and that perceptual learning involves detecting new information or "responding to variables of physical stimulation not previously responded to" (p. 34). The process of learning was one of discrimination rather than of association or making inferences. Perception was thought to change toward closer correspondence with the environment. This kind of perceptual change happens as learning in an adult, as perception becomes skilled and fine-tuned for certain occupations, such as tea tasting or differentiating qualities of snow or performances of ballet dancers. Most important, it has implications for development, as children in the normal course of growing up distinguish among more and more features of the world that they encounter. This theory was in the functional tradition, and the nature of developmental change was assumed to be not the building up of children's mental structures, but children obtaining information about the world and themselves. A contemporary version of this theory will be presented in the next chapter, and will serve as a framework for the later chapters.

Present-Day Theories of Perceptual Development

We turn now to three contemporary approaches to understanding perceptual development: information processing, present-day rationalism, and the ecological approach. There are fundamental differences in the underlying assumptions of these views.

The most important difference among present-day theorists is their assumptions about the nature of the *information* that is the basis for perception. On the one hand, there is the assumption common to both the information-processing and rationalist approaches, with their roots in enrichment theories and in earlier empiricist and nativist views, that the information available to sensory systems is impoverished, ambiguous, and otherwise insufficient to support perception. Consequently, these theories assume construction of representations or inferences to supplement the information.

On the other hand, the assumption of the ecological approach, rooted in functionalism, holds that information is normally ample and structured, and that it fully specifies the layout, surfaces, objects, and events of the world. Consequently, this theory emphasizes activities of exploration and processes of detection, selection, and abstraction for obtaining information about the world and about oneself.

Thus there is a major theoretical distinction between a *construction* view of the way perception develops and the *differentiation* view. Construction views, like their predecessors, assume that perception must be built up starting with input from the receptors to create a *representation* of the world. These present-day representational views have been much influenced by computer analogies. Input, sometimes likened to a representation on a computer screen in the case of visual perception, must be processed and various computational strategies and transformations brought into play to achieve a final representation of the world. David Marr, a representational theorist who proposed detailed stages of computation for the construction of a visual perception, is an influential example (Marr, 1982).

A contemporary version of this view that focuses on development and how young human infants learn is presented by C. Rovee-Collier. She retains the conditioning paradigms in earlier theories, but with a shift in the notion of what is conditioned. She eschews the earlier stimulus-response (S-R) terminology, arguing that classical conditioning is "a process by which organisms acquire predictive information about the structure of their environments" (1986, p. 143), a way for a species to learn the "essential relations that characterize their niche." She notes a general change in conditioning theories: "Current perspectives of classical conditioning focus on the nature of what is learned, its functional significance, how it is represented and under what conditions it is expressed" (1986, p. 140). Rovee-Collier's approach, stressing that infants learn the structure of their environment, is a construction approach insofar as representations of the world are hypothesized and much of the research is focused on memory of the representation acquired, rather than on perception.

There is no line of descent in our diagram from the response-oriented S-R theories of the 1950s to today, because even those developmental researchers who use conditioning paradigms tend to use cognitive terminology and emphasize learning of predictive relations between environmental events rather than S-R connections. Association as a mechanism is kept by some, however, along with the conditioning paradigm (Hall, 1991).

Under cognitively oriented theories in the 1990s, we locate present-day rationalism. The term "rationalist" here refers to an emphasis on inference, and also to what the premises for inference are thought to be. Unlike earlier Helmholtzian theorists, it is not primarily experience that is thought to provide the major premises. Instead, the premises are thought to be primarily innate. Such a view gained adherents in the domain of language acquisition, led by Noam Chomsky (1965). Chomsky thought that language is special to humans and that the basis for it is laid down innately in the form of abstract ideas providing rules for grammar. His views have been extended by psychologists (Gleitman, Gleitman, Landau, & Wanner, 1988).

The strong nativist view, with an emphasis on reason and inference, has been applied recently to the study of cognitive development, including perception, in infants. An example of a rationalist theory that is concerned with perception and its development is that of Spelke, who has performed many experiments on object perception by young infants. Spelke's research has led her to conclude that objects are perceived by young infants as having cohesion, boundedness, rigidity, and no possibility of action at distance (two surfaces move together only if they are in contact) (E.S. Spelke, 1990). She treats these properties as principles that guide infants' inferences about objects. These principles are the basis for infants' construction of representations of objects, and Spelke presumes them to be innate and unchanging over the course of development. Object perception, she says, reflects basic constraints on motions of physical bodies, and ability to perceive objects is thus closely related to ability to *reason* about objects and their behavior.

A further distinction between construction theories and the ecological approach is that neither information-processing nor rationalist approaches link perception with action. Except for Piaget, construction theories do not hypothesize a role for action in perceptual development. The ecological approach, on the other hand, emphasizes the fundamental reciprocity of perception and action.

At the present time, another approach, referred to as a dynamic-systems approach, is gaining influence, and this approach also stresses the role of action in development (Thelen & Smith, 1994). Though not concerned with perceptual development, this approach has important premises in common with the ecological approach, namely, that to understand development, the focus must be on the animal-environment fit, and that neither representations nor innate or preordained plans direct development. Instead, new abilities emerge because multiple dynamic forces of growth and the organism's own activity drive developmental change. We will consider research from this perspective in a later chapter on locomotion. First, however, we will present the ecological approach to perceptual development—a task to which we now turn.

2

✦ ✧ ✦ ✧ ✦

An Ecological Approach
to Perceptual Development

The ecological approach to visual perception (J.J. Gibson, 1966, 1979) provides the framework for the view of perceptual development we present here. It is a theory about perceiving by active creatures who look and listen and move around. It is a theory about everyday perceiving in the world, and it differs greatly from theories that begin with a motionless creature haplessly bombarded by stimuli. Perceiving creatures are part of a world from which they seek information and in which they use it. Perceiving begins at least as soon as an animal is born and well it should, for its function is to keep an animal in touch with the environment around it.

The Reciprocity of Perceiver and Environment

The ecological approach takes as its unit of study the animal in its environment, considered as an interactive system. The relations within this system are reciprocal, with the reciprocity including a species evolving in an environment to which it becomes adapted, and an individual acting in its own niche, developing and learning.

How does this reciprocity work for perceiving? The environment provides opportunities and resources for action, and information for what is to be perceived so as to guide action. Action has consequences that provide more information for the perceiver. The animal and the environment are dynamic players in the systemic whole. The dynamic system is a cycle that can begin with events in the world, such as a looming object like a predator or a truck, or with action instigated by the animal itself, such as driving the truck, since animals are animate and can act spontaneously. This cycle is truly one of mutuality. Animal and environment (including other animals) make a complementary whole. What the environment offers can be physical, such as a comfortable surface that provides babies with needed support, or pins pricking them that arouse cries of distress; or social, such as caretakers smiling and cuddling them or responding to their cries by feeding them or rearranging their clothing. Older children can change their immediate environments by seeking a more comfortable surface, discarding clothing, or seeking out caretakers.

To understand perceiving within this system requires accounts at three levels. First, we need to describe the *environment* in particular, what there is to be perceived. This description must be on a scale appropriate to the animal and its niche, in neither micromillimeters nor light-years. Such a description includes the *sources* of information for the layout, the objects in it, and the events that take place in it. Second, we need to describe the *information* for perceiving. The information consists of the energy changes in a physical medium corresponding to their sources—the layout, objects, and events of the environment. Finally, we must describe the process of perceiving, how the animal *obtains* the information about the environment and what it actually does perceive.

The ecological approach to perception, as envisaged by J.J. Gibson (1979), includes three major ideas that distinguish it from other theories of perception. One is the concept of *affordance,* the user-specific relation between an object or event and an animal of a given kind. A second is the concept of *information,* how events in the world are specified for perceivers in ambient arrays of energy. Third is the process of *information pickup,* how the information is obtained by an active perceiver and what is actually perceived. These concepts and their implications form the core of the theory.

Three Concepts

Affordance

We begin with affordance because the central tenet of the ecological approach is the complementarity of the animal and the environment. An "affordance" refers to the fit between an animal's capabilities and the environmental supports and opportunities (both good and bad) that make possible a given activity. For example, a chair affords sitting for creatures possessing a flexible torso and hip joints, and legs with knees that bend at the height of the chair's seat. A path affords traversal to a destination, and it may contain obstacles that afford collision or turning aside to avoid. Affordances are properties of the environment as they are related to animals' capabilities for using them. They include not only objects but layout properties such as surfaces, corners, and holes. Affordances are also offered by events, including social events such as a looming, loving, or angry face.

To perceive an affordance is to detect an environmental property that provides opportunity for action and that is specified in an ambient array of energy available to the perceiver. Since an affordance is an objective property of the environment, it exists whether or not it is perceived or realized. Affordances vary with species and with development. Water provides a surface of support for a bug but not for a human. What affords sitting for an adult human differs in size and scale from what affords sitting for a child. Affordances vary in availability with habitats, since potential tools and resources may be present in some climates and cultures but not in others. Furthermore, affordances ordinarily must be discovered through perceptual learning. Knowledge of affordances and the probability of using them varies, even among humans. Chopsticks afford carrying food to the mouth, and igloos afford shelter for all adult members of the human race, but the number of people who use them is limited by climate and social custom.

Fundamentally, the realization of an affordance requires that animal and environment be adapted for one another. Bipedal locomotion in humans is possible when they have the necessary anatomy, postural control, and strength for balancing on two legs and lifting their body weight with them, *and* when the terrain is tolerably flat, solid, rigid, extended, and relatively uncluttered.

There is a second reciprocal relation implied by the affordance concept: a perception-action reciprocity. Perception guides action in accord with the environmental supports or impediments presented, and action in turn yields information for further guidance, resulting in a continuous perception-action cycle. Realization of an affordance, as this reciprocity implies, means that an animal must take into account the environmental resources presented in relation to the capabilities and dimensions of its own body. Children begin learning to do this very early and continue to do so as their powers and dimensions increase and change.

We find awareness of body-scaling of resources even reflected in children's literature. Remember the tale, "The Three Bears"? Father Bear, Mother Bear, and Little Bear go for a walk while their porridge cools. They return to find their home raided, remarkably individualistically. All the opportunities have been explored, but only Little Bear's small portion of porridge has been eaten, the little chair sat in, and the junior-size bed slept in. The body-scaling metaphor is, indeed, the major point of the story, and little children always enjoy it. Even when they are not yet perfectly in tune with their own proportions, they realize that Goldilocks had more to learn; she didn't know how big she was and she broke the chair!

Affordances evolve in a niche unique to a species, and in this sense are anticipated for its individual members. But as we pointed out, this potential does not mean that affordances are automatically perceived and acted upon. Humans, at least, must *learn* to use affordances. We have emphasized that affordances reflect a fit between an environmental property and a possibility for action. But such a fit does not imply that the learning of affordances is necessarily simple or automatic. Some affordances may be easily learned; others may require much exploration, practice, and time. Darwin understood this, as his observation on the hand suggests:

> Although the intellectual powers and social habits of man are of paramount importance to him, we must not underrate the importance of his bodily structure. . . . Even to hammer with precision is no easy matter, as everyone who has tried to learn carpentry will admit. To throw a stone with as true an aim as can a Fuegian in defending himself, or in killing birds, requires the most consummate perfection in the correlated action of the muscles of the hand, arm, and shoulder, not to mention a fine sense of touch. . . . To chip a flint into the rudest tool, or to form a barbed spear or hook from a bone, demands the use of a perfect hand. (Darwin, 1974, p. 135ff.)

Even a universal affordance for humans, such as the graspability of an object of a given size and location, shows developmental changes that involve learning. Arms grow longer; posture and balance change, and so do ways of controlling the grasp. Children accommodate to such changes during growth, and their skills develop accordingly. Further development of expertise may involve learning to realize affordances unavailable to nonexperts. A three-inch-wide beam affords performing backflips for a gymnast, but the affordance is not realizable by others; rock climbers learn to use certain terrains for support that do not appear to others to provide a surface of support.

To study the development of perception of affordances requires both describing the objective basis for an affordance in the perceiver-environment relation, and describing the information that specifies the affordance and makes possible its perception.

Information

Information is the second essential concept in the ecological approach to perception. The way in which it will be used is similar to the commonsense meaning of information *about* something, but the term "information" is also used by others in different ways, so we review its history in psychology. The term was adopted in the 1940s by scientists in the Bell Laboratories for measurement of the amount of information that a channel could carry (Shannon and Weaver, 1949). They invented a system of measuring information in "bits," an either-or alternative especially suited to evaluation of communication systems. The notion was thought to be useful to psychologists, who found it a way of dealing mathematically with variability (G.A. Miller, 1956), uncertainty, or number of alternatives (Garner, 1962). It was applied extensively to attention (Broadbent, 1958), where the notion of a "channel" became popular. The practice of measuring information in this way continues, but in psychology the quantitative emphasis has been lost. The term, for many psychologists, has come to mean "input" that is "processed" in various ways after entering a cognitive system; hence the term "information processing."

The various uses of "information" were commented on by J.J. Gibson: "These meanings of 'information' contrast with the term 'stimulus information' that I wish to use, that is, specifying of an environmental source by a stimulus, i.e., the conveying of information about the world by ambient light, sound, and odor, and the information obtainable by mechanical means" (1962).

We use information in his sense, as the structured distribution of energy in an ambient array that specifies events or aspects of events in the environment (see J.J. Gibson, 1966, ch. 10, and 1979, pt. 2). The *sources* of the information are the events, objects, and layout of surfaces in the world. The correspondence of information with these aspects of the environment is one not of similarity, but rather of specificity. The optical disturbances created by an approaching car, for example, do not resemble the car; rather they uniquely specify it and its path of locomotion in relation to oneself. The specification relation is critical because if information is fully specific to its sources in the world, then perception of the layout and objects and events in it is possible without hypothesizing processes of supplementation such as intermediary concepts and representations. The possibility of perceiving a property of the environment directly, without supplementation, exists when there is sufficient information to specify it *and* a perceiver who is attuned to that information—again emphasizing the perceiver-environment fit.

Information is not punctate, instantaneous, or fleeting. It is spread over space and over time. Describing the information for an ongoing event is not a matter of identifying dimensional quantities of physical energy. J.J. Gibson called the description of visual stimulus information "ecological optics" to distinguish it from the optics of physics. It is a description of the distribution of light at a level appropriate for perceptual systems. Information is contained in arrays, for example, the ambient array of light surrounding us. It is structured by the surfaces, boundaries, objects, and layout of the environment. The order in the array is not lost. But this structured array is not static. It changes or flows as one moves one's head around, stands up, sits down, or walks about (see fig. 2.1). These changes are essential for extracting information about the relatively permanent aspects of the environment, since they are the result of continuously shifting points of view. Information that specifies the persisting layout is only made available by one's movement in the layout. Gibson referred to it as "invariant over transformation."

Identifying and describing the information that specifies constant and changing features of the world, over events as well as things, has been a major part of the research program of the ecological approach to perception (J.J. Gibson, 1979). One example is research on optical information that specifies "time to contact" in such events as an object looming or an observer approaching an obstacle or surface that must be contacted or not contacted in some way (e.g., a diving bird approaching water, a person avoiding a collision or about to jump

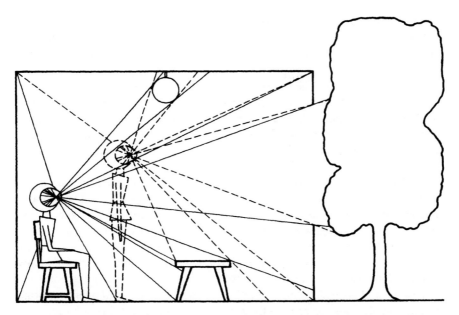

FIGURE 2.1. A structured array with an observer sitting and rising. The thin solid lines indicate the information in the ambient optic array for the seated observer, and the thin dashed lines the altered optic array after standing up and moving forward. From *The Ecological Approach to Visual Perception* (p. 72), by J.J. Gibson, 1979, Boston, MA: Houghton-Mifflin. Copyright © 1979 by Houghton-Mifflin Company. Reprinted with permission.

over a barrier). Lee (1980) showed that the ratio of the size of the projected image of an object to its rate of expansion for objects approaching at a constant velocity at any moment is a constant that specifies time-to-contact. He described this information as a mathematical constant (Tau). The information has wide generality, and animals (including humans) make use of it.

The transformations of the optical array during locomotion constitute information for objects and the layout. Such transformations are created both by movements of observers and by motions of objects. The perspective changes in optical structure revealed by one's own movement specify one's path of locomotion. Furthermore, as a person moves about, information is made available specifying persisting features of the environment such as sizes of things, and the solidity and shape of objects. When a person or object passes in front of us, our view of another object may be temporarily occluded, but as it emerges again, the accretion and deletion of optical texture elements at its edges specify its shape and permanence. As an object itself moves, it gives us information for its unity—all its parts move together.

A person's movements through the layout also provide information for the *self*: where one is, where one is going, and what one is accomplishing. Self-produced movement in the world yields information at the same time for events in the world and for oneself as an independent object interacting with it. J.J. Gibson said, "One perceives the environment and coperceives oneself" (1979, p. 126).

It is not only optical information for visual perception that we obtain through changes. As we handle things and move over the terrain, we bring about mechanical information in our joints. Acoustical information is produced by surfaces contacting each other. Information is available in mechanical, acoustic, and other modes of array, even in a changing array of smell against an existing background.

Information must be actively sought; it does not fall, like rain, on passive receptor surfaces. We move our heads to disocclude a portion of a temporarily invisible scene; we step forward to magnify a wanted view; we lean to peer around a corner or glance in our rearview mirror as we back the car. In sum, activities of observers result in changing points of view, perspective transformations, continuous occlusion and disocclusion of edges and boundaries, and flow patterns that specify one's continuously changing relation to objects, paths, obstructions, and goals. The function of perceptual activity is to obtain information. As we shall see, as soon as they are able, young infants bring objects closer than arm's length to scrutinize them or test them by mouthing, and they crawl around objects to explore them from all sides.

Pickup of Information

Animals, including humans, actively seek information for guiding their actions and knowing their surroundings, sometimes using elaborate strategies, as in the case of animals that seek prey or keep track of their whereabouts by echolocation. Bats do not guide their flight visually, as a human flier does. Their keen hearing is adapted to detect fine binaural differences and temporal gradients inherent in reflected sound from prey, obstructions, and open flight paths, a kind of structuring of the acoustic array. As they fly, they obtain the information by sending out high-pitched squeaks that are modulated by the objects and surfaces around them in relation to their own position and direction of movement. Their hearing systems are adapted, even, to distinguishing the two sound sources— their own squeaks and the echoes—to prevent interference.

Humans have an equally keen and unique perceptual adaptation. We can pick up an object and twist it about with our fingers, feeling it with different fingers and combinations of flexing and pressing that might seem (to a creature not possessing hands) random and aimless, but that nevertheless allow us to recognize the object. This skill (J.J. Gibson, 1966) is known as active touch, useful to all of us, with the potential to be developed as a virtuoso skill. We are impressed by persons who can read Braille; physicians who locate fractures and tumors by delicate prodding; graders of fine textiles; musicians; or blind watchmakers who can repair and even construct a delicate timepiece. Human infants have systems for obtaining information tactually, and they do it from birth, with emerging and developing skills.

We can differentiate two general kinds of active information pickup. Actions can be *exploratory,* functioning primarily to yield knowledge, such as when one fumbles in the dark for a light switch or when a blind or blindfolded person feels someone's face for impressions that will permit identification of it. Or an action can be primarily *performatory,* such as when one presses a clearly identified light switch, puts on one's coat, or inserts and turns a key in a lock. These performatory acts have certain expected results; they are performed to produce them. They depend on and confirm an already learned affordance. Of course, they may also yield knowledge and spur exploration, for example, when the key does not turn nor the lock yield and one must proceed to manipulate the key in a different manner or try other keys.

Exploratory activity is especially prevalent in infancy and is, as we shall see, spontaneous and striking. Exploratory activity yields knowledge about environmental possibilities, affordances, and one's own capabilities. Perception and action are closely intertwined in both exploration and performance, and learning is an important outcome of both types of action. Perception guides action; action makes information available for perception. Exploratory actions seem especially useful for learning by a novice, but the confirmational consequences of expectant performances are essential as well.

Action has a central role in cognitive development because of the intertwining of perception and actions. Much of the information that is essential for perceptual development cannot be obtained until appropriate action systems are functional. In later chapters we will trace the development of action and exploratory activity, showing how maturing perceptual systems interact with growth of postural control and how development of the systems potentiates perceptual learning, the very foundation of intelligence.

Perceptual Learning

Where does learning fit in the ecological view of perceptual development? Newborn infants are capable of very few performatory actions, but their perceptual systems, while immature in many respects, are functional and are used. Babies have a great deal to learn about—everything that the world has to offer—and perceptual learning is their way of discovering what particular things and people afford for them, where things and people are in relation to themselves, what is happening, what characterizes their permanent surroundings, and what they can do.

We can profit from comparative psychologists who have made intensive studies of what and how animals of many species learn early in life: for example, what songbirds learn about singing; what various species learn about foraging for food; what migratory species learn about finding their way (Gallistel, 1990). Learning goes on in the young of all species, but especially in the human species; what is learned is what is relevant to the animal's environmental niche and the kind of creature it is. Learning occurs along with general growth and maturing of action systems, so we should study it early, relating it to attainment of essential ways of adapting to the environment, as Johnston observes:

> Although it has been a frequent concern of learning theorists to draw a sharp line between learning and the rest of development, that is not a position from which the ecological approach can proceed. Successful adaptation requires that the entire life cycle of the organism, from conception to maturity, be able to cope with the demands of its environment, and processes of learning must be integrated with other developmental processes to ensure success. (1985, p. 18)

What is learned is the first question to ask, because the animal-environment fit has characteristic requirements depending on the animal and its way of life. Just as young birds may learn to sing and to fly, bees to forage, and migrating birds to orient by the stars, so human infants have their own developing behavior systems. The major behavioral systems that develop during human infants' first year are (1) communication and interaction with other people; (2) reaching, grasping, and manipulating objects; and (3) locomotion. Many affordances are learned as each system emerges and develops. We need to study what is learned and its necessary conditions as the development of each system proceeds. We will especially consider infancy, emphasizing development within the three domains, examining perceptual learning as it occurs in the context of development, and relating controlled observations and experimental research that help to reveal its underlying conditions. To do this, we will need to examine first the ways in which we can find out what an infant perceives, an achievement that eluded developmental psychologists until a few decades ago.

The task of infants is to learn about the affordances their world offers them. We will see that this happens in an orderly fashion. As growth provides them with more effective action systems and sensory equipment, their perceptual world is expanded and differentiated by their own activities. They have the motivation to explore with these systems, and exploration, spontaneously undertaken, is the crux of learning what the world offers and how to use it.

Development of Action

Since our major concern is with perceptual development, we must also consider the development of capabilities for action and its contribution to perceptual development. We noted that the perception-action relation is a reciprocal one, a kind of continuous cycle with perception guiding action, and action furnishing new information for perception—information about the animal itself, its own dimensional and dynamic properties, and the environmental consequences of its actions. Development is marked by growth of bodily dimensions and dynamic capacities, so there are many sources of change in this cyclical perception-action relation. Developmental changes in eyeball dimensions and interocular distance make visual adjustments imperative. When the body grows larger, or when a part of it grows larger or more capable in relation to the whole, potentials for action change. A shift in proportions as the child grows less top heavy and stronger in the legs are among the factors that make walking possible. The gradual achievement of control of posture underlies all forms of perception-action development.

Indeed, postural development is a leading factor in all behavioral development. At one time, psychologists tended to favor the rather simplistic assumption that action begins as individual reflexes and attains greater complexity by combining reflexes, as elements, through some associative process such as conditioning. But we know now that action, even the simplest, is always organized, related to what is going on in the rest of the body, potentially flexible, nearly always intentional, and frequently anticipatory, in the sense of preparing for later action.

Individual actions, such as an infant lifting a hand to the mouth, always occur against a postural background and, in fact, can occur only to the extent that the infant is supported and posturally stable. Differentiation of actions occurs as postural control develops, beginning with control of head and shoulders and proceeding downward, depending on growth of limbs and many other factors. As new actions become possible, infants' potential for exploring their surroundings and themselves grows.

The ecological approach to perceptual development is compatible with views of development expressed in recent years by naturalists and comparative psychologists. Learning should be studied in the context of development as it proceeds, starting as early as possible. Even prenatal development is part of the study to be undertaken, because it has become clear that the fetus is an active organism and that interaction with environmental factors is an essential aspect of growth during the gestation period, as well as from birth on. Internal (physiological, biochemical) and external environments affect the growing fetus as it differentiates. This position emphasizes that development is the result of interaction of genetic and other factors within a growing organism, and of the organism and its environment from the beginning. Development is a dynamic process, and an organism undergoes its own processes of organization and creation, so a simple dichotomy (or even interaction) of genetic and environmental factors cannot be separated out as discrete factors in the organism's ongoing transformations (Goodwin, 1990; Oyama, 1985; Johnston, 1987). Thus, it is the relation and interaction of the organism and its environment that we focus on and emphasize here.

What Is Perceived?

We have considered three general questions: What is there *to be* perceived? What is the information for perceiving? And how is the information obtained? A final question is: What *is perceived?* Not information—information is specification for its sources in the world. Not light, color, form, space, intensity, or other isolated sensory properties. We perceive what is in the world as it relates to us: (1) the *layout* of the environment; (2) the *objects* in the layout; and (3) *events* that go on over time, situated in the layout and involving the objects, in terms of what they afford for us.

What is meant by *layout?* It refers to the permanent arrangement of the surfaces of the world, which support and surround the objects that furnish the world and move around in it. The term "space" has often been used in textbooks to refer to the locations of things, but it conveys too strongly the notion of empty space (for which there is no specification). We perceive the surfaces that we walk on and the ceiling above us, and we perceive these surfaces as permanent places for situating ourselves, the objects, and the events that happen there. The ground, for terrestrial animals, is always perceived as stretching away from us, at our feet. We locate ourselves in this layout and locate other things in reference to us and to the ground that stretches under them as well as us. The layout is pretty circumscribed for an infant: the walls of a room and a ceiling, plus the surface the infant lies on, for the most part. But these basic, permanent, underlying and surrounding surfaces are perceived as background for everything else very early. As a child achieves first reaching and then locomotion, the layout of the world available to be perceived expands enormously, and how this happens has a big share in the story of perceptual development.

The layout we perceive around us is far from empty; it is furnished with *objects* of many kinds, animate and inanimate. Objects, on the whole, are moveable or move on their own, as is the case with animals. Some of them, like houses, do not afford moving by individual persons, some can be moved by a sturdy adult, and some small ones can be moved easily, but they are not permanently fixed in the sense that the ground or a mountain is. The categories of objects are many—people, animals, things to sit on, things to eat, pictures of things, and even symbols, such as letters and numbers. Learning to perceive the affordances and the features of all these things is a task that begins at birth and continues throughout life.

The third category of what is perceived is the largest—the *events* that take place within the layout. The events are the movements and actions that occur, some performed by ourselves and some external to us. They implicate objects and provide the dynamics of all scenes in the layout. Events have a special importance, because it is only through events that properties of things, including permanent properties of both things and the layout, are revealed. What is permanent is revealed through change and nonchange. When an object moves, parts of the object all move together, revealing it as a unit. I walk out my front door and down the sidewalk and what I am seeing—the vista ahead—is continually changing. But I can reverse the vista, walk back again, and the surrounding layout will look the same. My path could be shifted by a moveable object appearing or being thrust in front of me, but the basic layout is perceived as constant, revealed by my locomotion through it. The fact that perceiving is an active process, a search for information about the layout and what goes on in it, is in accord with the emphasis on movement and change. Perceiving is an event that provides us with changes that reveal the properties, permanent or impermanent, of things and places. We move our heads to see what something is, and we look back again to see if the order is the same.

Growing children learn to find their way around the layout, at some point using objects as landmarks to help them. But they must discover that such objects should not be very moveable if they are to be useful (a concept Hansel and Gretel had not yet mastered when they marked their path of locomotion with a trail of bread crumbs). They learn about the layout of a small world around them fairly early, but as they become able to move themselves to new places, creating larger events, the layout that can be perceived expands and the objects encountered are multiplied, and so are the events that can be witnessed.

Perceiving a layout, objects in it, and events going on is not a mere registration of presence. Perceiving involves both perception and action, inevitably, as we have stressed, and also involves perception of oneself in relation to everything else. It is an active process of obtaining information; even a newborn infant moves eyes and head in an exploratory searching fashion, turning the head to look, for example, when a voice speaks or a rattle is shaken at one side. These exploratory movements provide information about something in the environment. In later weeks, more and more kinds of activity are possible as a baby learns what the layout of the world and the objects and happenings in it afford. Learning about the affordances, objects, and happenings around us is a lifetime pursuit that begins early and elaborates as actions and environmental opportunities emerge and broaden. Our aim is to understand how this happens. How do we come to perceive the world so richly? And how do we, as psychologists, find out about this? Ways of finding out emerge from the properties of infant behavior and infants' own readiness and capabilities for seeking information about the environment and about themselves. We consider how this happens in the next chapter.

3
✦ ✧ ✦ ✧ ✦

Studying Perceptual Development in Preverbal Infants

Tasks, Methods, and Motivation

Babies cannot be questioned about what they see, hear, taste, smell, or feel, nor can they be asked whether they have only meaningless sensations. Perhaps for this reason, it was long assumed by many people that the world perceived by an infant is a chaotic patchwork of sensations, or even that infants are deaf or partially blind. William James, in an oft quoted statement, commented that a baby's world was a "blooming, buzzing confusion" (James, 1890). Now we know that James's opinion was mistaken; even newborns are capable of actively seeking information about the environment surrounding them.

We could not have made such a statement with assurance 30 years ago. Enormous advances in our knowledge have been made since that time, owing to new methods introduced and very effectively put to work by a number of researchers. What inspired this remarkable change? One reason was that developmental psychologists were spurred by ethologists who demonstrated the importance of an animal's ability to fit into and function in its normal habitat, so a promising way to ask the right questions might be to make use of infants' own spontaneous activity and the ways they naturally attend to the world surrounding them. We have already pointed out that perception is active, a kind of foraging for information. This activity is observable in behavior, for behavior itself is neither reflex nor random but marked by functional units that we call tasks.

Tasks: The Continuity and Segmentation of Behavior

In the past, there have been two views of the way a very young infant's behavior should be characterized. One was that it is random, disconnected, and quite without order or method; the other, that it is reflex in nature, structured, indeed, but in fixed, inherited patterns of responses to stimulation. Piaget, for example, held that the activity of neonates was reflexive, only gradually accommodating to ongoing events in a flexible way. A third way of characterizing young infants'—even neonates'—behavior is one that we favor: behavior (human activity) goes on continuously, segmented into units over time that may be referred to as episodes or events. In older children or adults we view these segments of behavior as functional directed units, having beginnings and ends, with smaller units nested within larger ones. We will refer to units of a size appropriate to some goal or end as *tasks*. As development proceeds, the directed, tasklike quality of these behavioral episodes is easier to identify, because goals tend to become more differentiated and specific. But even infants have simple tasks that are natural to them as living organisms, tasks that infants' structure and dynamic organization make both possible and necessary. Babies breathe, take in nourishment, move, sleep, and, when not sleeping, use their perceptual systems to make contact with the environment and so obtain information—all highly functional, directed activities.

Human infants have a long wait before they are ready to walk, talk, and follow directions. But they have tasks to pursue meanwhile, especially interacting with their surroundings and their companions. Their tasks are very broad ones to begin with, but their activity nevertheless has continuity, is segmented into functional episodes, and is spontaneous. Most important, infants have ways of attending to what goes on within and around them. Bouts of attending occur, sometimes spontaneous and sometimes instigated by environmental events.

What does the environment present for infants to attend to? The environment offers surfaces to rest on, objects that approach and sometimes touch them and can be touched, surroundings arranged in a layout that can be seen and heard, and, of course, caretakers who provide sources of nourishment, comfort, and social contact. The social contact is of the utmost importance, because it affords objects that act back, objects that are responsive to infants' activities, enabling them to learn to engage their activity in exchanges of information. These opportunities provided by the environment are what we termed, in the last chapter, affordances. A broad task of human infants is to learn to make use of affordances. Infants do so by engaging in exploratory activity, using all the perception and action systems available to them in perception-action cycles that are nested within the continuous stream of behavior. As babies begin to control simple perception-action cycles that realize affordances, their tasks become more specific and behavior more often appears controlled, initiated for a specific end. It looks, and is, intentional.

An Example

We illustrate the notion that a task differentiates and becomes more specific in the activity of a young infant with the following example of an experiment per-

FIGURE 3.1. Infant in a Jolly Jumper, discovering its use. From "Motor Development: A New Synthesis," by E. Thelen, 1995, *American Psychologist, 50*, p. 86. Copyright © 1995 by the American Psychological Association, Inc. Reprinted with permission. Photograph by Dexter Gormley. The original research was performed by Goldfield, Kay, and Warren (1993).

formed by Goldfield, Kay, and Warren (1993). They placed infants 6 months old in a piece of equipment called a Jolly Jumper (see fig. 3.1). The infants wore a harness that hung from a spring, with their feet just touching the floor. The babies were left to themselves to find out what would happen. It took several sessions for babies to discover, as they made a few sporadic kicks, that an organized kickup pattern would shift them from irregular bouncing to a sustained pattern of oscillation. Over the trial sessions, the babies discovered the task constraints imposed by the harness and the spring and by their own powers of pushing, and how it felt to reach a more economical, organized pattern of bounce that they could control. One could see an intentional, goal-directed system develop as the babies explored their own action systems in relation to the constraints of the spring system and the rigid floor beneath them. They discovered through kinaesthetic feedback the optimal rate for a "preferred" bouncing frequency. The variability of the bounces declined from one bout to the next until babies reached peak rate, evidence of increasing control. Exploring decreased, and the activity became more specifically patterned and intentional. The babies learned through exploratory activity what the spring afforded, and how to control their actions to reach a goal that was economical and attractive.

Intrinsic Motivation and Exploratory Activity

The term "task" carries with it the implication of motivation that instigates and ends a behavior episode. Anything that motivates the task has the effect of unifying the total episode. Such motivation need not imply an external direction, even though the dictionary definition of "task" implies an imposed requirement. Motivated activity in an infant is endogenous, functional, and implicit in the dynamics of an organism that possesses interacting systems for perceiving and acting. Young infants are geared to use all the capacities within their power. Their perception is purposive, in the sense that it is a search for information, a way of keeping in touch with what is going on. Moreover, the resulting interactions with the environment yield behavioral consequences that can be perceived by infants, supplying information about events in the world, simultaneous events within the organism, and their relation to one another in the ongoing cycle of action and events in the world.

Foraging for information is a kind of intrinsic motivation, spontaneously providing the foundation for the learning of affordances and the eventual control of behavior. It is just such motivation that has been used successfully by developmental psychologists to devise methods for studying infants' perception. One can observe babies in their quest for information by providing an opportunity and observing what ensues. Given a choice between what has already been explored and something novel, babies regularly attend to what is novel.

How do human infants explore? Their perceptual systems allow them to look around (especially at anything moving nearby), to listen (with a well-developed auditory system), to detect odors (of a caretaker, for example), to discriminate certain tastes (e.g., sweet versus bitter), to feel things that touch them, and, of major importance, to detect *their own movements*. As for action, they can use the mouth to suck for nourishment and also to explore substances, such as that of their own hands; they can turn the head to one side or the other; they can move their arms and kick their legs.

An experiment of Thoman and Ingersoll (1993) revealed an unexpected form of spontaneous activity. Premature infants (33 weeks conceptual age) were given a "breathing bear" in their hospital cribs, placed away from contact with the infant. The bear noiselessly simulated the regular rhythm of the baby's even breathing when quietly asleep. Over a 2-week period these infants learned to move in the direction of the bear so as to increase their amount of contact and reduced their latency to do so as compared with a control group given a nonbreathing bear. Even premature infants are apparently capable of organizing their movements sufficiently to achieve physical proximity to a nearby object that provides orderly rhythmic stimulation reflecting their own breathing rhythm. These babies subsequently showed more mature sleep patterns than control babies. Order in the environment is perceived as an affordance very early.

The spontaneous bodily activity of the baby, primitively organized as it is, brings changes in the baby's relation with the environment, eventually leading the way to *control* of the activity as its consequences are detected. The perceptual systems are actively playing a role in the task. An experiment by van der Meer, van der Weel, and Lee (1995) with babies 2 to 4 weeks of age confirms the readiness of the visual system for interaction in a perception-action cycle. Weights were tied to the babies' wrists, just heavy enough to provide resistance against lifting, but not preventing it. The babies were placed on their backs with their heads turned to one side, so that one hand could be viewed when lifted, but not the other. As babies attempted spontaneous moving of the arms, they gradually ceased moving the nonvisible limb but increased lifting the limb that brought a hand into view (see fig. 3.2). The ensuing hand-watching is an event with very adaptive consequences for the baby. The hand provides a standard for learning the scale of the layout in relation to the baby's own hand. This event also provides babies with an opportunity for learning about themselves as instruments of control, bringing something within sight on their own power.

The mouth too is an organ of great importance in early development. Babies bring their hands to their mouths with considerable frequency and explore substances put in their mouths with active mouthing (Rochat, 1987; Rochat, Blass, & Hoffmeyer, 1988). Butterworth and Hopkins (1988), observing the spontaneous activity of newborn infants, found that they can (and do) move a hand to the mouth, directly or indirectly, and open the mouth in anticipation of the hand's arrival. The hand sometimes made contact with the face before arrival at the mouth, moving on toward the mouth when it was in the neighborhood of the mouth. Indeed, observations by means of ultrasound have indicated that hand contacts with face and mouth occur prenatally, allowing for prenatal practice of this organization of an action system.

The major effector systems that are functional in newborns are moving the head and eyes to look, mouthing for both nutritional and exploratory purposes, and moving trunk and limbs. These systems have all been exploited by experimenters for investigating how perception and action together lead to gathering information, the major task of a healthy infant.

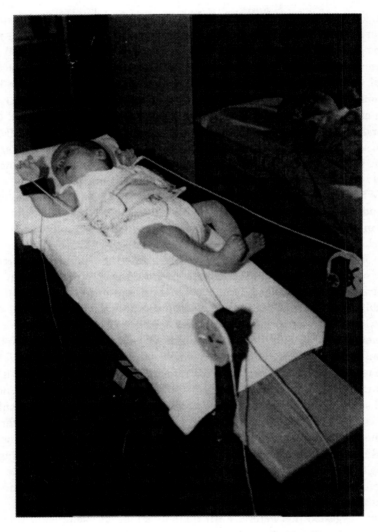

FIGURE 3.2. Neonatal infant lifting and looking at weighted hand. Only the visible hand was lifted, pulling against the weights. From "The Functional Significance of Arm Movements in Neonates," by A.L.H. van der Meer, F.R. van der Meer, and D.N. Lee, 1995, *Science, 267*, p. 694. Copyright © 1995 by the American Association for the Advancement of Science. Reprinted with permission. Photo courtesy of F.R. van der Meer.

Methods of Studying Perceptual Development
in Prelinguistic Infants

Even before the 20th century, "baby books" included studies of individual infants and how they developed, some containing excellent observations, such as Preyer's (1888, 1889). Early in this century, research with infants on a larger scale began and reached a climax with the research of Gesell (1946) and some of his contemporaries (e.g., McGraw, 1935). This research was largely observational, and while it provided a rich background of information on motor development, it yielded only limited information about perceptual and cognitive development. Learning experiments with infants during the 1930s and 1940s generally tried to impose classical conditioning methods on infants (Munn, 1946; Wenger, 1936; Sameroff, 1971), with disappointing results. The experiments followed from the notion that behavior is founded on reflexes, and that development proceeds via stimulus-response associations.

When developmental psychologists, encouraged by the work of ethologists, took advantage of the spontaneous attentional and exploratory behavior of human infants, new questions were asked and progress began to be made. What do babies look at? Listen to? How do they learn spontaneously? These were some of the questions. For studying learning, a different experimental paradigm replaced classical conditioning. If infants were allowed to perform a naturally occurring act spontaneously, the act would be repeated if it produced, predictably, some favorable or notable consequence. Such a procedure was originally introduced with animals and was referred to by Skinnerians as "instrumental conditioning." Similar research with infants was referred to by H. Papousek, an ethologist, as "appetitional behavior." Papousek used head turning, a natural exploratory act, as the instrumental behavior, and followed it with a squirt of milk to the infant's mouth. It could be preceded by an event, such as a bell sounding, to signal that orienting in one direction or the other would be followed by milk. Infants easily learned to perform this orienting behavior during the first three months of life. During the second three months, Papousek found that complicated routines could be introduced, such as alternating orienting to the left and the right for different signals. The infants not only learned to perform these routines, but continued to respond to a complicated routine after satiation, refusing the milk but continuing the experimenter's "game." This finding suggested that natural intrinsic motivation, for example, to solve the problem or test the predictability of an event, was involved. Papousek thought of these experiments as "a model for the analysis of the development of intentional behavior" (H. Papousek, 1967, p. 249).

Soon after Papousek's experiments with milk as the predictable consequence, it was found that consequences appropriate to a purely exploratory motive were at least equally effective. The consequences could be something novel to look at, or music or voices to listen to (Koch, 1962). A revolution in infant research on perception and learning was at hand. A number of methods, all exploiting a baby's endogenous motivation, resulted. Early ones included preferential visual attention to a fixed display, habituation, instrumental or operant conditioning of the kind devised by Papousek, and controlled observation of any spontaneous behavior under cleverly contrived experimental conditions. We describe these methods and some of their findings.

Preferential Looking

The systematic study of looking preferences of young infants was one of the first methods to be exploited. The assumption was that if a baby oriented toward one of two displays and attended to it significantly longer than to an alternative one, the baby must be capable of discriminating between the two. Pairs of displays were presented directly in front of the infant, and the time the baby looked at each member of the pair was noted by an unseen observer. The observer watched the baby's eyes and pressed a key as one or the other display was fixated, so a cumulated looking time could be calculated for a given period of presentation. This method was carefully checked for reliability and found to be easily replicable. An experimenter could pair displays to test some hypothesis, such as a presumed preference for inhomogeneity over homogeneity, for novelty over familiarity, complexity over simplicity, and so on.

The most productive pioneer with this method was Robert Fantz (1961). His procedure with infants from 1 to 15 weeks old was to place babies on their backs in an enclosed chamber, facing upward toward a pair of patterned designs. An observer peeked through a small hole, monitoring where the baby's gaze fell by watching for a reflection of one or the other target pattern on the baby's cornea and pressing a key to record the duration of the fixation. Fantz's main question was whether or not infants had an innate ability to perceive form. Targets included a bulls-eye paired with stripes; a checkerboard paired with a plain square; a cross paired with a circle; and a pair of triangles, one larger than the other. If the infants showed a preference for looking at one over the other (as was the case, for example, with the checkerboard over the plain square), it was inferred that the two patterns were indeed discriminated.

These comparisons seem, by now, rather ad hoc, but they led to more systematic experiments and more sophisticated questions. Fantz and his collaborators discovered that even the youngest infants prefer to look at a patterned display in preference to a plain homogeneously colored one; that the magnitude of patterning preference increases with age; that curved contours are preferred over straight ones; and that a three-dimensional spherical object is preferred over a flat, two-dimensional circle (Fantz, Fagan, & Miranda, 1975).

One of Fantz's most interesting findings concerned visual acuity and its development (Fantz, Ordy, & Udelf, 1962). Since infants tended to look longer at a patterned display than at a uniform one, they should prefer to look at a field that could be resolved into separated stripes, rather than at a uniform gray. Presenting pairs of striped displays of appropriately varied densities should then reveal the infants' potential to resolve the stripes by discovering the finest striping that would be preferred over a uniform field. This method revealed that acuity increases remarkably between 1 and 6 months. Teller (1979) described an ingenious preferential looking procedure for determining visual acuity in young infants, dubbed the forced-choice preferential looking technique. Infants are shown two fields of equal size and brightness, differing in patterning or lack of it. One field is a grating (stripes, which can be of variable width) and the other plain. An adult observer, unaware of the position of the grating, observes the infant's eyes and makes a forced choice, on each trial, as to the infant's predominant gaze direction. Grating densities can be varied and the highest spatial frequency required to yield a 75% correct (patterned) choice estimated, thus yielding a rough measure of acuity. The method can be adapted for use in practical, applied situations to assess developmental progress, comparing individual infants to known age norms.

The experiments so far described generally used static, two-dimensional displays, hardly approximating the visual scene customary in the everyday life of an infant. They showed, however, that babies do look for information in inhomogeneity, exploring with their visual systems even under very limited conditions. Later researchers have shown that the preference method can be adapted to a more natural situation, with babies well-propped in a comfortable infant seat, so that their heads can turn easily to look from side to side as they gain motor control. The baby's face can be videotaped for later coding and reliability checks, and more natural displays can be presented, such as real objects to scrutinize and videotapes portraying active, colorful events.

One of the most creative adaptations of the preference method was Spelke's. She not only presented videotapes of live scenes, she accompanied them with an audio recording appropriate to one of the videotaped events (E. Spelke, 1976). Infants are not limited to perceiving visual scenes. They smell, feel, and hear caretakers who pick them up, caress them, and talk to them. Do young infants perceive a visual event and accompanying speech as a single event, despite information being picked up multimodally, by both visual and auditory sensory systems? Spelke, using the preference method, presented infants with videotapes of two events, side by side. When the event was taped, so was a soundtrack of the audible accompaniments. In an experiment with 4 1/2-month-old infants, one of the events displayed was an adult female playing a peekaboo game. The other was a hand, playing a rhythmic beat on a small instrument. As the baby watched, only one of the soundtracks was played, with the speaker located between the two displays. The question was, would the baby perceive a unified event and, given a choice, look at the visual scene specified by the soundtrack being played? The babies did attend reliably more to the auditorily specified visual event, apparently identifying the event as a whole. This method has been used in many more recent experiments to ask diverse questions about the development of event perception during infancy.

Habituation and Dishabituation

The method of habituation was in use with animals before it became a standard method for investigating what human infants perceive. In a typical experiment a display is presented to an infant for a limited period; the display is then withdrawn, and, after a short interval, the display is re-presented. The infant's looking time is recorded for each presentation. As the presentations continue, the duration of visual attention tends to decline. This is the effect known as habituation. After a set number of trials, or when the decline reaches a predetermined fraction of the time spent looking during the first period (or perhaps the mean of the first two), a novel display is presented. If the baby detects the change, looking time increases. The increase in looking is known as dishabituation. Controls must be provided in which there is no change of display, since looking times fluctuate due to numerous uncontrollable factors (e.g., discomfort of the infant, distractions in the surroundings, etc.). Habituation may be followed by a preference test, comparing the now familiar display with a novel one. Babies may be expected to explore the novel one, if a difference is detected.

This procedure has been used in many experiments investigating infants' discrimination of two-dimensional patterns, much like early experiments with the looking preference procedure. We illustrate with experiments on the perception of outline forms by Schwartz and Day (1979), who were interested in whether young infants perceive relational information, and whether they perceive whole forms or only parts of them. (The question of part versus whole perception was hotly argued in the earlier days of research on infant visual perception). Their experiments examined discrimination of linear angular contours varying in degree of angle; discrimination of outlines of geometrical forms such as rectangles, diamonds, and incomplete triangles; and the effect of orientation of these figures in the two-dimensional display. The participants were 2- to 3-month-old infants. The procedure incorporated a habituation phase of successive 20-second exposures of one of the figures, A, separated from the next by an intertrial interval of 5 seconds. Then four test figures, A, B, C, and D, were presented for 20 seconds each, separated by intervals of 5 seconds. This was the dishabituation phase. An observer judged when the infant was looking at the figure, much as in the preference experiments. The difference in fixation time between the habituation figure and the test figure was considered the index of discrimination.

Figure 3.3 from Schwarz and Day depicts a habituation curve produced by a group of infants shown angles of different degrees and orientation. Circles at the right-hand side show that the test figures (B, C, D) were looked at longer than the habituation figure (A), indicating dishabituation. Difference in degree of angle accounted for the extent of dishabituation. Further experiments indicated that the angles could be rotated without disturbing the discrimination. The same pattern of results held when the experiments presented rectangles of different

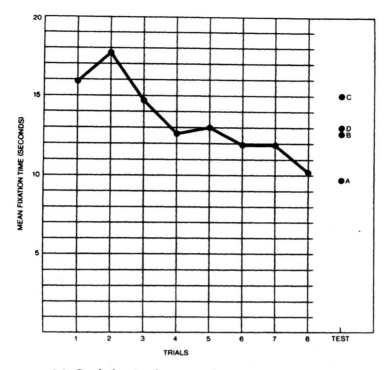

FIGURE 3.3. Graph showing the course of visual habituation of infants to a two-dimensional angular figure, followed by dishabituation (indicated by dots in right-hand margin). From "Visual Shape Perception in Early Infancy," by M. Schwartz and R.H. Day, 1979, *Monographs of the Society for Research in Child Development, 44* (7, Serial No. 182), p. 14. Copyright © 1979 by the Society for Research in Child Development, Inc. Reprinted with permission.

proportions. Triangles with gaps in the side of an outline could still be discriminated from other triangles. Overall, these experiments suggested that the infants were using relational information and may have perceived the outline shapes as wholes. We note also the extraordinary discriminatory ability of these infants; the differences in degree of angle, proportion of rectangles, and so on, were not very large.

There have been many investigations of developing discrimination of sensory qualities in infants, such as color (hue) of light and frequency (pitch) of tones, using a habituation method. The results can be compared with those obtained by other methods (e.g., preferences for one of a pair). For example, Bornstein (1976), using the habituation method, found that 3-month-old infants discriminated wavelengths in pretty much the same ranges as adults with normal trichromatic color vision. His evidence was disputed by investigators using other methods, but it now seems likely that by 3 months infants have an adultlike color sensitivity (see Banks and Salapatek, 1983, for a detailed discussion).

The major questions we raise in this book will not be concerned with sensory discrimination of two-dimensional patterns or of pure lights or tones. But it is possible to use the habituation method to investigate perception of properties of real objects and what they afford. For an example, we present research on infants' perception of an important property of objects, their substance—that is, their rigidity or hardness as contrasted with their manipulability or elasticity. This property of graspable objects provides numerous affordances, such as chewability or lack of it, or throwability, as with a dense, hard ball that can be used as a missile.

Information for object substance is not directly visible in a motionless object, but we can usually poke or squeeze an object to detect its rigidity or lack of it. However, events in which an object moves can reveal its substance by means of visible information in the way it moves. Gibson, Owsley, & Johnston (1978) used the habituation method to determine whether 5-month-old infants differentiated two types of motion—rigid or elastic—as invariant properties over three different events. The object used to present the events was a round disklike piece of foam rubber, dappled with black spots. The object could be manipulated so as to produce either rigid motion or deformation. All motions were produced by a trained experimenter who could not see the infant. Four rigid motions were displayed: rotation in the frontal plane, rotation around the vertical axis, rotation around the horizontal axis, and a loom-zoom movement. Movements were cyclical and continuous. Deformation (an elastic motion) was accomplished by squeezing the object, also cyclical and continuous. In the habituation series of the experiment, an infant was presented with a series of three rigid motions in separate trials; in the dishabituation series, the fourth rigid motion (as yet unseen) and the deformation were presented, each separately. The different rigid motions were counterbalanced over subjects.

Rather than present a rigid motion for a set time, an "infant control" procedure was used (Horowitz, Paden, Bhana, & Self, 1972), a procedure that has been found very effective. For any trial, the particular motion displayed was continued until the infant looked away for 2 seconds. Thus, the infant could control the duration of the presentation. After an intertrial interval, the next presentation occurred. This procedure was continued until the infant had met a criterion of habituation of one-half the first or second exposure time for that motion. All three rigid motions were presented until the criterion was met. After habituation, the dishabituation posttests were given. Infants dishabituated (increased their looking times) for both new motions presented in the posttest, showing that the rigid motions could be discriminated from one another. But dishabituation was significantly greater for the deforming, elastic motion than for any rigid motion. This finding tells us that these infants could perceive a property of objects, one we call rigidity, generalize it over a number of nonidentical rigid motions, and discriminate it from deforming motion.

Instrumental Methods

We referred early in the chapter to instrumental learning (or operant conditioning) in discussing the self-motivating nature of infants' search for information about the world and themselves. This method takes advantage of a spontaneously performed natural action of an infant and follows it up with an event selected by the experimenter. It is possible to compare different contingent events for effectiveness in prolonging an infant's spontaneous activity, telling us what the baby chooses spontaneously to make happen and observe again. As we saw, the method was first used with spontaneous head turning, followed by food; but it was soon discovered that novel, potentially interesting visual and auditory events were at least equally effective in instigating and prolonging an infant's spontaneous performance. The basic procedure has been used with sucking, head turning, and arm and leg movements. The procedure can be altered innovatively to shed light on other questions, such as discriminability of events presented as signals for the baby's activity. We illustrate with all these types of activity, beginning again with head turning.

As we noted, head turning to look at something (and also to position the head to hear best what is being viewed) is a natural exploratory activity. Hearing a sound at one side causes even newborns to turn their heads in the direction of the sound (Wertheimer, 1961; Alegria & Noirot, 1978). With an instrumental learning procedure, an older infant is quickly taught to turn to look at some interesting event when a signal chosen by the experimenter is given. The event of interest can be a person popping into view and "peekabooing" (Bower, 1966) or a toy appearing, such as a toy bear beating on a drum (Kuhl, 1991). After the baby has learned to look for the event, the signal can be modified and the baby tested for generalization to other similar signals. This procedure can give valuable evidence either of discrimination or of perception of something equivalent or "constant," as in the following experiment.

Kuhl (1991) used a head-turning procedure to investigate infants' appreciation of vowel sounds as equivalent ("constant") when uttered by different speakers. Babies need such an appreciation if they are to learn their native language spoken by more than a single speaker, since vowel sounds vary when spoken by males or females or people of varying age or language environment. In Kuhl's experiment, the babies (6 months old) sat on a parent's lap, placed so that they could turn to look at a target. An assistant engaged the babies' attention visually, while a speech sound, for example, /a/, was played repeatedly from a loudspeaker to the infant's left. When this sound changed to an /i/, a bear playing a drum inside a lighted box above the speaker was turned on. Babies learned quickly to look toward the box when the sound changed to /i/. The question was whether they would turn to look when new instances of modifed /a/ or modifed /i/ vowels were presented. Infants of 6 months did categorize the sounds: that is, they would turn at a change to a novel /i/ sound (i.e., one spoken by a man if they had been trained with a woman's utterance) but not to a novel /a/ sound. The continuous and changed sounds were counterbalanced, half of the infants hearing /i/ as the changed sound and half /a/.

Another action, sucking, has been used as the instrumental activity in a similar fashion for dozens of experiments on very early discrimination of the sounds of language, such as individual phonemes. Pioneers in this research were Eimas and his collaborators (Eimas, Siqueland, Jusczyk, & Vigorito, 1971). Their technique is referred to as "high-amplitude sucking." In their work with 1- to 4-month-old infants, a dry nipple, attached to a pressure transducer so as to produce a record, was placed in the baby's mouth. Whenever the baby's spontaneous sucking on the nipple reached a given amplitude, a consonant syllable, /ba/, was played on a tape. The sucking rate of these high-amplitude sucks typically rose, eliciting with each vigorous suck a contingent sound of the syllable. Eventually, the baby slowed down, satiated with the sound. At a set criterion of decline, the contingent sound was changed to /pa/. The sucking rate typically rose again, demonstrating the infant's ability to discriminate the consonant phonemes. It was also demonstrated that they were perceived categorically, over small changes, by infants as young as 1 month (see Aslin, Pisoni, & Jusczyk, 1983, for a discussion of categorical perception of phonemes). Later experiments using this method have tested discrimination of many other phoneme pairs, including ones not heard in an infant's own language environment, and have shown that neonates possess an astonishing ability to discriminate these constituents of speech and other properties of speech as well, such as intonation. We will consider how very early perception of speech develops in a later chapter. We stress here, once more, the motivating properties to the infant not only of the event of hearing the human voice, but also of controlling its presentation.

The high-amplitude sucking method can also be used to elicit visual events as so-called "reinforcers." Siqueland and DeLucia followed sucking at criterion amplitude with the appearance of a slide exposed to the infant's view on a lighted screen. Slides included geometric patterns, cartoon figures, and human faces, changing every 30 seconds. When the slides were withdrawn, sucking rate and amplitude declined. Simply presenting a group of infants with a changing pattern of slides, not contingent on their sucking, was ineffective. The authors concluded that "visual feedback of the type employed in these experiments was effective in supporting motivated exploratory behavior in infants as young as 3 weeks of age" (1969, p. 1146).

The instrumental method has been used with success with one other set of actions, arm and leg movements. These experiments have been focused less on discriminatory powers of the infant, and more on how control is learned and transferred. Piaget (1952) provided the first example of this method by attaching a string to the right wrist of his 2-month-old son, with the other end fastened to a rattle above his crib. The child learned to stretch his arm to make the rattle sound. At just 3 months, when Piaget attached the string to the left arm, the left arm swung while the right was barely mobile, so the learning "transferred" to the unpracticed arm. This method has been perfected and exploited in many experiments by Rovee-Collier and her colleagues (C.K. Rovee-Collier & Gekoski, 1979), who refer to it as the method of "conjugate reinforcement." Rovee-Collier has used a foot kick engaged by a cord attached to the ankle and also to a mobile so as to produce movement of the mobile. In her experiments, 2- and 3-month-old infants who received conjugate reinforcement (movement of the mobile, contingent upon their own kicks) rapidly increased their kick rate and then reduced it when the movement was made noncontingent. A moving mobile not controlled by the baby did not activate foot kicks. C.K. Rovee-Collier, Morongiello, Aron, and Kuperschmidt (1978) observed topographical response differentiation and reversal of it upon a contingency reversal to the nontrained leg. That is, the original diffuse kicking response was differentiated to activation of only the attached leg; and when conditions were reversed so that kicking the opposite leg operated the mobile, there was a rapid shift in leg movement. These experiments provide an elegant demonstration that very young infants can learn, if provided with the means, to control an environmental change even before their reaching and grasping abilities have matured. They are, in a sense, provided with a tool that extends their immature manipulatory systems.

These experiments also show that actions begun as exploratory can become controlled performatory activity when they lead to adaptive consequences. Learning may occur "online," so to speak, as exploration leads selectively to a gradually more controlled performance. Exploration thus becomes prospective and leads to controlled, intentional performance naturally, as consequences are perceived; performance in turn can become more skilled as the perceiver-actor observes and uses the means of control over the outcome.

Observation of Performance in Naturalistic Settings

One of our major ways of finding out about any kind of development is systematic observation of activity in natural, or simulated but still naturalistic, settings. If such a method is pursued developmentally, with objective methods of recording and coding what happens, it can be as uncontaminated by experimenter bias as physiological measures like heart rate. Videotaping and computing equipment have contributed greatly to such ecologically valid means of obtaining data.

Observing performance (including instructed performing) is the method generally depended on for studying behavior of older children and adults. But we can study it along with development too, as actions become possible. Crying, vocalizing, and smiling are activities that can be observed very early as a baby begins to communicate with caretakers. Reaching for things and gradually manipulating objects becomes possible and progresses at length beginning around 4 months, and a few months later, locomotion begins. But can these observable, natural actions tell us anything about perception? They can, indeed. We rely heavily on the development of normally observable behavior, both exploratory and performatory, in the chapters to follow. Now, we cite one example of how observation of performance in a quasi-natural situation, the "visual cliff," lends itself to experimental study. Babies presented with this situation are free to control their behavior, and as they do so we can learn a good deal about what they perceive.

Experiments with the visual cliff were first done with animals (Gibson & Walk, 1960; Walk & Gibson, 1961). In fact, the first experiment was a spin-off from another research project, which entailed rearing a number of rats in the dark. Dark rearing is a very troublesome endeavor, and the experimenters (Walk, Gibson, & Tighe, 1957) decided to make their labors pay by putting the rats to good use in another experiment, one they thought of as a depth perception test, as soon as the rats emerged from their darkened habitat. But the test could not involve a preliminary learning process or the carefully controlled rearing conditions would be undermined. It was decided to create a kind of visual void that the rats could walk out on over a glass surface or keep away from on an alternative patterned surface. A patterned surface was placed well below the glass on one side of a large space, identical with that directly under the animal's feet on the "safe-looking" side. Both dark- and light-reared rats were placed, one at a time, on a board between the two surfaces. All the animals behaved in the same way. They stepped down onto the patterned surface just under their feet and avoided the "deep" side. The rats reared in darkness apparently saw what the normally reared animals did, a surface to be walked on, on one side, but a drop-off on the other.

In a later experiment, kittens were reared in the dark (half of each of several litters) and brought out when the light-reared siblings had opened their eyes and could walk about. The dark-reared kittens initially behaved indiscriminately on the visual cliff, wandering aimlessly about from side to side. The kittens were maintained after this initial experience in the usual lighted laboratory environment and tested again daily on the cliff. By the third day of testing, 80% of them avoided the deep side. By the seventh day, all of them did. This shift in behavior could not be due to learning to avoid a cliff because of punishment, like falling, since they had the opportunity to learn that walking on the glass over the deep side was perfectly safe in that respect, and they were given no opportunity to fall. We know, however, that visually guided locomotion in kittens requires self-guided practice, a way of acquiring perceptual control of the action (Held & Hein, 1963).

Experiments were conducted on the cliff with human infants, all having the ability to crawl. An infant was placed on a center board that horizontally bridged the apparatus similar to the one just described (see fig. 3.4). The baby's mother stood alternately at the edge of each side, facing her baby, twirling a toy, and urging the baby to come to her. In the original cliff experiment with infants, 30 out of 33 refused to crawl over the deep side. These infants varied in age in

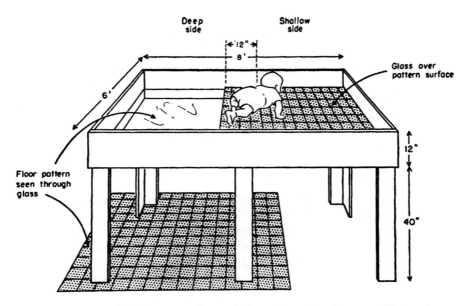

FIGURE 3.4. A visual cliff for testing human infants. From "Development of Perception: Discrimination of Depth Compared with Discrimination of Graphic Symbols," by E.J. Gibson, 1963, in J.C. Wright and J. Kagan (Eds.), "Basic Cognitive Processes in Children," *Monographs of the Society for Research in Child Development, 28* (2, Serial No. 86), p. 11. Copyright © 1963 by the Society for Research in Child Development, Inc. Reprinted with permission.

months and in length of crawling experience. More recent experiments have examined the role of crawling experience, age, and other factors. It is likely that crawling experience plays a role in avoiding the cliff in human infants; the baby must have good visual control of locomotion, certainly as much as the kitten (see fig. 3.5).

This experiment reminds us again of the concept of affordance. The surface for locomotion on one side of the cliff presented a visually safe substrate for locomotion. For the other side, visual information specified an area to be avoided. How such information comes to be perceived and used is the chief problem to be dealt with in the following chapters. We shall rely heavily on observations of performance in natural and simulated situations that can tell us about development of perceived affordances in fulfilling the tasks of infancy over the first 2 years.

Summary

We began this chapter with a discussion of the flow of behavior, stressing its continuity and at the same time its segmentation into units of varied length,

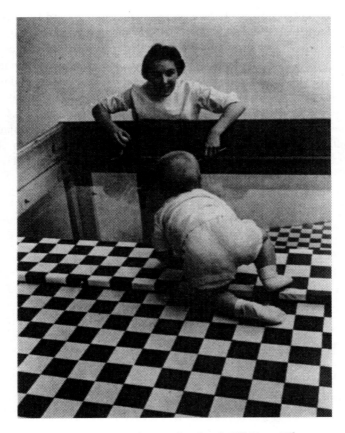

FIGURE 3.5. A human infant on the visual cliff. From "The Visual Cliff," by E.J. Gibson and R.D. Walk, 1960, *Scientific American, 202,* p. 65. Copyright © 1960 by Scientific American, Inc. Reprinted with permission.

some longer and some shorter ones embedded in organized fashion within the longer ones. We frequently refer to the longer units as tasks, meaning that they are initiated to serve some function and are terminated when an appropriate endpoint or goal is attained. In older children and adults, it is easy to mark task organization within the behavior flow, as goals become more specific and tasks are readily identified as intentional or perhaps required by external and social pressures. Identifying tasks in young infants is not so easily done, but natural requirements for maintaining a living organism in its environment are present from the beginning. These include making contact with the environment, getting information about it (exploratory activity), and acting on that information as the infant begins to learn about the affordances of the environment and how to control them.

Motivation for making contact with the environment and learning to perceive its affordances is spontaneous, intrinsic, and observable even in neonatal behavior. Psychologists have devised methods for making use of such motivation in experimental paradigms. We have presented examples of the major behavioral methods, showing how they can reveal the functioning of developing perceptual systems. We go on in the next chapters to investigate the way the perception-action cycles operate developmentally to furnish needed information about the affordances of surroundings, the effective powers of the infant to use them, and the evolution of tasks in more elaborated organizations of nested units. Perceptual learning about the world and the self is at the root of the whole story.

4

✦ ✧ ✦ ✧ ✦

Development and Learning in Infancy

Order in Developmental Tasks

The next three chapters are concerned with the three major, extensive tasks of infancy: learning to communicate with others, learning about objects and what they afford, and learning to move around in the world. These tasks have a natural order for their beginning. Communication comes first, because newborns are ready to look at and listen to their companions, and they are able and motivated to respond appropriately in limited ways; they can activate their facial musculature responsively, and they can vocalize. Attending to and learning about objects begins about 4 months later, when the action systems for reaching and manipulation are ready to go. Locomotion only begins at the half-year mark or later, when growth of the lower limbs makes crawling possible. Readiness of action systems promotes readiness to learn about new affordances. There are other constraints that combine to influence these processes, but babies are prepared to seek and attend to new information as it becomes available, and to learn to control their emerging action systems adaptively. Action systems lag behind sensory systems, so order of perceptual development during the first year is strongly influenced by the development of new possibilities for action.

We suggested earlier that learning can be studied most profitably in the context of continuous development, as it happens in real life. Perceptual learning is especially prominent during infancy, before language is available. We will take a close look at some tasks of infancy where learning is readily observed, in order to discover the essential conditions for learning and to uncover the role of other developmental factors in promoting it. Many developmental factors facilitate and constrain learning. Everyone knows that a day-old infant cannot be taught to speak a sentence or even a word. But perceptual learning about speech starts at least that early. We note here just a few of the structural and dynamic factors that have a prominent role in instigating and contributing to perceptual learning and development.

The Role of Posture

Posture is a constraining factor that exerts a prominent effect during the first year, limiting and pacing what an infant can learn about. All movement takes place on a background of posture, the whole body reorganizing for a single act like reaching and picking something up (Rochat & Senders, 1991; Rochat & Goubet, 1995). There must be prospective changes like tensing abdominal muscles and straightening the back before even a simple reach begins (see fig. 4.1). But posture is a long time developing and therefore necessarily sets limits for emergence of many new skills, among them reaching, grasping, and handling, and after that locomotion, skills that we will treat in some detail. Control of posture begins in the newborn with the head: newborns can move their eyes to look at an object (especially a moving one) and can rotate their heads if supported (though jerkily and with limited control) to assist in getting a glance to the right place. The precision of head turning to keep the gaze on a moving object increases between 11 and 28 weeks, when it reaches near adult control (Daniel and Lee, 1990). Head rotation happens for a moving object that can be followed with the eyes, and also at the instigation of a sound at one side of the head, an event that leads infants to open their eyes and turn toward the sound source. It has been shown (Amiel-Tison & Grenier, 1986) that providing support to a newborn baby's neck, head, and upper back when presenting a scene for visual pickup of information greatly facilitates the quality and amount of information the baby obtains.

Posture is a fundamental requirement for specific actions, because it functions to maintain the body in a stable relation to gravity. As an individual grows, this relationship changes. The legs acquire a greater mass with respect to the head and torso, and muscular growth takes place in the limbs. Activity of the growing parts, meanwhile, is spontaneous and becomes gradually more organized to achieve adaptive functions and control the movement.

Action systems develop on this background of posture, as bodily growth and postural control allow a new system to emerge and act on and in response to the environment. The reaching-grasping-handling system, for example, develops as the trunk and upper limbs permit individual limb and head function to differentiate and to be controlled independently. As this happens, infants begin to be interested in objects, to reach for them, bring them close, and obtain haptic information by handling. As control of the trunk gains strength and sitting without support becomes possible, the hands are freed for more elaborate exploratory and active uses. Eventually, as postural control extends to the legs,

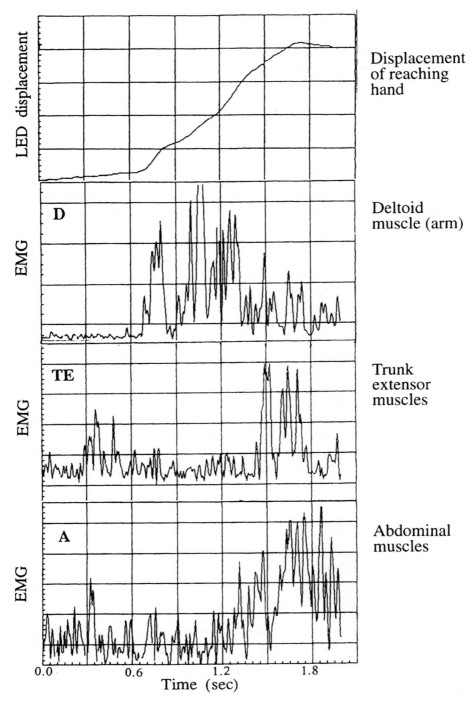

FIGURE 4.1. Postural preparation for reaching. From "Prospective Control: A Basic Aspect of Action Development," by C. von Hofsten, 1993, *Human Development, 36,* p. 263. Copyright © 1993 by S. Karger AG. Reprinted with permission.

locomotion becomes possible, first crawling, which is the less difficult balancing act, and finally upright locomotion, which demands virtuoso control of equilibrium of the whole body and at the same time opens up the world for exploration of its useful offerings and its geography.

The Perceptual Systems

As the body changes in its motor capacities for effective action, so do the *perceptual pick-up systems*. Major changes occur, especially in the visual system, resulting in more ways of obtaining optical information about the layout and the things and people in it. Acuity in the newborn infant is poor, especially in the foveal region, whereas the adult fovea is rich in cones and provides the sharpest focus for examining detail. During the first few months after birth, cells migrate toward the fovea from the peripheral retina, and acuity gradually improves (see Banks, 1988; Banks & Salapatek, 1983; Aslin, 1988). The peripheral areas of a neonate's retina are functional, however, and movement of objects in the nearby environment is detected quite well. Information for depth, at this early age, can be obtained from movement; but stereoscopic vision, which is dependent on foveal vision (both eyes necessarily focused on the same object), does not function adequately until 4 months or later (Held, Birch, & Gwiazda, 1980). Yet the young infant is by no means visually incompetent or impervious to depth, as the following experimental example makes clear.

P.J. Kellman (1984) investigated the development of three-dimensional form perception, comparing infants aged about 3.5 months with adults. Infants at this age generally do not perceive depth from static views, even when the static views are presented stereoscopically, but they are able to use information in optical transformations of objects—that is, the continuous optical transformation of an object over time—to detect the three-dimensional form of an object. Kellman showed that motion-produced transformations revealed an object's shape to the babies, whereas different static views did not, showing the importance of motion-carried information from the beginning (see chap. 6 for details).

Other changes that occur in the visual system include changes in thickness and shape of the lens, serving accommodation, and the position of the eyes in the head (the eyes grow farther apart, thus changing the angle of convergence of the two eyes). These changes in the visual system, we believe, are integrated with simultaneously occurring changes in the postural and finer motor systems as growth continues, before a new perceptual-motor system such as grasping a perceived object is ready to go.

There is growth of sensitivity in other perceptual systems, too: in the auditory system (see Aslin et al., 1983), touch (Kisilevsky, Stack, & Muir, 1991), the vestibular system, and perhaps smell and taste. We know much less about postnatal development of these systems, except for the auditory system. Hearing is quite well developed in newborns, however; in fact, hearing is sufficiently developed even before birth for a fetus to hear sound in the external world (see chap. 5).

This sketchy reference to development of some separate systems leads us to the process of development that relates the different perceptual systems to each other and to adaptive synergies of action. Such development characterizes multiple changes following birth. Organizations of perceptual and motor systems exist in a newborn, but big changes will occur as the baby grows older. As an example, consider development of occular-vestibular-kinesthetic-motor organization, a coordination of information from several perceptual systems with the muscular systems that enable us to control posture in relation to gravity. A human adult can stand or walk on two legs, maintaining an upright posture despite the pull of gravity. Information that makes this feat possible is provided by an interacting complex of perceptual systems—kinesthetic, vestibular, and visual.

Upright posture is very actively maintained, although as adults we are not usually aware of the small adjustments we are constantly making. We know that the visual system is normally of great importance in controlling these adjustments, from experiments devised by Lee (Lee, 1974; Lee & Aronson, 1974) in which conflict between the visual and the vestibular and kinesthetic systems was created by placing people in a small floorless room that actually moved around them (the "moving room" experiment). When the room is moved forward, "optical flow" patterns are created that inform one (incorrectly) that one is falling backward, despite the fact that the floor is still solid and unmoving. Adults respond by leaning forward, adjusting their posture to the visual stimulation. Lee and Aronson presented this situation to 12-month-old new walkers. These infants also made compensatory adjustments to room movement. In fact, young walkers tend to overcompensate and fall down as a consequence. B. Bertenthal and Bai (1989) found that 7- and 9-month-old infants who were not yet walking responded compensatorily when seated in such a room. Even neonates appear to be sensitive to optical flow (Jouen & Lepeqc, 1989). As new postural and action systems such as sitting and walking become active, multimodal information about oneself in relation to the environment must be organized within them.

Coordination of Perceptual Systems

Coordination of information among the perceptual systems is the rule at later ages, as we see, hear, and feel objects simultaneously in multimodally perceived events. Some coordinations exist at birth, but as new action systems come into play and more information becomes available from perceptual systems, learned adaptations occur in new organizations of behavior. These new organizations, eventually used in the service of realizing affordances offered by the environment, constitute important instances of perceptual learning. How this reorganization might occur has been studied in experiments subjecting adults to artificial rearrangement of optical information, for example, placing prisms over the eyes (E.J. Gibson, 1969; Hay & Pick, 1966), but there are few studies of its natural occurrence in development as anatomical structures change with growth. Many studies will show, however, the importance of multimodal information in directing attention to an event, even in very young infants.

Learning as a Developmental Process

The three following chapters concern the development of three modes of behavior that underlie and profoundly affect all the complex activities, both cognitive and performatory, that ensue as a human life progresses. These are communication with others; reaching for, manipulating, and using objects; and locomotion—getting around in the environment. In discussing these topics, we shall stress learning, showing how it is both instigated and constrained by maturing perceptual and action systems, and how it changes the relations of a developing baby with the environment. Learning always involves a change in the relation between an active organism and some affordance of the environment, especially the use of information about the environment in relation to the organism itself—its potential for perceiving and achieving the affordance. We call this "perceptual learning."

Learning can affect changes in task, in what is perceived, and in the form of an activity, both exploratory and performatory. The changes are typically toward greater *specificity*. A task, for example, may change from a very general goal of looking around (What is going on?) toward searching for a desired person or object, or toward making something specific happen, such as making a mobile twirl. The change may be an economical reduction in the information used to assess a situation offering a potential affordance, such as pushing or pressing a surface to test its supportability; or it may be a shift to an alternative means (a more adaptive action) to reach a desired object or place.

Learning in the course of development typically involves both perceptual and action change. Even if the change appears to be primarily in the form of the action, such as a motor skill, the action itself informs the perceiver about what is going on, as well as about himself or herself—what is being achieved—and thus introduces perceptual change and knowledge. In later cognitive learning, these changes may be too subtle for observers to detect, but during the first year they are often quite overt, giving us a unique opportunity to study the way learning occurs. (We address this question and offer a theory in chapter 8.)

The Environment

As big changes in perception and action occur during the first year, the accessible environment changes. A greater scope of action provides a broader world to explore, a world that is richer in information to be detected and that offers more potential affordances. Changes in the environment include important changes in the social environment. The social environment "acts back"; that is, it responds to an individual's own actions. As adults note that an infant is responding to their speech and is showing attention to objects, for example, they begin to provide objects for the baby's attention or grasp, and eventually they provide names for them. Adults create a special kind of learning environment for children, but it will become evident that even very young babies engage spontaneously in a vast amount of self-education. Locomotion for instance, is not taught by adults, is spontaneous on the part of the infant, and leads the infant on to new and crucial knowledge about surfaces, places, and obstacles, and about how to get to a desired spot in the world.

Organization of Chapters 5, 6, and 7

In the following three chapters, we present a great deal of substantive material on the development of communication, perceiving and using objects, and locomotion. There is a rich background of research to be set in an appropriate framework, so in each of these chapters, several common themes will be addressed. One theme is *what is to be perceived*. This theme includes the relevant properties offered by the environment and the information for them. A second theme has to do with *how this information is picked up*. What are the exploratory systems by means of which we search for and detect the information? A third theme is *what actions (or interactions) take place.* How do the action systems develop in relation to the environmental properties that support them, and what relevant affordances are thus provided to be learned about? These themes are inherent in the ecological approach. Finally, we consider the consequences for *knowledge*. It becomes clear that in the process of obtaining and acting upon the information presented, babies are at the same time obtaining information about the world for a *self* in *control*. The knowledge being acquired, in the end, pertains to that self acting adaptively in the world, which is what the ecological approach is about.

5

✦ ✧ ✦ ✧ ✦

What Infants Learn About

Communication

Human infants are born into a world in which they are completely dependent upon others to meet their needs and guarantee their survival. Yet newborns are by no means passive recipients of the nurturance of others. They are already active perceivers, and they are participants in social interactions from the start, creating conditions for learning from other people. Infants require many months to learn their language well enough to use it themselves, but communication nevertheless begins in the crib by other means. Although infants will not begin to use words until their second year, the groundwork for language learning begins to be laid even before birth. The human infant has a potential action system—use of the vocal cords for speech–although a long ontogenesis precedes making use of it with maximal effectiveness. This ontogenetic history has many aspects, including earlier means of communicating. Infants are receptive to information in communications by means of gesture, facial expression, vocalization, and action events that come to carry meaning, such as an adult putting the infant down and going away.

The human infant's total dependency on adult care makes social interaction imperative, and the baby has a role to play in keeping the care coming by interacting. Infants are motivated from the start to attend to kinds of information provided by adults and are even ready to respond actively to offers of engagement. We will consider the information available and responded to in communicative exchanges, and the means for communicating that are at infants' command during the first couple of years. The course of learning to communicate with others during infancy involves learning to act on the affordances offered by other people.

Readiness to Learn

By the time they are born, full-term human infants have been hearing certain sounds for several weeks (Querleu, Renard, Versyp, Paris-Delrue, & Crepin, 1988; Querleu, Renard, Boutteville, & Crepin, 1989), and they have already begun to learn about their social world. They can hear voices in utero, especially their mothers', but others too; for newborns just 1 day old their mothers' voices are more reinforcing of nonnutritive sucking than are their fathers' voices or the voice of another woman (A. DeCasper & Fifer, 1980; A. DeCasper & Prescott, 1984).

Besides learning to recognize their mothers' voices, infants learn other things in the speech they hear prenatally. For example, they recognize a story read aloud by their mothers before they were born. In an investigation by A. De-Casper and Spence (1986), twice daily during the last 6 weeks of pregnancy, mothers read aloud one of three stories. Following birth, their infants heard a tape recording either of their mothers reading both the story they had heard and another story, or of another woman reading both stories. Recognition was tested by reinforcing sucking with one or the other story tape. The stories heard prenatally were more reinforcing than were the stories the infants had not heard before. Furthermore, the infants showed the same preference for the familiar story whether they heard their mothers or a different woman reading them. After they are born, babies continue to learn about their mothers' voices as they are nurtured and cared for. By 1 month of age, babies have learned the unique intonation pattern of their mothers' voices; babies will suck to produce her voice if it has normal intonation, but not if it is monotonous (Mehler, Bertoncini, Barriere, & Jassik-Gerschenfeld, 1978).

Newborns have already learned to detect some characteristics of their native language. In the earliest investigation (Mehler, Jusczyk, Lambertz, Halsted, Bertoncini, & Amiel-Tison, 1988), 4-day-old French infants were habituated to a recording of a bilingual woman speaking either French or Russian. The infants who first listened to the woman speaking Russian subsequently dishabituated when they began to hear her speak their "native language," French. Another group of 4-day-old French infants listened to recordings of another bilingual woman speaking English and Italian. These infants did not dishabituate when they began to hear the woman speak in the second language. Thus, they discriminated between their own and a "foreign" language, but not between two foreign languages. In a subsequent investigation, Moon, Cooper, and Fifer (1993) assessed newborns' preference for their native language. Two-day-old infants, born to either Spanish-speaking or English-speaking mothers, participated in a contingent reinforcement procedure in which they listened to recordings of a woman speaking Spanish or English. The infants engaged in longer sucking bursts when listening to their native language than to the non-native language.

It is interesting to consider what information these newborns could have picked up that generalized to other voices, even voices speaking different words. Nazzi, Bertoncini, and Mehler (1998) have found that newborn French infants discriminated between sentences from "foreign" languages belonging to different rhythmic "classes" (Japanese and English), but not between sentences from "foreign" languages belonging to the same rhythmic class (Dutch and English). Four different female native speakers of each language produced the recorded sentences, so the infants' discrimination (or lack thereof) was not based on specific speaker characteristics. The characteristic tonal patterns and rhythms of the utterances must be responsible, since symbolic meanings of the language could play no role. These patterns exist only over time and evidently have invariant properties that appear recurrently, can be detected by the newborn infant, and are recognizable after birth in another speaker. This is convincing evidence both that information for perception is given over time, and that there is perceptual pickup of properties that are invariant and abstract from the beginning

Neonatal Exploratory Systems for Detecting Information for Communication

As with inanimate objects and events, information specifying other people is multimodal and redundant. Babies come to know their mothers by looking, by listening, and even by smelling. Infants who are being breast-fed learn to discriminate the unique odor of their own mothers' breast pads from those of other lactating mothers within the first few days of postnatal life (Porter, Cernoch, & McLaughlin, 1983). Breast-fed infants also orient longer to their mothers' axillary (armpit) odors than to the odors from other lactating as well as nonlactating mothers at least as early as 2 weeks of age (Cernoch & Porter, 1985).

More than a decade ago, it was reported that newborn infants recognized their mothers' faces by sight after having spent only a few hours with them (T. Field, Cohen, Garcia, & Greenberg, 1984). In the procedure of this study, the infants were first presented sequentially with their mothers' and strangers' live faces, and they looked longer at their mothers' faces. Next, the babies were habituated to their mothers' faces, and in the dishabituation phase of the procedure, they looked longer at the strangers' than at their mothers' faces. Another group of investigators suggested that the newborns' apparent visual recognition of their mothers might, instead, be recognition of their odor, since, as we have seen, breast-fed infants do recognize their mothers by means of smell at a young age. However, when an olfactory "mask" (air freshener) was used, precluding recognition by means of smell, the babies still looked longer at their mothers' than at the strangers' faces (I. Bushnell, Sai, & Mullin, 1989). Furthermore, when the women's odors were not masked, but their faces were occluded by gauze, the infants did not discriminate between their mothers' and others' faces.

How might infants detect information specifying their mothers' faces in the hours after birth? We may see here evidence of very early coordination of visual and auditory exploratory systems. Since babies begin learning about their mothers' voices even before they are born, their early interactions with their mothers, hearing her voice as they are held up to her face, may facilitate their attention to her face as the apparent source of her voice. An investigation of somewhat older infants' recognition of their mothers' faces, accompanied or not by their voices, provides an example of such coordination of visual and auditory exploration (Burnham, 1993). Infants aged 1, 3, and 5 months were videorecorded while participating in a visual-preference procedure with their mothers and strangers. The infants saw their mother and a stranger seated side by side in front of them. On no-speech trials, the mother's and stranger's faces were inert and their expressions neutral. On speech trials, their faces were accompanied by the precorded voice of mother or stranger reciting an excerpt from a nursery rhyme, while both faces were seen silently miming synchrony with the sound track. The video displays of the infants were then shown to adult observers, who were told to watch the infants and decide where their mothers had been sitting, that is, to the infants' right or left. When they watched displays of the 1- and 3-month-olds, the observers were more accurate when the faces had been accompanied by voices, especially when the sound tracks had been the mothers' rather than the strangers' voices. The infants were responding to their mothers' voices and not just to their lip movements. Observers more accurately judged "Where is Mother?" when watching babies who could hear their mothers' voices while seeing their faces, than when watching babies seeing their mothers' and strangers' silent faces with lips moving. Thus, voices can be said to recruit young infants' visual attention to their sources, providing circumstances for exploring and learning. The infants' responsiveness to their mothers' speaking faces is evident by the observers' successful judgments of where the infants' mothers had been located. It seems natural that these two aspects of one person should be united in specifying an important affordance for an infant, as well as allowing differentiation from others.

Information for Social Objects and Events

Even newborn infants behave in ways that encourage speech directed toward them. They afford being communicated with. Rheingold and Adams (1980) recorded samples of speech to newborns in a hospital nursery, and they observed that most of the staff—both men and women—talked to the infants, making extensive, grammatically well-formed comments on the infants' characteristics and behavior, and on what the adults were doing.

The Special Attraction of "Motherese"

When adults interact with and communicate with infants, they typically speak in a manner sometimes termed "motherese." Such infant-directed speech differs from ordinary adult-directed speech in having somewhat higher pitch, wider pitch range, exaggerated intonation, and slower tempo (Fernald & Simon, 1984; Fernald, 1985; Cooper & Aslin, 1990). This speech has special appeal for infants and may function to maintain infants' engagement in interaction with caregivers.

Fernald (1985) recorded samples of several mothers talking to their infants and talking to another adult. Then, using an operant auditory preference procedure in which head turning produced speech samples, she found that 4-month-olds showed a marked preference for listening to infant-directed speech compared to adult-directed speech. In a more recent investigation, Cooper and Aslin (1990) found that infants prefer infant-directed speech at an even younger age. Their measure of preference was infants' looking time at a checkerboard pattern when it produced either infant-directed or adult-directed speech. One-month-old infants, and even newborns, looked longer at the pattern when it was the apparent source of infant-directed speech.

How widespread is infant-directed speech as the manner in which adults interact with young infants? Is it specific to a particular language or culture? Fernald, Taeschner, Dunn, Papousek, Boysson-Bardies, and Fukui (1989) conducted a cross-language study for which they recorded samples of mothers and fathers speaking to their month-old infants and speaking to another adult. The adults were native speakers of one of six languages: French, Italian, German, Japanese, British English, and American English. Across all six languages, both mothers and fathers spoke with higher and more variable fundamental frequency, shorter utterances, and longer pauses when speaking to their infants. There were also differences; mothers, but not fathers, used a greater fundamental frequency range when speaking to their infants. What was striking, however, was the remarkable similarity in the manner in which adults across these languages spoke to their infants. Grieser and Kuhl (1988) found similar features in samples of Mandarin Chinese mothers talking to their 2-month-old infants and to adults. The infant-directed speech of these mothers, too, was characterized by higher and wider range of fundamental frequency, shorter utterances, and longer pauses than in adult-directed speech. Thus even in this tonal language, in which differences in pitch contour convey differences in word meaning, higher and wider-ranging fundamental frequencies are features of the special manner in which mothers talk to their infants.

What are the specific acoustic features of infant-directed speech that affect infants' preference for such speech? Fernald and Kuhl (1987), using an operant auditory preference procedure, assessed 4-month-old infants' preferences for samples of infant-directed and adult-directed speech in which one or another characteristic feature had been isolated and other features eliminated. The features tested were fundamental frequency pattern, amplitude pattern, and duration pattern. The infants demonstrated a preference for the fundamental frequency pattern of infant-directed speech compared to adult-directed speech, but they showed no preference for the amplitude or duration patterns of infant-directed speech.

Cooper and Aslin (1994), using the measure of fixation time to a checkerboard pattern, found that, although 1-month-olds could discriminate the isolated fundamental frequency pattern of infant-directed speech from that of adult-directed speech, they did not look longer when they could listen to the isolated fundamental frequency pattern of infant-directed speech. However, these young infants did show a preference for a natural recording of infant-directed speech compared to the recording of its fundamental frequency. Thus, it seems to be a characteristic quality of a human voice that functions early to engage infants' attention.

Initially, it is the mother's voice that is special. Cooper, Abraham, Berman, and Staska (1997) found that 1-month-olds who prefer infant-directed speech spoken by a stranger show no preference between infant-directed and adult-directed speech spoken by their own mothers. By 4 months of age, infants do show preference for their mothers' infant-directed compared to adult-directed speech. The preference for their own mothers' infant-directed speech develops in the context of communication and caretaking interactions during the early months.

What is the specific appeal for young infants of infant-directed speech? What function does it serve for maintaining caretaker-infant interaction, and what meanings are conveyed by it? Fernald (1984) suggested that the characteristic pitch contours of infant-directed speech elicit infants' attention. She also noted that high and wide-ranging fundamental frequencies are associated with emotional activation and suggested that the appeal, for infants, of infant-directed speech may be its affective expressive characteristic (Fernald & Kuhl, 1987, p. 291).

The intonation patterns of mothers' infant-directed speech vary depending on what they are trying to achieve in interacting with their young infants. When soothing infants, mothers use more falling than rising pitch contours; when eliciting eye contact and their infants' attention, mothers use more rising than falling pitch contours; when maintaining infants' attention and positive affect, mothers' contours are bell shaped (Stern, Spieker, Barnett, & MacKain, 1983).

Fernald (1989) hypothesized that mothers' communicative intent is conveyed in the intonation patterns of infant-directed speech. She recorded speech samples of mothers and fathers when talking to their 10- to 14-month-old infants and to another adult in five different situations: soliciting attention, prohibiting some action, conveying approval, comforting, and playing a game. The content of the samples was filtered out, so only the rhythm and intonation patterns could be heard. After the five situations were described to a group of adults, they listened to the samples and judged with which situation each speech excerpt was concerned. They were more accurate at judging what intention was conveyed in the infant-directed speech samples than in the adult-directed speech samples. In fact, their accuracy was not better than chance for

some of the adult-directed speech samples. Meaning is carried by verbal semantic content to a much greater extent in speech directed to adults than in
speech directed to infants. For infants, the intonation patterns or "melodies" of
others' speech to them are the first sound-meaning correspondences detected.

The intonation patterns conveying intent in infant-directed speech are not
specific to American English. J. Papousek, Papousek, and Symmes (1991) videorecorded interactions of American and Mandarin Chinese mothers and their 2-
month-old infants in several naturally occurring situations: encouraging infants' attention, turn taking, and play; discouraging some behavior; or soothing
infants. Acoustic analyses of the mothers' speech revealed characteristic intonation patterns quite specific to the mothers' different intentions. Further, those
intonation patterns were similar in American English and the tonal Mandarin
Chinese language. Long before infants begin to acquire linguistic meaning specific to their language, they participate actively in communicating with their
caregivers in vocal interactions in which meaning is exchanged, and intentions
are conveyed and responded to. This is a prime example of perception and action engaged in the attainment of a major affordance of a baby's environment.

Facial and Vocal Affective Expressions

The affective expressiveness of caregivers and others toward infants has important meaning for infants. Mother's happy, loving face and voice afford soothing and comfort for an infant, whereas angry or fearful voices and facial expressions may portend avoidance or distress for an infant, or perhaps being
seized suddenly, or being handled roughly or without comfortable support. Perceiving affect in others directed to oneself is an important achievement, and infants begin to develop sensitivity to vocal and facial affective expressions from
an early age. There is information for affective meaning in the intonation,
rhythm, and stress patterns of speech, and infants as young as 3 months discriminate some vocal affective expressions. Using a habituation procedure,
A. Walker-Andrews and Grolnick (1983) presented 3- and 5-month-old infants
with either a happy or sad vocal expression along with a slide of a concordant
happy or sad face. After habituating to one vocal expression, half of the infants
were presented with the other vocal expression while they continued to see the
same face. Infants of both ages increased their looking when the vocal expression changed, demonstrating they differentiated the two vocal expressions.

Babies even younger than 3 months have been found to discriminate among
facial-vocal affective expressions displayed by their own mothers. Haviland and
Lelwica (1987) observed 10-week-old infants' reactions when their mothers displayed joy, anger, and sadness. The infants responded systematically differently
to their mothers' different expressions. They expressed joy to their mothers' joy-
ful expressions; they increased their mouthing movements to their mothers' sad
expressions; and they ceased moving and sometimes expressed anger (or burst

into tears and had to be removed from the situation and be soothed) to their mothers' angry expressions.

By several months of age, infants respond to some vocal expressions of meaning conveyed by speakers of their own as well as of unfamiliar languages. Fernald (1993) presented 5-month-olds from English-speaking homes with excerpts of adult females vocalizing approval or disapproval in English, Italian, or German. The infants showed positive affect when hearing infant-directed speech expressing approval in all three languages, and they showed negative affect when hearing infant-directed speech expressing disapproval in the same languages. The infants were not differentially responsive to adult-directed affective-expressive vocalizations. Thus, the infants gave evidence of having learned to perceive the meaning of the special kind of affective-expressive speech they hear in communicative encounters.

Some investigators have suggested that infants discriminate affective expressiveness of voices prior to discriminating vocal and facial affective expressiveness (e.g., A. Caron, Caron, & McLean, 1988). However, A.S. Walker-Andrews and Lennon (1991) noted that the experimental circumstances in which young infants have shown discrimination of vocal affective expressions have included slides or photographs of faces that the infants watched while hearing the vocal expressions. These experimenters further demonstrated that 5-month-olds' discrimination of happy and angry vocal expressions depended on the presence of appropriate facial representations. When the infants could look only at a checkerboard display, they did not differentiate the vocal affective expressions. Thus, it seems likely that—rather than perceiving voices and faces as distinct entities and then associating them—young infants come to perceive the affordances of the multimodal communicative events in which they participate. These affordances, made available in the context of social interactions, include caregivers conveying the same affective expression through facial and other bodily gesture and concomitant vocalization.

Walker-Andrews's earlier research on the development of intermodal perception of expressive behaviors established that during the first several months, infants develop sensitivity to information specifying correspondence of adults' facial and vocal affective expressions. By 5 months, infants look longer at a video display of an actress's facial expression that is synchronous with a sound track conveying the same affect (e.g., happiness or anger) vocally (Walker, 1982). By 7 months, infants show the same preferential looking behavior even when the sound track is asynchronous with the ongoing facial/gestural expression of the same affect (Walker, 1982). Thus, these older infants detect correspondences specific to the meaning of the ongoing event in addition to the synchrony of the visual and vocal affective expressiveness. They are differentiating the information specifying the affordance of the event rather than simply matching visible lip movements and voice sounds, since when the lower portion of the actress's face was occluded, 7-month-olds still looked preferentially and appropriately at actresses expressing happy and angry affect (A. Walker-Andrews, 1986).

By the second half-year of life, infants distinguish happy and angry expressive behaviors on the basis of information specific to these important communicative events. Soken and Pick (1992) showed 7-month-olds point-light displays of actresses expressing happy or angry affect. A point-light display (Johansson, 1950) is a visual display that is dark or homogeneous except for points of light placed on muscles or joints. The display is moving in some characteristic way, but no pictorial details are present. The infants simultaneously heard sound tracks of different actresses expressing one or the other affect vocally. Since the infants saw only patterns of moving lights specifying the facial gesturing of one actress while they heard the voice of another actress, any preferential looking at the concordant displays would have to be based on facial motions specific to each of the two affects. The infants did show appropriate preferential looking at the concordant displays. Thus, they distinguished happy and angry facial expressions on the basis of facial motion information, while the intermodal correspondences they detected were specific to happy and angry expressions conveyed by different persons.

The affective expressiveness of adults in communication events with young infants conveys important information for the infants' well-being, and infants learn to perceive these expressions and their meaning in the faces and voices of those with whom they interact. By 7 months, they distinguish angry and happy expressive behavior communicated by different persons (Soken & Pick, 1992). Are these infants distinguishing positive from negative affective expressiveness in general? Or are they sensitive to information specific to particular affective expressions? Soken and Pick (1999) concluded that, at least by 7 months, infants distinguish among vocal-facial affective expressions of happiness, anger, sadness, and interest. An important topic for future research would be the development of this specificity of intermodal perception of affective expressions during the first months of life. As they participate in communication bouts with caregivers, do infants first broadly distinguish expressions of positive and negative affect conveyed by caregivers, along with what those expressions portend for themselves? Or do infants learn the meaning of specific affective expressions from the start? Perhaps both go on as development proceeds by processes of differentiation on the one hand and unification on the other.

In addition to the properties discussed, infants continue to learn to perceive many properties of people that are relevant for their own behavior and nurturance. For example, by 4 months of age, babies show sensitivity to intermodal information specifying facial gender (A. Walker-Andrews, Bahrick, Raglioni, & Diaz, 1991). Infants were presented with video displays of faces of a man and a woman speaking accompanied by synchronous sound tracks of the man's or the woman's voice. Both 4- and 6-month-old infants demonstrated significant looking to the sound-specified faces of appropriate gender. Also, 4- and 7-month-olds are sensitive to intermodal information specifying adult and child faces and voices of the same gender (Bahrick, Netto, & Hernandez-Reif, 1998).

Development of Communicative Actions and Interactions

Early Imitation of Voices and Gestures

The active participation of infants in interacting with others is strikingly revealed in a particular mode of interacting, namely imitating. The actions of infants imitating others' gestures demonstrates the coordination of perceiving and acting from an early age. One of the first investigations of infants imitating vocalizations concerned pitch matching (Kessen, Levine, & Wendrich, 1979). For the procedure of this study, experimenters and mothers engaged in a variety of vocalization exchanges involving pitch-matching with the mothers' 3- to 6-month-old infants in the laboratory and at home. The procedure extended over several weeks and involved three standard pitches, all within the infants' normal vocalization range. The data for analysis were 15-minute audiorecorded segments, obtained in the laboratory, of presentations of an adult's vocalized pitch sounds followed by the infant's vocalization. A group of professional music teachers rated the match or mismatch of the infants' vocalizations. Strikingly, all of the infants had more pitch matches than mismatches and vocalized at the presented pitch significantly frequently. The investigators noted that the infants were actively engaged in the task; they "watched the experimenter closely and they vocalized to her often and energetically" (Kessen et al., 1979, p. 96). The interaction and turn taking of this imitation task appeared to promote focused communication between infant and adult.

That infants' imitation of adults' vocalizations is an essentially social-communicative action is apparent from a more recent investigation of the role of vision and audition in young infants' imitation of adults' speech sounds (Legerstee, 1990). Three- to four-month-old infants heard audiotaped sequences of one or the other of two vowel sounds. Following each sequence of presentations of a vowel was a silent period during which the infants' vocalizations were recorded. Simultaneous with the audio presentation, the infants saw a female adult silently and synchronously mouthing either the vowel being presented, or the alternative vowel. Half of the infants participated in the matched condition, and half in the mismatched condition. Only the infants in the matched condition imitated the vowels they heard, demonstrating the importance of inter-modal information for eliciting infants' speech production as well as for their perception of speech (e.g., P. Kuhl & Meltzoff, 1984). For the infants, detecting the correspondences of facial mouthing and vocal information may serve to engage them to attend closely to the adult with whom they are interacting.

When and in what circumstances do infants begin to imitate? Meltzoff and Moore presented the first empirical report of visual (gestural) imitation by newborn infants (Meltzoff & Moore, 1977). Their report was greeted with some skepticism, but within a few years, it was firmly established that even newborns will, indeed, imitate some gestures they see others perform. The particular gestures the babies imitated in Meltzoff and Moore's study were mouth opening and closing, and tongue protrusion and withdrawal (Meltzoff & Moore, 1983). In a subsequent study by the same investigators, newborns also imitated head movements, demonstrating that their gestural imitation is not restricted to oral actions (Meltzoff & Moore, 1989).

The general procedure used by Meltzoff and Moore involves an adult modeling a gesture for the baby for a period of time, followed by a period when the adult's face remains passive, followed by another modeling period. Some investigators have used a somewhat different and less successful procedure in which the adult models a gesture continuously. Meltzoff and Moore (1989) suggested that infants may detect a disruption of ongoing activity when the adult who has been gesturing becomes passive. If so, then matching the adults' gesture may function, for the infants, to reengage the interaction. In other words, in this interaction situation, the passive phase encourages the infants' participation more than when the adult continuously displays the gesture.

Newborn infants have to see the gestural action itself, not a static display of it, in order to imitate it. Vintner (1986), using a procedure like that of Meltzoff and Moore, presented newborns either with gestural actions of tongue protrusion and hand opening, or with static versions of the same gestures, that is, a protruded tongue and an open hand. Only the infants who saw the gestural actions imitated them. The infants shown the static displays visually fixated the facial and manual models, but they did not imitate them. Within a few months however, infants do imitate static displays produced by a live model (Meltzoff & Moore, 1992).

For infants to imitate actions, the actions must be those of a person, not of an object. Legerstee (1991) conducted a study with older infants (5- to 8 months old) who watched an adult engaging in tongue protrusions and mouth openings, or an object presenting similar actions. Only the infants who watched the person gesturing produced the same gestures, demonstrating that for them the context for imitation is one of social interaction and communication.

Can we be more specific about how infants are communicating when they imitate adults' gestures? We have already noted the turn-taking aspect of the circumstances in which young infants' imitation is most easily elicited. Meltzoff and Moore have suggested that infants are engaging or "probing" the adult with whom they are interacting when they mimic the adult's gestures (1992, p. 483). Their studies involved 6-week-old infants, their mothers, and a male stranger, with the mothers and stranger each modeling one of two gestures, mouth opening and tongue protrusion, in succession. In pilot work, the investigators observed that frequently when the second adult appeared, the infants imitated the gesture modeled by the first adult, especially when the infants had not watched that adult going out of view. The procedure of a subsequent experiment ensured that the infants would watch the first adult come into view from one side of the testing room and, after the gesturing phase was completed, go out of view on the other side of the testing room, followed by the second adult coming into view from that side. In these circumstances the infants matched the gestures of each adult present more frequently than they reproduced the gestures of the out-of-sight adult. In retrospect, these findings are consistent with the suggestion that the infants in the pilot study who had not seen the first adult go out of view and the second adult come into view were reproducing the first adult's gestures to engage the second adult. The infants acted in an exploratory way so as to promote communication with and know the adult, as if to ask, "Are you a tongue protruder? Will you communicate?" Jones (1996) has recently argued that young infants' matching of adults' oral gestures is a precursor to the kinds of exploratory actions infants will engage in when they can reach for objects and bring them to their mouths.

Face-to-face Interaction

Young infants gaze at their mothers' faces during communication events. It is clear that the communication events in which infants learn to perceive affective expressions of their caregivers are not settings in which the infants are passive recipients of those affective expressions, conveyed to them by adults. From early on, infants are active participants in face-to-face interaction, and there is bidirectional influence on the organization of such events (fig. 5.1). Condon and Sander (1974) provided some of the first observations of coordinated face-to-face interactions of caregivers and newborns. They conducted frame-by-frame analyses of filmed episodes of parents speaking to their infants and described the infants' behavior as being tightly synchronized with and entrained by the adults' speech. Although the description of infant-parent communicative events as precisely synchronized has been disputed by more recent observational analyses (e.g., Cohn & Tronick, 1987; Fogel, 1988), the coordinated nature of such interactions is clear. Infants as young as 6 weeks become distressed if their mothers interrupt face-to-face interaction by becoming passive and nonresponsive, but not if their mothers interrupt face-to-face interaction as though their attention has temporarily turned to something (or someone) else (Murray & Trevarthan, 1988).

Cohn and Tronick (1987, 1988) observed face-to-face interaction episodes in 3-, 6-, and 9-month-old infants and their mothers. The regulation of the interactions varied across this age range. For example, the interactions with 3-month-olds began when the infants looked at their mothers and when looking was reciprocated by the mothers. However, the mothers of 6- and 9- month-old infants elicited their infants' attention to initiate an interaction. The mothers of the infants at the two youngest ages assumed a positive expression prior to their infants' assuming a positive expression, but infants at the oldest age were equally likely to become positive prior to their mothers. In any case, the mothers and

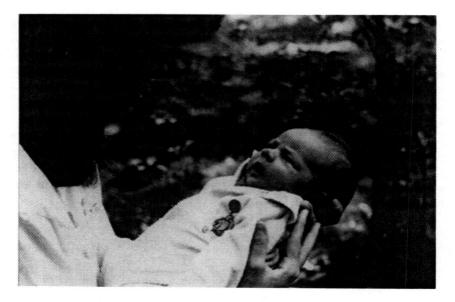

FIGURE 5.1. Interaction of mother and 6-week-old infant. Note the eye-to-eye directed gaze and and mouth opening of both participants. Photo courtesy of Sally Ann Carey.

infants did not change affective states simultaneously, as would be suggested by Condon and Sander's entrainment hypothesis. Rather the dyadic system is characterized by mutual behavior regulation with considerable variability inherent in the organization (Fogel, 1988).

Not only does the nature of the regulation of mother-infant face-to-face interaction change over the course of the first few months of life, but the roles of the participants in early interactions anticipate how interactions are subsequently regulated. Gable and Isabella (1992) observed infants interacting with their mothers first when the infants were just 1 month old, and the same infants later when they were 4 months old. Some of the mothers' regulatory actions (state and level of physical activity) with their one-month-olds were positively associated with the infants' own arousal regulation in terms of gaze behavior and affective expression at 4 months.

Infants' interactions with caregivers become finely tuned during the first year in ways that are perceivable (if not describable) by observers of those interactions. Frye, Rawling, Moore, and Myers (1983) recorded silent 1-minute episodes of infants 3 and 10 months old who were alone or in the presence of their mother or an object displayed by their unseen mother. In the latter cases, the mother or object was either passive or interacting with the infants. At both ages, observers watching displays of the episodes could discern whether or not the infants were alone, whether they were in the presence of an active or passive object/person, and whether their interaction was a greeting (first 20 sec of the episode) or a withdrawal (last 20 sec of the episode). At 10 months, but not at 3 months, observers could also discern whether the infants were with an object or their mother. In the "object" conditions, the object was made to interact (or be passive) by the mother, so the object/mother distinction made by observers of 10-month olds may reflect the observers' sensitivity to infants' responses to active inanimate versus animate objects.

Infants' participation in "protocommunication" interactions with caregivers is also reflected in systematic facial, vocal, arm, and hand activity (Fogel & Hannan, 1985). Legerstee, Corter, and Kienapple (1990) recorded the facial, hand, and arm actions of infants engaged in interpersonal and nonsocial interactions. The infants were observed longitudinally from 9 to 15 weeks of age as they interacted with their passive and active mother, and with a passive and active doll. In the latter case, the suspended doll danced and sounded when the infants looked at it. When the mothers were active, talking to their babies as though at home, the babies pointed while smiling and gazing and opened their hands while gazing with a neutral expression. When the mothers were passive, the babies closed their hands with their arms at their sides while facially expressing distress, and when they vocalized, they curled their hands with their arms at their sides. With objects—both passive and active—the babies gazed with a neutral expression and showed a variety of hand and arm gestures. Even at the youngest age, the infants showed different organized facial, hand, and arm actions in the social and nonsocial contexts.

In the course of their first months of life, infants acquire sensitivity to the typical interaction contingencies that are specific to their own interactions with their mothers (and presumably also the contingencies of their interactions with their fathers). Bigelow (1998) observed 4- and 5- month-old infants interacting with their mothers and with strangers. She found that the infants were most responsive to strangers, in terms of smiling and vocalizing, when the strangers' degree of contingent responsiveness was most like that of the infants' own mothers.

What are infants learning about themselves as they become skilled participants in social interactions with their caregivers? Face-to-face interactions provide opportunities for young infants to use their facial, vocal, and arm and hand actions, and to learn about their consequences for reciprocal regulation of the ongoing interaction. The adult participants in these interactions can disrupt infants' opportunities for acting on affordances for interpersonal interaction, for example, by becoming passive or nonresponsive, and they can enhance infants' learning affordances of interaction by their actions to initiate and maintain dialogue (Fogel & Thelen, 1987; Weinberg & Tronick, 1994, 1996).

Infants' emerging skill at controlling their own posture and actions contributes to the nature of their participation in face-to-face interactions with caregivers. Fogel, Dedo, and McEwen (1992) observed 3 to 6-month-old infants interacting with their mothers while the infants were sitting in infant seats, reclining (at 45°), or lying supine. The infants looked most at their mothers' faces when they were lying down, and least when they were sitting upright. Further, infants who could reach looked less often at their mothers' faces than infants who could not yet control reaching for objects. Had there been objects (toys) available, it is likely that the older, reaching babies would have demonstrated their newly emerging exploratory skills.

The Emergence of Joint Visual Attention

Joint visual attention, the circumstance in dyadic interaction when infant and adult can direct their gaze toward the same object or event, is an important achievement of the latter part of infants' first year and the beginning of their second year. The establishment of joint visual attention is important because it provides a basis for further communication and learning, both language learning and learning about the affordances of the object of shared attention.

Joint visual attention involves coordinating attention toward a partner and toward the object or event of mutual interest, and it appears to evolve from young infants' participation in face-to-face interaction, in the following period of intense exploration of objects (see chapter 6), and finally, in coordinated attention with a partner to an interesting object or event. Bakeman and Adamson (1984) observed systematic developmental changes in how infants from 6 to 18 months and their mothers interact with toys. The youngest infants were often engrossed in exploring the toys, showing little attention to their mothers. Conversely, these youngest infants showed more engagement with their mothers only (without the object) than did the older infants. As infants' engagement with their mothers only declined with age, the infants' coordinated joint activity with their mothers and with the toys increased with age. The infants also engaged in more coordinated joint activity with their mothers than when a same-age peer was their partner, suggesting that their mothers supported or promoted joint coordination.

Early in the achievement of joint visual attention, infants' caregivers will follow the infants' gaze, adjusting their gaze to look where the infant looks in order to maintain the shared experience (Collis & Schaffer, 1975; Collis, 1977). Infants as young as 2 months have been reported to readjust their gaze to look toward an object their caregivers are attending to (Scaife & Bruner, 1975; Butterworth & Grover, 1990). Later work sets about 10 months as the age when joint visual attention reliably appears (Corkum & Moore, 1998). Once again, we see that infants' interactions with others are characterized by coordination and reciprocity.

From many experimental investigations of the development of joint visual attention, it has been found that infants can direct their gaze toward a location in front of them toward which their caregiver is looking before they will direct their gaze toward a location outside of their visual field, for example, behind them (Butterworth & Cochran, 1980; Butterworth & Grover, 1990; Butterworth & Jarrett, 1991). Butterworth has argued that infants initially do not represent space outside of their immediate visual fields, that is, they do not appear to know that interesting objects or events might be located out of their sight, and until they do acquire this representational understanding, they do not follow another's gaze to look for an object not presently in their view (Butterworth, 1991). However, recent findings suggest that infants are not disposed to look behind themselves in this case because the caretaker's gesture toward an out-of-sight object is difficult to discern (Deak, Flom, & Pick, in press). In the usual experimental situation for observing joint visual attention, the adult and infant sit facing each other. In this circumstance, when the adult gestures toward an object behind the infant, the adult's deviation from gazing directly at the infant is minimal compared to when the adult gestures toward an object in front of the infant. However, when 12- and 18-month-olds and their caregivers are seated at right angles to each other, the infants are as likely to look at an object behind them as at one in front of them, when the adult's gestures are of equivalent magnitude.

In many early experimental investigations of the emergence of joint visual attention, the adult indicated the intended object of attention simply by gaze direction, and the question was asked whether infants could follow the adults' line of gaze. Not surprisingly, when adults point to as well as look toward the intended object of joint attention, infants are more likely to follow the adults' gesture and achieve joint attention (e.g., Butterworth & Grover, 1990; Deak, Flom, & Pick, 1995). However, the development of comprehension of the pointing gesture is itself an achievement of young infants in the service of communicating with the adults and others in their world. Infants of 6 to 9 months of age are as likely to look at their mother's finger when she points to an object as in the direction of the object itself; by 12 months, infants understand the indicational nature of finger pointing and can follow the direction of their mother's point to look at the object (Butterworth & Grover, 1990). Such pointing is itself a social, communicative gesture. Leung and Rheingold (1981) noted that 1-year-old infants typically look toward where others point, and they also have learned they can direct others' attention by pointing. Furthermore, such pointing rarely occurs silently; rather infants vocalize and look toward the adult whose attention they seek to direct by pointing.

Achieving control of coordinated attention with another sets the stage for sustained exploration and learning about the object of shared attention. There is abundant evidence that language learning is promoted in the context of shared attention. For example, Tomasello and Farrar (1986) observed naturalistic interactions and conversations of infants at 15 and 21 months of age with their mothers. During episodes of joint visual attention, the mothers and their children engaged in longer conversations with longer utterances than during episodes not characterized by joint visual attention. Joint attention enables infants to know what object in a cluttered array is being referred to by an adult who is labeling it or talking about it. Baldwin (1991) investigated the function of joint visual attention in new-word learning by infants 16 to 19 months old. The infants participated in two conditions: in one, they were told the names of unfamiliar objects when they and the experimenter were both attending to the same object. In a second condition, the infants were told the name of an unfamiliar object when the experimenter was looking at that object but the infant was attending to another object. Thus, the infants in the first condition were engaged in joint visual attention whereas those in the second condition were not. The infants learned the new names only in the first condition. More important, the infants in the second condition did *not* apply the new name to the object *they* had been looking at when they first heard it. They perceived the *adults'* line of regard and understood its relevance for knowing the referents of new object names.

Social Referencing

The achievement of joint visual attention—the coordination of attention toward both a social partner and an object or event of mutual interest—provides infants with a new means of using their social partner to regulate their own activity. This manner of using the caregiver to regulate the infants' own activity is illustrated by the phenomenon known as "social referencing," in which infants use their caregivers' facial affective expressions to modulate or regulate their own actions. Sorce, Emde, Campos, and Klinnert (1985) experimentally investigated infants' use of social referencing to regulate their own behavior in the well-known visual cliff situation. Twelve-month-olds were placed on the shallow side of a visual cliff while their mothers faced them from the other side, smiled, and encouraged them to proceed toward an attractive toy located near the mother. The optical depth of the "deep" side of the cliff was 30 cm, a drop-off distance ambiguous for affording safe crossing or falling for most crawling 12-month-olds. When the infants approached the drop-off, most hesitated and looked back and forth between the lowered surface and their mothers' faces. At this point the mothers posed a static affective expression (which they had previously practiced under an experimenter's guidance): either happiness, fear, interest, anger, or sadness. None of the infants whose mothers posed fear crossed to the deep side, and most retreated from the edge. Likewise, nearly all of the infants whose mothers posed anger paused and then retreated. Conversely, most of the infants whose mothers posed happiness or interest proceeded across the divide to retrieve the toy and join their mothers. The infants whose mothers posed sadness provide an interesting illustration that the infants are not simply responding to their mothers' positive or negative affect but instead are using the meaning of the specific affective expression in relation to the circumstances to guide their own behavior. Although some infants whose mothers posed sadness eventually crossed the cliff (more than in either the anger or fear conditions), most continued to look back and forth between their mothers' faces and their potential path of locomotion over the cliff. Sadness conveys no clear meaning in this situation—neither promoting nor prohibiting continued locomotion—and the infants acted as though they were searching for the meaning of their mothers' affect in relation to their ongoing behavior.

One other condition of this study (Sorce et al., 1985) further demonstrates that the infants were not simply responding to their mothers' affective expressions in an associative fashion but rather were using those expressions to regulate their own ongoing activity in relation to the cliff situation. A new group of babies participated in a condition in which their mothers posed a static fear expression as before, but in which the cliff was "shallow," obviously affording safe crossing. In this situation, most babies showed no social referencing but simply crossed over the cliff and proceeded toward their mothers and the toys. Furthermore, those babies who did pause at the edge to look back and forth at their mothers' fearful faces and at the path of locomotion simply proceeded to cross over the cliff. Perceiving safe passageway to the goals of mother and toy guided the infants' locomotion toward those goals, and their progress was unimpeded by their mothers' conveying otherwise.

Instrumental Use of Others: Learning Control

From an early age, infants play an active role in managing structured interactions with adults, and their actions clearly serve a communicative function. Ross and Lollis (1987) observed infant-adult pairs longitudinally at four ages: 9 months, 12 months, 15 months, and 18 months. At each session the adults engaged the infants in a series of structured games such as peekaboo, and stack and topple blocks. Periodically, each game was interrupted by the adults' failure to take a turn, and the infants' communicative actions during interrupted and noninterrupted phases were observed. At all ages the infants increased their communicative behavior during the interrupted phases. Their actions were many and varied. Overall, during the interrupted phases, the infants did more vocalizing to the adults, alternating gaze between adult and toy, touching or pointing to the adult, showing or giving the toy to the adult, and repeating their own or the adult's turn.

The infants' behaviors reflect their perceiving the game as involving coordination of their own and another's actions on the objects. During the noninterrupted phases, the infants smiled more and directed more laughter toward the adults than in the interrupted phases of the games. The number of actions during the interrupted phases as well as the variety of actions increased developmentally. Thus at the youngest age, the infants frequently alternated gaze between adult and toy and touched or pointed to the adults. At the oldest age, they were likely to usurp the adult's turn or give the toy to the adult, both examples of increasing clarity of the communicative actions. But even the youngest infants' actions reflect intentions to promote coordinated or joint action. Mosier and Rogoff (1994) have recently documented that infants as young as 6 months use adults (their mothers) as agents for gaining access to an out-of-reach toy or for demonstrating how a toy works.

Infants' instrumental use of others in social interactions with objects may serve multiple functions for infants learning about objects. First, information about the action possibilities, the affordances of the objects, are revealed, and communicative interaction about the object and its affordances are facilitated. Further, coordinated social actions themselves—passing a ball back and forth, stacking and restacking blocks—may emphasize circumstances in which learning about objects and events is enhanced, promoting the development of the infants' own exploratory actions. Such coordinated social interaction with objects also promotes the learning of social routines, for example, that offering a toy to another is followed by "thanking." Thus, the action possibilities infants learn in communicative interaction contexts are many and varied.

Imitating Actions on Objects

Imitation is a specific kind of learning that sometimes occurs in contexts of communicative interaction. When we considered young infants' imitation of others' oral gestures (mouth opening and tongue protrusion) earlier in this chapter, we suggested (following Meltzoff & Moore, 1992; S. Jones, 1996) that matching others' gestures may be a rudimentary means of exploring others and engaging their attention and communication. The fact that infants imitate others' gestures also emphasizes the close coupling of perceiving and acting. At least by late in the first year, infants can learn too how to perform specific actions on objects by watching others. This kind of learning has also been called learning by imitation, or observational learning, and it demonstrates the significance of interaction with others as a context in which learning about affordances of objects takes place (see chap. 10).

Meltzoff has conducted the most extensive investigations of infants learning specific ways of interacting with objects by observing others' actions. In an early study (Meltzoff, 1985), 14- and 24-month-olds watched an experimenter perform a specific action with an unfamiliar toy—the adult pulled the toy apart and put it back together several times. Then the children were presented with the same toy either immediately or after 24 hours, and their actions on the object were observed. Children of both ages were highly likely to perform the same action on the object, both immediately and after 24 hours. But might they not have performed the same action without having seen the adult do it? Meltzoff typically uses two control conditions to help interpret what it is the children have learned. In one condition, the children are simply presented with the object to see what they will do with it on their own (baseline control condtion). In a second condition, an adult manipulates the object (e.g., moves it through a circular path several times) but does not perform the "target" action (specific functional use) with it (the "adult manipulation" control condition). Thus, this condition tells us what infants will learn about the object by seeing it manipulated, but not in the specific way that other infants see someone acting on it.

The children in the imitation conditions—both immediate and deferred—showed a reliably higher frequency of the specific target action on the object than did children in either control condition. Thus, the children in the imitation conditions learned the specific behaviors by watching them performed by the adult. In other studies, Meltzoff has found that 14- and 24-month-olds can learn to pu'l apart and put together an unfamiliar toy by observing a video display of an adult performing the action (Meltzoff, 1988a), and that 14-month-olds (and presumably older children as well) can perform observed target actions performed by a live adult after a delay of one week (Meltzoff, 1988b). In the latter study, the children initially observed different actions on each of six objects. One week later, most of the children in the imitation condition (11 of 12) performed appropriate target actions on at least three of the six objects.

What is being communicated to and learned by the children in the imitation conditions of these studies? The target actions are functions specific to each object, but are the children learning entirely novel ways of acting on objects? We suggest not. Rather, the opportunity of observing another perform the actions promotes realizing the utility of a behavior for an observed consequence. It provides a way of emphasizing a specific means to an end and thus enhancing the possibility that the infants will perceive and act on it. It is a way of learning a functional relation that might, over time, be detected without the adult's modeling. The control conditions of Meltzoff's (1988b) study provide interesting evidence for this interpretation of what infants learn by observing others acting in specific ways on objects. Most of the infants in the two control conditions performed some of the target actions on some of the objects (8 of 12 infants in the baseline control condition, and 9 of 12 infants in the adult manipulation condition). Furthermore, some of the specific actions on objects (e.g., pushing a button on a particular toy) were performed nearly as frequently by infants in one or the other control condition as by infants in the imitation condition. One target action, making a toy bear dance, was performed more frequently (though not significantly more) by infants in the adult manipulation control condition than by infants in the imitation condition. Thus, it seems the imitation condition provides opportunity to discover a specific affordance for an object that may not be discovered at once through the infants' own initial exploratory actions with the objects. An important way of discovering affordances of objects is observing others realizing the affordances in the course of interacting with objects. Discovering the affordance of a tool is a case in point (see chap. 10).

Meltzoff (1988c) has further shown that even 9-month-old infants can learn to perform specific actions on at least three different objects and can act on those affordances at least 24 hours after first observing them performed. Bauer (1996) and her colleagues have shown that infants of 12 months can learn and perform a specific sequence of actions on objects after seeing the sequence modeled several weeks earlier. Thus, from an early age, observing others acting to produce an event—using a specific means to an end—facilitates discovery and learning how to produce and reproduce that event oneself.

Observational learning to perform actions on objects is quite sophisticated behavior that presupposes infants' capability to reach for, obtain, and manipulate objects, as well as to perceive properties of objects that identify them and specify their affordances. Social interaction at the level of observational learning about objects and their uses must be preceded by development of infants' ability to perform actions on objects. In the next chapter we will consider the development of perception and action in infants' attainment of object use.

Perceptual Learning in the Linguistic Environment

Early in life, infants can distinguish many, perhaps all, of the basic speech sounds, or phones, used in human languages. Initially, infants are sensitive both to the phonetic contrasts that are meaningful in the language they hear around them, and to those that are not. During the first year, however, infants' speech sound discrimination becomes more selective, reflecting their particular linguistic environment (P. Kuhl, Williams, Lacerda, Stevens, & Lindblom, 1992). Polka and Werker (1994) used an infant head-turn procedure to assess 6- to 8-month-olds' and 10- to 12-month-olds' sensitivity to two German vowel contrasts. The infants' families were English-speaking, and the contrasts distinguished meaning in German, but not in English. Most of the younger infants, but few of the older infants, were able to achieve a discrimination criterion for the German contrasts. However, both the younger and older infants achieved a discrimination criterion with English contrasts. In a second experiment, 4-month-olds and 6-month-olds participated in a habituation-dishabituation procedure using the same contrasts. Both groups discriminated the English contrasts, but only the younger group showed evidence of discriminating the German contrasts. Similar results have been found across language communities, and for consonant contrasts as well as vowel contrasts (P. Kuhl et al., 1992; Werker, Gilbert, Humphrey, & Tees, 1981; Werker & Tees, 1984; Werker, 1989). During the second half of the first year, infants discriminate speech sounds with increasing selectivity and specificity to the language they hear around them and will eventually learn to speak. Their earlier sensitivity to all speech sounds develops toward sensitivity to those sounds relevant for communicating in their own language.

During the second half-year of life, infants differentiate other features of adults' vocalization in communication with them. One example is a pause at a clause boundary, which is a more consistent feature of infant-directed speech than of adult-directed speech (Broen, 1972). These pauses might help infants segment the speech directed to them, and there is evidence that clauses do become perceivable units for infants. Hirsh-Pasek, Nelson, Jusczyk, Cassidy, Druss, and Kennedy (1987) recorded episodes of a mother interacting with and telling stories to her young daughter. Then two types of excerpts were constructed from these episodes. The "natural" excerpt that began and ended at a sentence boundary had 1-second pauses inserted at all clause boundaries. The "unnatural" excerpt that began and ended midclause had 1-second pauses inserted between words in the middle of the clause. Seven- to ten-month-old infants listened to the two types of excerpts played from speakers at either side of their heads, and they showed a clear preference for the natural excerpts by orienting to them much longer than to the unnatural excerpts. These infants detected and differentiated units in a mother's speech that would be relevant for their subsequent language learning.

Young infants not only hear people talking to each other and to them but see people talking as well. Information about at least two aspects of speech is made available by watching a speaker's lips and mouth. Mouth openings and closings correspond to syllable rhythm. Place of articulation of phonetic units is also discernible by watching mouth movements (P. Kuhl & Meltzoff, 1984). Adults are sensitive to the intermodal information for these specific aspects of speech, and by the time infants are about 5 months old, they also detect this information. P. Kuhl and Meltzoff (1984) presented young infants with side-by-side video displays of the faces of two female talkers, each articulating a different vowel in synchrony. Sequences of one or the other vowel, synchronous with the talking faces, were heard from a speaker midway between the two displays. The infants looked at the faces throughout most of the procedure, but they looked significantly longer at the faces corresponding to the vowels they heard than at the faces inconsistent with the heard vowels. Thus, they demonstrated knowledge that these specific speech sounds are produced by mouths moving in a corresponding manner. That the speech sounds the infants heard directed their looking was demonstrated in a second experiment in which the video displays were presented silently, accompanied by pure tones preserving some of the vowel characteristics. Specifically, they preserved the temporal characteristics and amplitude pattern of the original vowels. The tones became louder as the mouths opened wider, and less loud as the mouths were closing. In these circumstances, infants again looked at the faces throughout the procedure, but they showed no preferential looking at one or the other face. Thus, the infants' sound-specified looking in the first experiment was based on the spectral rather than temporal characteristics of the vowels they heard. Subsequent studies have extended these effects to other vowel sounds (P. Kuhl & Meltzoff, 1988).

In studies designed to identify the specific speech sound information sufficient to detect the correspondence between intermodal mouth movement and speech sounds, P. Kuhl, Williams, and Meltzoff (1991) presented adults and infants with side-by-side talking faces, and sound tracks of single features of the vowels. Adults, but not infants, showed sound-specified looking in these conditions. Thus, during the first half-year of life, infants *learn* to recognize correspondences of speech sounds and mouth movements. They will gradually further differentiate these correspondences, becoming able to detect invariants of mouth movements and speech sounds when presented with only minimal information for them. But even the infants in these studies demonstrated the results of their perceptual learning by detecting the correspondences in the presence of incomplete information, since what they saw were video representations of faces rather than the solid, live faces themselves. Mastery of one's native language is clearly grounded in the early months of life as infants' perception of speech directed toward themselves as well as others becomes both more selective and more differentiated, a nice example of perceptual learning.

What Is Learned: Affordances and Consequences for Knowledge

Well before they learn to speak, and from their earliest days, human infants are learning to participate in the world of other people. Infants differentiate themselves from others, discovering, anticipating, and promoting responsiveness of their partners in interactions. Infants learn to discern the emotions and moods of their caregivers, which have prospective meaning for what will happen next. From the consequences of others' facial and vocal expressions for the infants and their well-being, they are learning about intentionality in their reciprocal interactions with their caregivers, both their own intentionality and that of others. For example, by 6 months, infants distinguish between "comforting" and "approving" verbalizations of adults directed toward them (Moore, Spence, & Katz, 1997). Thus, they detect the meaning in the verbalization that specifies the current mutual relationship in an ongoing interaction with a caregiver. Finally, as infants achieve capability for regulating and controlling interactions themselves, they begin to learn about properties of objects and events, as well as people, through communicative interaction. What infants learn about objects and what they afford is the topic to which we now turn.

6

◆ ◇ ◆ ◇ ◆

What Infants Learn About

Interaction with Objects

We have seen that infants engage in perceptual learning that promotes communication with other people even before they are born, and that they respond actively to other human beings and initiate communications themselves, soon after birth. The case is different, however, for inanimate objects, for the first several months of an infant's life. Objects become easily accessible as infants gain control of reaching and manipulation. They become the focus of intense scrutiny and exploratory activity as new actions become possible, making new affordances discoverable. Very young infants do engage in exploratory activity by means of mouthing, and they feel substances like hair and blankets with their fingers, but active engagement in displacement and lifting waits upon development of manual control. Nevertheless, infants are surrounded by objects and perceive many of their properties as their first lessons in learning about the world. Impressive research in recent years has shown us that babies pick up information specifying *properties* of objects surprisingly early, often long before they are able to use them as specification for the *affordances* the objects offer to more mature members of the species. Perception often waits on development of posture and action systems to discover and act on the affordances of objects.

We describe first the astonishing discoveries of recent developmental research on infants' perception of object properties and then go on to discuss how perception of affordances develops, relating properties that specify objects to the child's developing abilities. Finally, we refer briefly to the controversy over when a child perceives the continuity of objects—the fact that they continue to exist over time although they may be presently out of sight, hearing, or touch.

Properties of Objects and the Information for Them

Material objects, said James Gibson, are "substances in the solid state . . . specified by the textures and contours of the optic array. . . . There is internal pattern, . . . shape as well as contour, . . . colour, . . . [patterns of] deformation of
contour and internal pattern which may specify [them] as animate. . . . In so far
as an animal can discriminate these variables of the optic array, he can discriminate the properties of objects which render them not only bump-into-able
and walk-on-able, but also . . . get-underneath-able, or edible, or likely to cause
pain" (J.J. Gibson, 1958, p. 190). These latter are the affordances of the object
that render them meaningful, as well as specific in terms of the object's properties in relation to the abilities of the animal.

Consider briefly what defines an object. Objects are *detachable*, segregated
from the self, external, and located in the world. They are not only detachable,
they are *moveable* and can be in different places. Their moveability separates
them both from the self and from the surfaces of the permanent layout on which
they rest and are located. Since they are located somewhere, they take up space,
have *solidity* or three-dimensionality. They are *segregated* from other objects.
Just as all objects have solidity, they also have *unity* or wholeness, and when
objects move, they move as a unit. An object with parts may have parts that
move in such a way as to deform its contour (in which case it may be *animate*),
but it all moves together if it changes location. Objects vary in *size* (an important property for growing infants), in *substance*, in *shape* or contour, in *weight*
and *temperature*, in *noise-making* properties (related, of course, to substance,
animacy, and other properties), and in surface properties such as *texture* and
color. We discuss research on some of these properties as they are detected early in life, keeping in mind that objects are moveable and stressing the role of
motion of both object and perceiver in detecting information for an object's
properties.

Unity

All objects possess unity. All their parts move together when they move or are
moved. They are, furthermore, perceived as a unit, as a whole. They have surfaces, like the layout of a place, but the surfaces are closed and continuous, making a single object. There has long been a controversy among psychologists over
whether learning is required to perceive that an object is a unit or whether the
wholeness of an object is perceptually primitive, as Gestalt psychologists maintained. Research with infants has centered on a paradigm in which an infant is
presented with an object in motion with a portion of it covered (see fig. 6.1). The
infant is allowed to gaze at the object for a time, and then presented with a
choice between the whole, unbroken object no longer occluded, and two segments of the object with a break where the occluder covered the original. If the

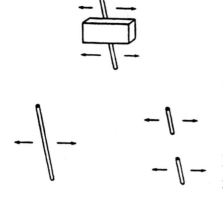

FIGURE 6.1. Objects used in demonstration of perceived unity of partly occluded object by 4-month-old infants. From "Perception of Partly Occluded Objects in Infancy," by P.J. Kellman and E.S. Spelke, 1983, in *Cognitive Psychology, 15*, p. 489. Copyright © 1983 by the Academic Press, Inc. Reprinted with permission.

baby gazes longer at the broken figure, presumably the object was perceived as a unit and the infant is surprised at the break. P.J. Kellman and Spelke (1983), observing 4-month-old infants, found that they looked longer at the broken object (a rod), evidently having perceived the occluded, moving rod as a whole. Control infants who were habituated to a stationary occluded rod, on the other hand, showed no preference for gazing at either the whole or the broken display, even when the parts were of similar shape and color and were aligned behind the occluder.

Motion of the occluded object is an essential condition for revealing its true unity to infants of 4 or 5 months. As long as the visible pieces of the occluded object in the habituation display undergo common motion, the infants dishabituate to the broken display. If the visible parts of the occluded object are seen to move separately, or if they are presented in static displays, then the infants do not appear to perceive the unity of the object. The infants detect common and independent motion of surfaces, perceiving a unified object in the first circumstance and not in the second (E. Spelke, 1988). In general, motions of objects or movements of the observer are crucial for revealing valid, permanent properties of an object and its layout.

Other experimenters have confirmed these results and have attempted to determine whether even younger infants detect unity of a moving, partially occluded object. Newborn infants (A. Slater, Johnson, Brown, & Badenoch, 1996) do not appear to perceive the unity of the occluded moving object, and in fact they look longer at an unbroken rod during the test period. By 2 months, however, infants give evidence of perceiving the unity of the occluded rod, given ample information for a depth difference between rod and occluder, a small occluder, and good motion information (S.P. Johnson and Aslin, 1995).

Perception of object unity with partial occlusion of the object thus develops during the early months. It is not yet known however, whether objects in full view and unoccluded are perceived as units from an earlier age. By 4 months at least, infants perceive the unity of bounded objects that move relative to their background or that can be seen as separated in depth relative to the perceiver (von Hofsten & Spelke, 1985). By this time, infants have had every opportunity to observe that an object moves as a unit, whatever its configuration, and in fact continues to be single and whole when they themselves are moving, still segregated from themselves and from other objects.

Adults generally perceive even stationary, partially occluded objects as units, given good continuation of contour and shared surface coloring and texture. Ability to use static information to perceive unity was found by Craton (1996) to develop at about 6.5 months, but infants did not use information such as edge alignment and contour to perceive the forms of an occluded object until 8 months. Ability to use different kinds of information to detect object properties develops at different times during the first year of life, with motion information having priority. Perceiving an object as segregated from another is specified by separate movement of the object before an infant can actively explore manually.

Segregation

If an object is perceived as a unit, it is presumably also perceived as segregated from other nearby objects. Separate movement, as discussed, would effectively segregate an object from an array of things. However, discrete objects in an array are normally perceived as segregated from surfaces surrounding them even when they are not in motion. Individual objects have boundaries and occupy a different space from nearby objects. They generally have some distinctive features that they do not share with other objects around them. It appears, however, that infants use features such as shape, color, or texture considerably later than motion information both for perceiving objects as units and for segregating objects (P.J. Kellman & Spelke, 1983; Craton, 1996).

A number of experiments have investigated the detection of two objects as segregated or attached in infants of 3.5 to 4.5 months. The typical measure used for an infant's perception of segregation has been a "surprise" response: time of looking at *movement* of two objects separately, or as a single unit, following familiarization with the pair in a *stationary* presentation. Looking time is presumably longer, for example, for a pair of objects perceived as a single unit, then observed to move apart separately.

On the whole, infants younger than 4 months tend to view stationary, contiguous surfaces as a single unit, and discontinuous surfaces as separate. From 4 months, a number of experiments suggest that information about features (color, shape, texture) may begin to play a role in perceived segregation. Visual attention to objects plays a role by 5 months and probably earlier with very familiar objects.

Recent examples of experiments of this genre are Needham (1998) and Needham and Baillargeon (1998). Needham (1998) performed developmental comparisons of infants' use of information about features to segregate adjacent objects, asking at what point between 4 and 8 months of age infants begin to use dissimilar features of two adjacent objects to perceive them as two distinct units. Infants were shown a display of a yellow zigzag-edged cylinder next to a tall blue box. After a familiarization period, the infants saw the two objects either move together when one was pulled or move apart when one was pulled, leaving the other stationary. Infants were assumed to look longer when the incident violated their expectations than when it confirmed them. In this experiment, 6.5-month-old infants looked equally long at both events, but at 7.5 months, infants looked longer when the objects moved together, presumably expecting them to move separately. In a further experiment, Needham used simpler objects in a comparable procedure with 6.5- and 4.5-month-old infants. Both groups were apparently able to segregate the objects (of both contrasting shape and color) into separate units. Needham concluded that they could make use of "configural knowledge" in perceiving objects as segregated units. They expected "different-looking surfaces" to belong to different units.

The experiments by Needham and Baillargeon (1998) investigated the role of infants' prior experience with an object in their ability to segregate it from another. Infants of 4.5 months were shown a cylinder next to a tall blue box. Following a brief familiarization with the two adjacent objects, a hand appeared and pulled the cylinder, in one instance moving it away from the box and in another, drawing the box with it. Time of looking at these incidents was equal, suggesting that the infants had no preliminary expectation of separate objects or a single one. But when infants were shown either object alone for 5 to 15 seconds before the two test events, they looked longer when the objects moved together, evidently perceiving them as separate objects. This expectation was confirmed even when the tests occurred 24 hours later, leading the authors to conclude that experience with a single object played a role in segregating it from an adjacent object in a later demonstration.

It seems, then, that infants before 4 to 4.5 months, when they begin to handle and explore objects, do not decompose an array of objects into segregated units on the basis of featural differences, whereas they begin to do so between 4.5 and 6.5 months. Prior experience with one of the objects, even in a different setting, facilitates segregation of the object from an adjacent one as early as 4.5 months. Normal experience with objects in daily use seems likely to render these objects easily perceptible as segregated units by the time a baby is ready to reach for things.

A related and even more interesting question concerns whether infants perceive *themselves* as separate, independent units, segregated from the layout and the objects in the world around them. Independent motion appears to facilitate segregation of an object from a surrounding array. What happens when an infant is moved? Do infants distinguish object motions from their own movements? Do objects in the layout appear to move with them? Or are objects in the surround identified as separate and located? A very clever experiment tells us

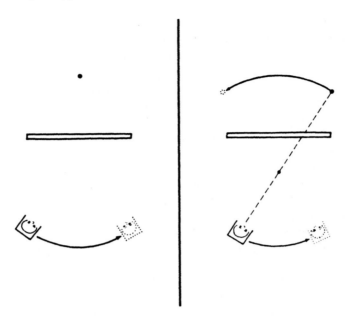

FIGURE 6.2. Conditions used for demonstration of differentiation of object and observer motion; infants perceived own motions as separate from moving objects (Kellman, Gleitman, & Spelke, 1987). Figure from "Kinematic Foundations of Infant Visual Perception," by P.J. Kellman, 1993, in C.E. Granrud (Ed.), *Visual Perception in Infancy* (p. 133), Hillsdale, NJ: Erlbaum. Reprinted with permission.

that, at least by 4 months, the latter is the case. P. Kellman, Gleitman, and Spelke (1987) habituated 4-month-old infants to a rod moving behind an occluder. But this time, the infants were moving also. They were seated in moveable chairs that swung back and forth in an arc as they viewed the occluded, moving rod (fig. 6.2). After habituation they were tested alternately with an unoccluded complete rod, or an unoccluded display with two separate pieces of rod. A second group of infants had the same tests, except that they had been habituated, while being moved, to a stationary occluded rod. Since the rod and the occluder were separated in depth, the rod underwent an optical (but not real) displacement from the moving infants' viewing position. Results of the tests showed that these infants could distinguish real motion of the occluded rod from optical displacement produced by their own movement, since the group observing real movement looked longer at the broken rod, as expected, whereas infants shown the static rod did not. The infants, furthermore, looked longer when shown the moving rod during habituation, as would be expected if they detected real motion of the object. Perception of unity thus depended on real motion. By 4 months, infants do indeed perceive objects as segregated from themselves and can detect their own and objects' real movements in space.

It was discovered some years ago that not only do infants perceive objects as segregated from each other, they also discriminate visually between arrays of objects differing in number. Strauss and Curtis (1981) found that, by about 1 year, infants distinguished between arrays of two versus three items. In their experiment, 10- and 12-month-olds were habituated to a series of slides in which the type of item varied as well as size and spatial arrangement, but the number of items remained the same. The infants subsequently dishabituated to displays in which the number of items changed—from two items to three, or from three items to two. Other differences in number (three vs. four, or four vs. five) were discriminated by the infants.

In a more recent study of infants' visual perception of number, van Loosbroek and Smitsman (1990) assessed 5-, 8-, or 13-month-olds' discrimination of number in displays of randomly moving figures. Using a habituation procedure, these investigators found that even the youngest infants discriminated small number differences, and that by 8 months, the infants discriminated differences of four versus three and four versus five. This is another example of the importance of object motion in revealing object properties to young infants.

Solidity

The experiments on segregation tell us that objects are seen as occupying a unique place in the layout, different from the infants' own and from that of other objects. Are the objects themselves also perceived as solid and three-dimensional? If so, what is the information? Once again, we find that motion of the object, such as being turned over or moved to another location, plays a role. An experiment by P.J. Kellman (1984) with 16-week-old infants provides convincing proof that these infants perceived the three-dimensional property of objects, provided that kinematic (motion) information was available. Kellman habituated infants to videotaped displays of a single object rotating in depth. Two different axes of rotation were alternated during habituation, with the same object always rotating. After habituation, the infants were tested with a videotape of the same object rotating in a new (third) axis, or with a videotape of a different object rotating around the same axis. The optical representations of the habituated object were thus different, although the object remained the same. To test the role of motion, the kinematic condition was compared with two groups of infants shown sequential stationary views of the same objects, all taken from the rotation sequences at 60° intervals or at 15° intervals (see fig. 6.3). The results demonstrated clearly that infants who were habituated to the kinematic condition generalized to the same object in the new rotation, gazing longer at a new object, whatever its axis of rotation. In contrast, the infants who were habituat-

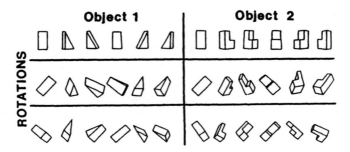

FIGURE 6.3. Schematic views of objects and axes of rotation used in demonstration of perceived object solidity. All views in the same column are of a single object; views in the same row are from a single axis of rotation. From "Perception of Three Dimensional Form by Human Infants," by P.J. Kellman, 1984, *Perception and Psychophysics, 36*, p. 355. Copyright © 1984 by the Psychonomic Society, Inc. Reprinted with permission.

ed to stationary sequences of the same objects showed no difference in response to the new test object compared to the old one in a new rotation. This result held even for static views 15° apart.

Would a similar result hold if the object itself does not move, but the observer obtains a continuously changing view of it by moving around it, thus providing the same motion perspective information? Kellman and Short (1987a) investigated this question by rotating infants in a chair that moved in an arc around a stationary object. The 16-week-old infants again generalized habituation to the same object presented in a new rotation, but not to a novel object; nor did they differentiate objects when presented with multiple static transformations of the object.

Solidity may also be detected by means of stereoscopic information (binocular disparity), but this information is not used before 4 months, at the earliest (Held, Birch, & Gwiazda, 1980). Infants who are sensitive to disparity (stereoscopic information) are already sensitive to kinetic information for depth (Yonas, Arterberry, & Granrud, 1987). Kinetic information providing a view of continuous transformations is of primary importance in development of object perception.

Size

The size of an object is obviously of importance to an infant beginning to reach out for things. How early are size differences among objects discriminated? As objects move toward or away from a viewer, or the viewer toward or away from objects, the visual angles subtended by the objects change, although of course their sizes do not. The objects' changing distances must be detected in relation to their constant sizes. Studies of size constancy over spatial displacements of an object have confirmed that infants as young as 18 weeks detect true size (see Day, 1987, for a summary).

Even newborns have been found to detect the size differences among otherwise identical objects located at varying distances (Granrud, 1987; A. Slater, Mattock, & Brown, 1990). Slater, Mattock, and Brown (1990) familiarized infants visually to either a small or a large cube placed at varying distances over a number of presentations. Following familiarization, both cubes were presented in a test trial, located so that they subtended equal visual angles. No matter which cube had been familiarized, infants gazed longer at the novel one. Since the cubes were stationary on each trial, no object motion information for distance was provided. However, the infants' own eye-head movements would have provided information for the relative distance away from themselves of the two objects. It may be that convergence (turning inward of the two eyes to focus on nearer objects) also is informative from birth, although evidence for its operation before 8 weeks is weak (P.J. Kellman & von Hofsten, 1992).

Size of an object can be detected haptically as well as visually. Small objects can be mouthed and size differences (of nipples, say) detected. When objects can be grasped, by 5 months or so, information for size can be actively obtained manually. We return to this ability shortly when we discuss development of exploratory activity.

Substance

The substance of an object, even more than its size, is apt to be revealed by way of haptic information, for example, whether an object is soft or hard, squishy or rigid. Young infants can and do obtain information for substance by mouthing. Rochat (1983) found that infants could detect differences between nipples varying in substance and rigidity at 1 month; by 3 months, they could distinguish nipples varying in shape or contour, as well.

Rochat (1987) compared newborns' discrimination of object substances by means of their mouths and their hands. He presented the infants with either a hard plastic object or a soft sponge-rubber object. For different groups of infants, the object was placed in their mouths or in their hands, and the infants' "squeezing" actions on the objects were recorded via pressure transducers attached to the objects. The infants squeezed the elastic object more than the rigid object with their mouths, but they squeezed the rigid objects more than the elastic object with their hands. Thus, the infants responded differently to the object substances, and their differential responding was specific to the two exploratory action systems—manual and oral. Newborns' early mouthing actions are dominated by sucking, and a spongy object provides better affordances for sucking than does a rigid object. Conversely, newborns' manual actions are more or less limited to grasping and clinging, and they exerted more such actions on the rigid than on the elastic object.

Substances can often be differentiated visually as well as haptically. Fabrics can be seen to differ by certain surface properties such as texture and reflection. However, the best optical information for substance is provided by applying pressure to the substance, thus displaying its resistance by the type of motion resulting. Hard substances move only rigidly, resisting deformation, whereas soft substances deform, exhibiting elasticity.

The difference between elastic and rigid substances can be detected through information given in the contrasting optical transformations by infants at 5 and even 3 months (E.J. Gibson, Owsley, & Johnston, 1978). Infants were shown a display of a foam-rubber object that could be manipulated so as to produce either rigid motion or deformation in different patterns. In one experiment infants were habituated to three rigid motions from a set of four (rotation in the frontal plane, rotation around the vertical axis, rotation around the horizontal axis, or looming, that is, displacement on the axis perpendicular to the infant). Following habituation to the three rigid motions, the infant was presented with displays of the fourth (as yet unseen) rigid motion, and of an elastic motion produced by squeezing the object. A pretest had revealed the two as equally interesting, but in the posttest the elastic motion elicited significantly longer looking times, indicating generalization of the four types of rigid motion. A comparable experiment habituating infants to different examples of deforming motion indicated generalization of motions characteristic of elastic substance (Walker, Owsley, Megaw-Nyce, Gibson, & Bahrick, 1980).

As further evidence for visual detection of these contrasting properties of substance, the shape (contour) of the object undergoing rigid motion was changed following habituation (E.J. Gibson, Owsley, Walker, & Megaw-Nyce, 1979). For one group of infants, the same rigid motion habituated was continued; for a second group, a new rigid motion was presented; and for a third, a deforming motion was presented. Habituation persisted for both groups presented with a rigid motion, despite the shape change, but there was dishabituation to the deforming motion. In a second experiment infants were habituated to one object undergoing two different rigid motions, followed by a different object undergoing the same rigid motions. The infants dishabituated to the new object, showing that they were in fact capable of distinguishing a shape change.

Not only can object substances be differentiated visually, as well as haptically, but substantial properties are often—perhaps most often—detected by means of more than one modality simultaneously. An experiment by L. Bahrick (1987) demonstrated young infants' differentiation of object substances by sight and by sound. Infants from 3 to 6–7 months saw and heard two objects in motion. Both objects were clear cylinders; one contained one large marble and the other contained several small marbles. As the objects were rotated repeatedly, the sounds of the marbles impacting the bottom surface differed, reflecting their differing composition (one vs. many marbles). Likewise, the visible impacts of the marbles in the two objects differed, as one or multiple marbles were seen hitting the bottom surface. In various conditions, the sound tracks of the event were presented in synchrony with or asynchronous with the visible event. Bahrick found that the older infants, but not the younger infants differentiated the objects' substances when the objects were seen and heard impacting the surface in synchrony as well as when the visible and audible impacts were asynchronous. These results document once again the importance of object motion as information for infants' perception of object properties.

Shape

Shape, or contour, refers to the surface layout of an object (J.J. Gibson, 1979). The experiment of E.J. Gibson and others (1979) discussed earlier (as well as P.J. Kellman's 1984 experiment, also discussed) indicates that infants detect an object's shape even as the object is undergoing perspective transformations that result in optical change. In other words, the object's shape is perceived as invariant or constant under motion transformation. The mean age of the infants in the experiment of E.J. Gibson et al. (1979) was about 3 months. Those infants perceived both the substance of the object and its shape, both the type of motion specifying substance and the continuous series of perspective transformations revealing the invariant shape of the object.

Shape constancy has been demonstrated by other investigators in infants of 3 or 4 months (A.J. Caron, Caron, & Carlson, 1979). Bornstein, Krinsky, and Benasich (1986) habituated infants to an object slanted at varying orientations and found that the infants subsequently discriminated the same object in a new orientation from a different object at the same slant. They also showed that the infants could discriminate relatively fine differences in object slant after the object had been presented repeatedly at one slant.

Shape constancy may even be present in newborns. A.M. Slater and Morrison (1985) familiarized newborns with a square presented at different slants over a number of trials. Familiarization was followed by a looking preference test, the square in a different slant contrasted with a trapezium. The infants looked preferentially at the novel shape. Object rotation in depth, a perspective transformation, can apparently be detected at birth. It is not clear what the information is, at that time, for detecting the change in slant, but it is clear that the baby is perceiving a world laid out in depth, containing moveable, solid objects.

Shape can be detected manually as well, by 5 months or so. We return to this subject shortly as we discuss exploratory activity in the service of discovering affordances.

Surface Properties

All of the properties so far discussed are best detected under conditions that provide motion transformations produced by object motion or observer movement in a spatial layout. Surface properties of objects, principally texture and color, can often be detected visually in stationary objects. Texture, especially, can be explored haptically, thus yielding the best information for roughness, smoothness, and so on.

Infants' sensitivity to color and brightness of surfaces has been studied extensively (see Banks & Shannon, 1993; Teller & Bornstein, 1987). Newborns are sensitive to some hue differences (Adams, Maurer, & Davis, 1986; Adams, Courage, & Mercer, 1994; Adams & Courage, 1998), and hue sensitivity increases over the next few months. Hue may be less important in advertising the affordances of objects than other properties that are mainly dependent on motion, and as a consequence are more attention getting as well as informative about useful properties of an object.

Obtaining Information about Objects and Their Affordances

Exploring Objects

Information about object properties and especially about what they afford is actively obtained by *exploring,* and after a few more months by actively using objects. Exploring objects and discovering how they can be used is the way meanings are learned. Discovering that something can be put in the mouth and sucked, even a finger, and that it affords alleviation from teething pains is indeed acquiring meaning. Meanings may be discovered first for people as social, interacting objects, because exploring by looking and listening are available from birth. But as new action systems emerge, new information can be obtained and new affordances are perceived and acted upon.

This general principle was demonstrated by Eppler (1995), observing both manual exploration and attention to objects by infants aged 3.5 and 5.5 months. They saw and heard pairs of video displays that portrayed social events (a woman playing hand games, and another woman speaking and smiling), contrasted with events in which an object was manipulated (a rattle being shaken, a spoon being banged on a metal surface). Times of looking at the two types of events were monitored, and the babies' manipulatory skills were evaluated during an opportunity to explore several objects manually.

As might be expected, both groups of infants looked and listened attentively to the social events. But when they were given the objects to explore, the older infants engaged in much more, and more sophisticated, manual exploration than the younger group. Furthermore, as predicted, the older group looked and listened attentively to the object-manipulation events on the videotape much longer than did the younger group. In fact, they looked as long at them as they had at the social events. Evidently, the emergence and refinement of new exploratory systems promotes attention to and thus learning more about the affordances of objects appropriate to them.

The exploratory systems available very early are mouthing, listening, and looking. Exploration by looking becomes increasingly effective as postural control of the eye-head-trunk systems is gained. This control progresses from the head downward, starting with eye movements, extending to gradual control of head movement to turn the head and gaze toward a sound source, and following that, control of the trunk and shoulders. All of this progress precedes control of the arms to grasp an object, although stretching an arm toward an advancing object has been observed in neonates (Bower, Broughton, & Moore, 1970).

The object-exploratory system that emerges around 4 to 5 months gives the appearance of a radical change in the infant's behavior. The new exploratory system combines a number of factors that have each been maturing at its own pace and that now come together in a system that makes possible the discovery of multiple new affordances. Major components are the increasing capabilities of the visual system, postural control of the torso, and development of muscular components of reaching, grasping, and fingering. Visual acuity as well as the motor components of fixating and tracking are fully competent for visual exploration by 4 to 5 months, and stereopsis is generally mature, extending information for depth from motion information to more precise information about stationary objects brought close-up for examination. At 4 to 5 months, an infant's exploratory strategies for examining objects—oral, visual, and manual—are ready to go and look very intentional. Babies begin to reach eagerly for things and bring them close. A whole new set of actions is opened up. Objects can be displaced, banged, shaken, rattled, squeezed and thrown, all actions providing information about an object's properties.

Multimodal Exploration

Infants' exploratory actions on objects are increasingly *multimodal*. A baby looks at an object as it is seized, brought closer for inspection, and handled and of course listens for any audible information such as rattling or scraping if the object makes contact with a surface. Noise-making toys will eventually be shaken, like a rattle, calling attention to substance, shape, size, and sound properties all at once. Shape, size, and substance (including weight) are all haptically accessed at once. Whether this plethora of modal information has to be "integrated" to build a schema of an object, as Piaget (1954) once taught, is doubtful. We have seen that object unity is detected visually from object motion information. There is also compelling evidence that information for object unity is made available by multimodal exploration of objects in motion.

Early experiments by Spelke and colleagues (E. Spelke, 1976; E. Spelke & Owsley, 1979) demonstrated that 4-month-old infants detect the synchrony of the sights and sounds of visible sounding objects. Infants watched two visible events occurring side by side, and they heard a sound track specific to and synchronous with one or the other event. The infants looked longer at the event whose sound track they were hearing, and they also searched for that event (looked to the side where they had previously seen it) when they heard its sound. In subsequent experiments (E. Spelke, 1979, 1981; E. Spelke, Born, & Chu, 1983), it was shown that 4-month-olds detect both the common rhythm and the simultaneity of what they see and hear in synchronized audible and visible events. In one experiment, the infants saw two toy animals moving up and down at the same rate, and the infants heard one repetitive sound when one toy impacted a surface and a different repetitive sound when the other toy impacted a surface. These infants showed preferential looking toward the event whose sounds corresponded to the impact and change of direction of movement of the object on a surface. In another experiment, the infants saw the two toys moving at different rates, and they heard repetitive sounds corresponding to each rhythmic motion, but the sounds did not occur simultaneously with the impact and change of direction of movement of the toys. In this case, the infants showed preferential looking toward the event whose repetitive up-and-down motion matched the tempo of the rhythmic sound they were hearing. Thus, the infants detected both the common tempo and the simultaneity of sights and sounds of the objects they saw and heard. Synchrony of sight and sound is a powerful invariant specifying the unity of an event that is seen and heard—for young infants, as well as for older members of the species (as is evident when we perceive performances of ventriloquists).

How do infants learn about object properties by means of more than one modality? Do infants detect the correspondences of what is perceived by multimodal exploration? Or must they learn to associate what is perceived by different modalities about the same object? An experiment by L.E. Bahrick (1988) provides evidence about the nature of intermodal learning. Bahrick presented 3-month-old infants with two filmed events that were heard and seen. One visible event was a transparent plexiglass cylinder containing one large marble being rotated. The sound of this event was one discrete impact as the marble hit the bottom of the container. The second visible event was an identical cylinder containing a number of small marbles being rotated. The sound of this event was an ensemble of multiple impacts as the marbles hit each other and the bottom of the container. Thus the composition of the visible event in each case corresponded to a unique, appropriate accompanying sound pattern.

Several groups of infants were familiarized with different versions of these events. One group watched the visible events synchronized with the appropriate sound tracks. A second group saw the events synchronized with the inappropriate sound track. Two other groups saw the events and heard either appropriate or inappropriate sound tracks not in synchrony with the visible events. If the infants were learning to associate the sight of the impact event with its sound, then both groups of infants presented with synchronous visible and audible impacts should have learned to perceive a unified visible and audible event. On the other hand, if intermodal learning involves detecting invariant correspondences, then only the infants who saw and heard the appropriate and synchronous impact should have learned to perceive a unified event. In fact, in the subsequent preference test, only infants who had been familiarized with films that were both synchronized and appropriately related visibly and audibly to the composition of the objects looked longer proportionally to the sound-specified film during the test, thus showing evidence of intermodal learning. The infants' learning involved detecting invariant correspondences rather than association, since infants familiarized with inappropriate sound tracks synchronous with the visible events showed no evidence of any intermodal learning.

Bahrick's results show that both synchrony and specificity of the visible and audible information are important for detecting the unity of a seen and heard event. The synchrony of motion and sound may direct the infant to the intermodal information that, in turn, makes possible detection of the common structure specifying the composition of the object and its concomitant impact sound.

One way to investigate the development of infants' intermodal perception of object properties is to ask whether information for object properties specific to more than one modality are discriminated and transferred intermodally as soon as infants can detect them. Experimental evidence has varied with the method employed, and especially with the developmental level of the exploratory skills involved, since different exploratory systems do not develop at the same rate. E.J. Gibson and Walker (1984) found evidence of transfer of mouthing (haptic) information about an object's substance to a visual presentation, at 1 month of age. Either a rigid or an elastic (sponge rubber) object, both cylindrical, was placed in the baby's mouth and the baby allowed to mouth it (sucking or moving the tongue and gums). Following a familiarization period, the object was withdrawn and a similar object, somewhat larger, was presented at easy viewing distance for the baby's visual regard. This object was either moved rigidly or squeezed in a pattern of elastic movement by a concealed experimenter. Babies showed a preference for looking at the novel substance, whichever one had not been familiarized via mouthing.

Obtaining haptic information from handling an object is not fully developed until much later than mouthing. Streri (1987) investigated intermodal transfer of object shape information from touch to vision and vice versa in 2- to 3-month-old infants. The infants were presented with an object either for visual or for manual exploration. Following habituation, the infants were presented with the same or a different object in the same or a different modality. The infants showed evidence of transfer to the visual modality of knowledge gained manually, but not the other way around. This asymmetry in infants' early recognition of object properties may reflect the infants' still immature control of manual exploration strategies. Infants of 5 months showed some transfer, but in the opposite direction (Streri & Pécheux, 1986). The visual and manual exploratory systems are apparently developing at different rates and are not yet obtaining the same information, at least about the shape of very small objects. By 6 months, infants have been shown to recognize visually the shape of objects they have explored manually (Ruff & Kohler, 1978; Rose et al., 1981).

The property of object unity appears to be amenable to visual-haptic transfer earlier, as Streri and Spelke (1988) demonstrated with 4- to 5-month-old infants. The infants explored haptically two objects (metal rings), one in each hand. The rings were connected either by a rigid rod, or by a flexible elastic band. Pulling with the arms moved the whole rigid structure in the first case, whereas the rings moved separately when pulled in the second case. Infants were habituated to one or the other of these conditions and then were presented visually with two displays of the objects: in one, the rings were moving together as a unit, and in the second, the rings were moving separately. Infants who had been habituated to the rigidly connected objects looked longer at the objects moving independently. Conversely, infants habituated to objects connected only by the elastic band looked longer at the objects moving as a unit. Thus, infants who explored the rigidly connected rings detected the common motion of the object's surfaces and perceived a single object, whereas the second group of infants detected the independent motion of the rings' surfaces and perceived distinct objects. Later studies (Streri et al., 1993) demonstrated the importance of *active* exploration of the objects for haptically detecting the common or independent motion of their surfaces.

When the same property, for example, object unity, can be detected by more than one modality or exploratory system, the information is often referred to as amodal, implying that it is abstract and invariant over sensory modalities. Information may indeed have a temporal structure that is invariant over different modalities. Visible object size and audible amplitude, for example, change in a corresponding fashion with approaching and receding distance from a perceiver. Walker-Andrews and Lennon (1985) found that 5-month-old infants detect this auditory-visual invariant relation. They presented infants with two visible displays, side by side, one of an automobile approaching, and the other of an automobile receding in distance across a landscape. Simultaneously the infants heard one of two sound tracks, an engine (of a lawn mower) either increasing or decreasing in amplitude. The infants looked longer at the retreating display when it was accompanied by the decreasing-amplitude sound track, and they looked longer at the approaching display when it was accompanied by the increasing-amplitude sound track, demonstrating awareness of the optical-acoustical invariant specifying changing distance. These infants had had previous opportunity to detect such information as they experienced walking, talking people approach them or recede from their view. Temporal synchrony is a ubiquitous amodal invariant. It should be noted that objects provide amodal information only when they are involved in an event, either self-produced or external to the perceiver.

Young infants are remarkably sensitive to auditory-visual correspondences of objects participating in events. By 7 to 9 months, they demonstrate sensitivity to such correspondences of some musical events (A. Pick, Gross, Heinrichs, Love, & Palmer, 1994). In this experiment, infants saw side-by-side visible displays of two musical instruments being played in synchrony, and they heard a sound track in synchrony with both displays, but specific to only one of the instruments. The instruments of each pair were from different musical instrument families and had overlapping pitch ranges and sizes. For example, one pair was a trumpet and a flute, another pair was a cello and a clarinet, and a third pair was a trumpet and a viola. The infants looked longer at the sound-specified members of a pair, evidence that they detected corresponding properties of the sight and sound of the instruments when they saw and heard them being played.

The *affordance* of an event may be specified by information for two or more modalities, such as the sound, appearance, and feel of a rattle, the sound of a musical instrument and its visible substance and manner of being played, or the sound and sight of someone approaching who is bringing prospective comfort. The consequences of these events when multimodally specified serve to unite them and specify the same meaning. The dynamic information in an event either witnessed or self-perpetrated by exploratory activity is essential.

Coordination of Exploratory Systems

Multimodal exploration may begin as independent exploitation of each exploratory system, as illustrated by Rochat's (1987) observation that newborn infants explore differently objects of various substances put in their mouth versus in their hand. During the infants' following months, we can see the development of coordination of exploratory systems for learning about objects. Rochat (1989) observed the development of coordinated exploratory behavior in infants from 2 to 5 months. The infants were given a hard blue rubber object of graspable size having several protuberances, each of a different texture. The object promoted multimodal exploration, having affordances for looking, mouthing, and manipulating. There were systematic changes over the infants' age range in the duration of their exploration and in the kinds of exploratory activity they engaged in. Simply grasping the object with one hand decreased, while looking at, mouthing, and fingering the object increased with age. From 2 to 4 months the infants did more grasping with both hands, and from 4 to 5 months they increased their frequency of transferring the object from one hand to the other and transported it frequently from their mouths to look at it, or vice versa. In a further study, the infants were given two objects to explore, one the same chewable nubby object as before, and the other one contrasting in shape, color, size, and texture. These infants showed some object differentiation, engaging in more transfer of the larger object from their mouths, and scratching the larger but not the smaller object.

Coordination of mouthing with grasping becomes particularly apparent by the middle of the first year. Whyte, McDonald, Baillargeon, and Newell (1994) analyzed records of 4- to 8-month-old infants' haptic exploration of brightly colored plastic cups of varying size. Even the younger infants grasped the cups differently depending on their size. Whether the infants mouthed objects they were already grasping depended on the objects' size and the infants' age—mouthing increased in frequency from 4 to 5 months and remained fairly stable after that. Larger objects (across the size range sampled—cups ranging in diameter from 1.2 cm to 9 cm) were mouthed more frequently than smaller objects. Furthermore, the way in which the infants grasped an object, that is, their finger grip configuration, differed depending on whether they subsequently transported it to their mouths or continued exploring it manually. This is another example of prospectivity in exploratory activity, wherein the manner of grasping an object promotes realizing certain actions on it, in this case, exploring it further in the mouth.

The auditory and visual exploratory systems are perhaps the earliest to engage in obtaining information about the world, and we have considered their important role in initiating communication. Their cooperation in specifying social events and the persons engaged in social interactions is established very early. The auditory and visual systems, along with the proprioceptive system, also function to specify properties and affordances of objects, including their location relative to oneself. In a longitudinal developmental study, R.K. Clifton, Muir, Ashmead, and Clarkson (1993) observed infants from 6 to 25 weeks of age as they reached for objects in the light and as they reached for objects that either sounded or glowed in the dark. Although the infants varied in the age at which they first began to reach for and grasp the objects, their onset of obtaining the objects was similar for objects in the light and in the dark. That infants reach as early for visible objects in the dark as in the light means that they need not rely on visual guidance of their hands to obtain an object. They are sensitive to proprioceptive information for the location of their hand and arm in relation to an object that is within reach. However, the development of sensitivity to proprioceptive information for location may rely on the many ongoing opportunities for infants to see their arms while reaching for objects. Clifton and colleagues also noted that blind infants do not begin reaching for sounds until they are several months older than the infants in their own study.

At least by 6 months, infants can reach accurately toward sounding objects in the dark if they have had opportunity to see, hear, and reach for them in the light. R.K. Clifton, Rochat, Litovsky, and Perris (1991) presented infants with two sounding objects, differing in size, in light and in darkness. The objects made different sounds, congruent with their sizes. In both light and darkness, the infants reached with both hands for the larger object, and with one hand for the smaller one. From seeing, hearing, and reaching for the two objects, each with its distinctive size and sound, the infants learned that the information from all three sources specified a unique *affordance*—how to reach to obtain a particular object. This activity is controlled and intentional and has become possible by way of multimodal exploration over a period of time in everyday activities. Even just one of the sources of information specifying the object's affordance eventually suffices to initiate the activity (R. Clifton, 1998).

For a normal, growing infant all these sources have been serving to provide information in parallel for ongoing events in daily life. New control for each modality may emerge at different times (e.g., head turning for listening, greater efficiency of saccadic movements of the eyes), but these developments converge to promote coordinated multimodal exploratory activity.

Development of Exploration in Later Infancy

Exploration of objects continues to develop throughout the first year, as grasping, handling, fingering, and then coordinating all the exploratory systems mature and gain experience. As the exploratory activities differentiate, so do the properties that provide information specifying particular affordances. Texture, for example, is explored best when fingering becomes skilled, much later than simple touching and handling. Surface properties of objects, indeed, are far less worthy of attention to infants who are busy developing good eye-hand coordination than are sizes and substance of things, or even such a property as temperature, which is important for specifying an affordance of comfort to an infant. E.W. Bushnell, Shaw, and Strauss (1985) investigated the relative importance of color and temperature of small, manipulable vials to 6-month-old infants. The infants were allowed to handle a single vial of a given temperature and color, examining it at length both haptically and visually. Then they were presented with a novel vial, differing either in color or temperature. When temperature was changed, there was a significant increase in both handling and looking, but when color was changed, there was no increase in either type of exploration. Color sensitivity is already well developed by 6 months, but color does not appear to be an important property in specifying affordance for handling. Finding warmth is a different matter.

Differentiation of exploratory actions develops in relation to distinctive properties of objects that specify affordances important for the growing child. Palmer (1989) found that exploratory actions relevant to significant properties of objects differentiated between 6 and 12 months. In a first study, she presented 6-, 9-, and 12-month-old infants with an array of objects, one at a time, for free exploration. The objects varied in size, substance, texture, sound, contour, and so on. Some actions, such as mouthing, accidental dropping, and fingering (of some objects), decreased with age, while other actions, such as banging of hard objects on the tabletop, increased with age. Many actions were specific to object properties. For example, only a toy mouse was dangled (by its tail); a rattle and a bell with a clapper were waved, but a bell without a clapper was not. In general, across the age range, the infants demonstrated a wide range of actions, and they increasingly discriminated among specific object properties.

In a second study, Palmer (1989) presented infants across the same age range with an array of objects that afforded less diversity of actions, but in which contrasting action-relevant properties were more controlled. For example, pairs of objects presented contrasts of weight (a light and heavy bottle, air- and water-filled balloons), size, substance (sponge-rubber and wooden blocks), sound, and so on. For this experiment, the objects were presented for exploration on one of two surfaces, either a hard wooden table or a table covered with a layer of sponge rubber. In addition to the age effects in the first study, Palmer observed specific effects of contrasting properties on the infants' actions. They waved and mouthed lightweight objects more than they did the heavier objects, they squeezed and scooted the heavier objects on the hard table more than they did the lighter objects, and they mouthed and squeezed the elastic objects more than they did the rigid objects.

Infants' exploratory actions on objects vary with the nature of the object, and changes in their exploratory systems lead to increasing specificity of actions on objects. By 6 months, infants have well-developed mouthing skills; by 9 months, they show vigorous waving and banging of objects, as well-controlled arm movements are achieved. By 12 months, they have increasing control of fine hand movements, enabling exploration by fingering and squeezing. Ruff and her colleagues, as well, have observed development of specificity in infants' exploratory actions with objects, with decreases in exploratory actions as infants became familiar with an object, and then corresponding increases in the same actions when infants encountered a novel object (H. Ruff, Saltareli, Capozzoli, & Dubiner, 1992).

Increasing specificity and economy of what begins as purely exploratory activity marks a shift toward actions directed at exploiting a particular affordance. Learning specific affordances for objects makes possible planned, directed action. This learning often begins with exploratory activity, and as knowledge is acquired, intentional, goal-directed action becomes more evident and frequent.

Control of Reaching, Grasping, and Manipulation

Exploratory activity has the function of obtaining information and, as we saw, becomes more skilled, better controlled, and more highly differentiated in relation to specific properties of objects. Activity has other functions as well, such as getting nourishment or seizing an object (food, perhaps) for a specific purpose. Such behavior is not only intentional and controlled but actively prospective, planned ahead. Action is reciprocal with perception, so we need to consider how actions upon objects develop. Using objects implicates quite specific, directed actions such as reaching, grasping, and manipulation that become skilled and efficient over many months. There is a large literature on so-called motor development, dating back to the 1930s, recalling such sources as Arnold Gesell and Mary Shirley. We confine our discussion here to actions as they relate to perceiving and using objects.

Individual acts such as orienting the head to look, reaching, and even aspects of communication are all constrained by posture, maintaining a balance with relation to gravity. Posture is the background for independent exercise of the head, arms, torso, and other body parts. Postural control comes first and, as the classical research demonstrated so well, develops from the head downward and from the central spinal section outward, culminating at length in emergence of upright stance and bipedal locomotion at about one year of age. Maintaining a balance with respect to gravity is highly dynamic, and specific movements of parts must be integrated with the whole body.

Infants, obviously, are dependent on external bodily support, provided by surfaces like beds and by the clasping arms of adults. "Functional action patterns" (see Rochat & Bullinger, 1994) such as turning the head to look at a sound source or a moving object, visual tracking of a moving object, or even extending a hand or arm toward that object at first requires firm support. Support of the head provided by an experimenter has been shown to permit what appear to be precocious manifestations of orienting and reaching (Bower, 1989). Normally, this development must wait upon gaining postural control so that action of a subsystem will not cause toppling over.

Progressive control of posture promotes functional actions, often intermodal ones such as hand-to-mouth-sucking. Visual tracking of objects is one of the first exploratory actions to emerge; even this is severely limited in the beginning by postural state. An asymmetrical posture that anchors the infant permits tracking but also limits its extent. By the second month, posture permits wider tracking, especially if the baby is well supported in an infant seat. The infant tends to lean to one side, with the head turned in the opposite direction. By 3 months, the trunk is stable while the head moves to follow the target's motion.

Consider what it means to *reach* successfully for a moving object that is being visually tracked. One must reach not for the location of the visible object, but rather for the location of the object when it intersects one's hand. To catch a ball successfully, one must aim for where the ball will be when it is at a catchable location—not out of reach, and before it collides with one's body; not too high, and not on the ground. To reach successfully for a moving object requires achieving prospective control of one's action. The optical information that specifies where a moving object will intersect with oneself is contained in its trajectory, and to catch such an object means adjusting the movement of one's arm and hand to the object's motion as specified by its trajectory. Clearly this is a remarkable achievement, and it reaffirms the reciprocity of perceiving and acting.

What is the course of development of prospective control of reaching during infancy? Von Hofsten (1982, 1993) has observed that even newborn infants, supported in a sitting position, show rudimentary eye-hand coordination and can reach toward a brightly colored object moving slowly in front of them. In a longitudinal study of infants from about 5 to 8 months of age, von Hofsten (1991) investigated the development of skilled reaching. The infants again were presented with a brightly colored object moving in front of them from one side to the other. The object moved at different speeds and videorecordings made with two cameras (one above and one in front of the baby) permitted calculation of the aim of the infant's reach in relation to the object's speed. From the youngest age, the infants reached predictively; most of their reaches were aimed ahead of where the object was located when the reach began. The observed developmental changes were not in the infants' predictive skill, but rather in the agility of their reaching and their success in catching. Their reaching became more economical and flexible, with fewer "steps" and midcourse corrections. As they gained agility, some of the oldest infants adopted a chasing strategy in which they did not aim at the meeting point of their arm with the object but instead moved their arm fast enough to catch the object.

How do infants guide their reaching for moving objects? What information do they use to control reaching? These questions were investigated by A. van der Meer, van der Weel, and Lee (1994) in a longitudinal study of infants from 5 to 11 months of age. The infants saw an attractive object move at varying speeds crossing in front of them. At some point along its path of motion, the object disappeared temporarily from the infants' view, passing behind an occluder and reappearing from its other side. Even at the youngest age, the infants looked ahead of the object's location and began to reach for it before it disappeared from view, demonstrating the hand-eye coordination observed by von Hofsten. The infants also anticipated the reappearance of the object from behind the occluder by gazing ahead of its location even while it was out of sight. It was only at the later ages that the infants also anticipated the reappearance of a fast-moving object by reaching for it; but by 11 months, infants can coordinate their reaching actions to the speed of an object's trajectory even when it disappears for some distance along its path of motion. The timing of the infants' reaches were precisely tuned to when the object would arrive at a catchable location. Achieving precise prospective control of catching involves coordination of optical information linking the timing of object motion with the timing of one's own movement.

Increasing efficiency and changes in the organization of the reaching action may follow from increasing postural control as the infant gains ability to maintain a sitting posture. Maintaining balance while sitting independently gives the infant a greater scope in the three-dimensional layout, which is extended still further when the infant can lean forward without falling. This development was studied by Rochat and Goubet (1995), who found that infants who had achieved self-sitting had a greatly expanded prehensile space, which increased their ability to explore and to control and plan behavior.

Obtaining an object in the layout requires not only reaching accurately for it, but grasping it effectively, a coordinated skill that has its own course of mastery. Von Hofsten and Ronnqvist (1988) made detailed observations of infants and adults opening and closing their hands as they prepared to grasp objects of different sizes located in front of them and within reach. Adults and infants of at least 9 months began closing their hands around the object before they touched it, and the timing of their preparatory closing depended on the size of the objects. Younger infants also began closing their hands before they touched the object, but their preparatory closing began when their hand was very near the object, and their timing was not related to the size of the object. Butterworth, Verweij, and Hopkins (1997) observed infants from 24 to 83 weeks as they grasped a small cube. All of the infants, even the youngest, displayed a variety of grips; developmental changes involved selecting from the variety of grips and using the most efficient grips most frequently. (Later we will see that the same developmental course is demonstrated by infants learning to grip a spoon in a functional manner so as to use it as a tool for eating.)

Reaching an object in the layout, either by touching and grasping or by locomotion, implies knowledge of how distant it is. It is interesting to ask about the origins of this ability, because there is good evidence that scaling sizes and distances of objects and layout begins early, based on the baby's own body dimensions and capacities for action. These dimensions and capacities change as a child grows and need to be continually updated, but exteroceptive information from joints and muscles is detected through exploratory activity and used effectively very early to establish a bodily frame of reference for action. Even newborn babies seem to be learning about body dimensions and capabilities as they watch their own moving arms (A.L.H. van der Meer, et al., 1995).

It has been known for some time that as babies begin to reach reliably for objects around 4 months of age, they are far more likely to reach for an object presented within reach, and to reach with decreasing frequency as the object's distance increases (Cruikshank, 1941; Field, 1976). Yonas and Hartman (1993) asked specifically when babies learn to perceive the affordance of contact, that is, when a proffered object is within touching distance with arm and fingertips extended. They found that they had to divide their group of 5-month-old infants into "leaners" and "nonleaners," since some were already able to control posture so as to lean forward and extend reach. The toy offered as a target was placed at exactly fingertip length, and also at two nearer positions and two farther. If the infants used arm length as an index of contactability, there should be an abrupt drop in reaching attempts as the fingertip boundary was passed. The nonleaners did indeed show such a boundary; they nearly always reached when the toy was well within and just in reach, but their frequency of reaching decreased suddenly as the object was just beyond their reach. The leaners reached out farther, their reaches peaking at 5 cm farther out than the fingertip boundary.

Yonas and Hartman (1993) also observed a group of 4-month-olds in the same procedure. The frequency of reaching by these younger infants also decreased as the toy was placed out of reach, but the decline was not nearly as steep as for the older infants. The difference between the two age groups reflects the increasing precision of perceiving an affordance, in this case the affordance of contact, as control of the appropriate action system is mastered. These investigators did not assess whether the infants had achieved independent sitting, but from Rochat and Goubet's (1995) findings, we would expect that the infants of either age who had explored their own reaching capabilities having achieved

independent sitting would display the most precise knowledge of the reachability of objects. In fact, Rochat and Goubet (1993) found this to be so. They
grouped 6-month-olds in terms of whether they had achieved independent sitting, "near"-sitting, or nonsitting and found their perceived reachability to be
highly related to their sitting status.

In a further study, McKenzie, Skouteris, Day, Hartman, and Yonas (1993)
found that by 8 months of age, infants perceive a boundary between objects that
can be contacted without leaning and those that cannot. These investigators offered infants of 10 to 12 months an implement (a wooden spoon) that would extend the region of contactability if wielded properly. The older infants, more often than the younger ones, made contact with the toy when the implement was
provided. Maintaining postural control while leaning and also wielding the implement may yet be beyond the capability of 10-month-olds.

These studies of the relation of increasing postural control and increasing
reaching precision all demonstrate how the layout is scaled in terms of perceived bodily constraints and abilities. As posture develops, enabling emergence of new actions for exploration and control of behavior, infants progressively discover the affordances of the world they live in, learning about the
objects and events around them and at the same time learning about their own
capabilities for using them.

Using Everyday Objects: Toys and Tools

It is interesting to consider what objects infants normally handle as reaching out
and grasping is mastered. A bottle and the breast are obvious ones and are made
easily accessible from birth. Soon, parents begin to offer toys such as rattles and
stuffed animals. Simple toys are indeed educational, since they permit exploration of surfaces and potential noise-making properties. Palmer (1989), whose
work was mentioned earlier, provides a descriptive picture of normal development of object use during the second half-year of life.

A big step comes, however, when an infant begins to use an object as a tool.
This is at least a two-step process, since the affordance of the tool and its use
must be perceived, as well as the more distant goal of acting on the final object
and achieving whatever it affords. Infants readily transfer objects and food such
as bits of toast to their mouth by hand, but using a spoon to do so requires a
number of steps and a well-planned series of actions. This is a "means-end" pattern of actions, analogous in one way to the classic task of allowing the baby to
look for an object hidden in one of two containers or covered by a cloth, so that
the baby must first reach into the container or remove the cloth in order to retrieve the hidden object. Infants do not usually accomplish this task easily until they are 8 to 10 months of age, even after they can remove the cloth or open
the container. After retrieving the target object once, they tend to approach the
same hiding place again, even when they have watched the object being placed

in the alternative one. Piaget, who invented the task, interpreted the baby's behavior as wanting in a notion of "object permanence" (Piaget, 1954), meaning that the baby considered the object as existing only when it was in view. There are many other interpretations of the behavior. Also, babies learn a simple routine very easily (e.g., "go to that place where toys are found"), and learning in a particular, unusual situation seems to be rather inflexible in early months.

Spontaneous use of a tool requires more skill than the "object permanence" task. Complex, serial acts of manipulation take practice and a plan for execution. Tool use that does not require such manipulation takes place early, for example, crying or fussing that instigates another person to provide a desired object or service. It is not the ability to control or predict an event that is wanting. If the tool is provided for the baby and rigged so that the behavior is easily consummated, as happens in the task of pulling on a string to activate a mobile (C.K. Rovee-Collier & Gekoski, 1979), the baby easily achieves control. But in a true tool-using operation, the tool has an affordance in relation to the goal, and this relation must be perceived. The affordance of the tool itself must be discerned first and then its actual functioning mastered (see Adolph, Eppler, & Gibson, 1993b; Smitsman, 1997).

Tools vary greatly from culture to culture, even ones for extension of reaching and grasping, such as tools for eating. Chinese children frequently start with spoons and are then given extensive practice with chopsticks in day-care situations.

Mastery of spoon use for eating requires coordinating several skills: the spoon must be inserted into the container, filled with food, and rotated as it is transported toward the mouth; the mouth must be opened at the appropriate time, and the spoon inserted into the mouth, depositing the food. Connolly and Dalgleish (1989) observed a group of children longitudinally from about 10 months onward as they learned to use a spoon. The children tried out many grips before eventually selecting those most effective for accomplishing the goal of carrying food to their mouths. Detecting the affordance relation of the spoon to the food is probably easily accomplished through observation, but the acquisition of skill in trajectory of movements, method of grasp, and temporal structure takes long exploration and practice, even when the goal is clear.

Siddiqui (1991) investigated infants' perception of the relation of spoons and containers—the fit of the spoon size and container opening. The infants were 8 and 12 months old. Eight-month-olds, of course, are not yet using spoons to feed themselves; instead they are banging and waving spoons. However, they have been fed with spoons for some time, providing opportunities for observing the relations of spoon sizes and bowl or jar openings. The infants were presented with sets of spoons and jars (containing a favorite food) in which both the spoons and the jar openings varied in size. In each set there was only one combination that would work; in the other cases, the spoon bowl was too large for the jar, preventing retrieval of food. The older infants reached toward jars with spoons much more often than did the younger infants, who presumably were engaging in other actions with the spoons. However, the infants in both age groups accurately selected spoon-jar combinations that would work. They perceived the functional relation of the spoon size and jar opening well before they could master the coordinated task of feeding themselves with a spoon.

We spend much of our lives acquiring new perception-action skills—drawing on paper, writing, using objects such as knives, scissors, and needles. Using musical instruments demands still greater intermodal coordination of vision, hearing, haptic skill, and touch. Manipulating objects and using tools is an endlessly developing human skill, which we return to in the last chapter.

Identifying Particular Objects

By the time infants can manipulate a toy in an appropriate fashion or use a simple tool, these objects have surely been identified, even if they cannot as yet be named. Objects are identified when they can be differentiated from other objects, and their affordances perceived to be specified by their distinguishing properties. This achievement involves perceptual learning (see chap. 8). Learning what properties specify a particular object's affordance is typically discovered in the course of an event in which the object is moving about, being moved by someone else, or, being moved in an exploratory fashion by oneself. An object may have numerous properties—color, shape, substance, internal details, weight, sharpness or smoothness, and so on. But only certain ones of these may be critical for distinguishing it as affording some interesting consequence or differentiating it from another object. Consider a comb, for instance. It is small enough to be held and manipulated, has teeth, and is fairly rigid. Other properties, such as its color, do not identify it and are immaterial for distinguishing it for its intended use (although it may have other uses). Babies perceive this object as part of an event and by 8 to 10 months may attempt to wield it on a head.

For many years, theorizing about identification of objects began with the assumption that at first, all object properties are subject to "stimulus generalization": another object possessing similar properties, such as shape or color may, by a generalizing process, be included in the identification. The original widespread generalization would have to be narrowed down through broader experience, as the perceiver discovered the truly distinguishing features of the object (E.J. Gibson, 1969). Discovering distinctive features of objects must indeed eventually occur, but this characterization of the course of identification now seems too simple, for several reasons. One is that objects in daily life are characterized by multimodal properties; furthermore they are normally perceived as part of an event with some sort of dénouement or consequence that draws attention to the object's affordance. The affordance, which gives the object meaning, is specified by a complex of properties combined in a unique way. Furthermore, early learning of this kind in infants is turning out to be more specific to a particular set of properties than originally thought (Hayne, MacDonald, & Barr, 1997). It might be that only a red comb, as originally presented, would be perceived (mistakenly) as a comb. However that may be, differentiation of truly identifying features occurs as objects are encountered in more varied contexts, and with opportunities for contrast with other objects. Information specifying truly distinguishing features will eventually be discovered and may be very economical, as in the case referred to earlier of infants reaching for a particular object in the dark, when only auditory information was available to specify it.

Perceiving the Continuity of Objects

Finally, we address a question that has been warmly debated in recent years: how early do infants know that objects continue to exist when they are occluded for brief intervals? To most people, the question must seem odd. Of course a table exists, even when someone walks past it and it is briefly out of sight (or even longer out of sight). But Piaget (see chap. 1) wrote that perception in infants is "fleeting" and consists of only the briefest images, sensorial and "figurative." Only after an infant has passed through the sensori-motor stage and finally attained the ability to represent things in memory, many months later, could that infant know that objects continue to exist over time. But research has now made it manifest that, in this respect at least, Piaget was wrong. Infants of 3 to 5 months, and probably much earlier, do expect objects to continue to exist, despite temporary occlusion. Research by Baillargeon (1993), among others, has called attention to this fact. But how do young infants know about the continuity of objects? Some psychologists have suggested that knowledge of continuity is an innate belief (e.g., Spelke, 1991).

We stress, however, that there are more than ample opportunities from birth on to learn about continuity of objects and of events, too, over time. Events continue over time, and so does perception, as we have frequently pointed out. It is the invariants over time that make perception of relations possible. If there is one thing that infants attend to, it is an event—motion, change, something happening. Information for continuity—continued existence—of objects and places is made available hundreds of times a day by a baby's own actions, such as raising an arm or kicking a leg. As the arm, hand, or leg is raised, it occludes momentarily whatever the baby is looking at, whatever may be in the field of view. That could be the mother's face as the baby is nursing, or any piece of furniture or appurtenance of the surrounding room. Deletion of optical structure (or texture) occurs as the limb occludes the scene, followed by a continuous accreting of the same structure as the hand moves on and the structure is disoccluded. This event is powerful information for the continued existence of objects (and also for their unity).

While this opportunity is guaranteed by the baby's own activity, it is also often presented by the movements of other people and things across the field of view. No reasoning or endowed "belief" is necessary; the information is easily and many times over obtained by perceptual systems that are ready to go at birth. Even before birth, continuity of the sounds of language are available to the fetus. Invariant patterns and rhythms are heard and perceived, as we know. Furthermore, the redundancy of multimodal perception provides information for continuity. An object can often be heard and even felt as it is briefly out of view. There are numerous occasions for a baby to learn quickly to expect continuity of things and events in the world.

Conclusion

The development of object perception provides a lesson for us as well as for infants as they learn about the affordances of objects. They are building a rich knowledge of themselves and of the world around them even before they begin to speak. Well before the end of the first year, they are interacting with other human beings, have explored and detected the uses of many objects, and have good ability for finding out about other ones. They begin by listening to and looking at their caretakers and the scenes of activity around them. They can mouth bottles and the breast, finger blankets and their own bodies, and get a hand to the mouth. From about 4 months on, reaching and grasping for nearby objects rapidly increase in frequency and skill. And as postural control extends downward, permitting sitting alone, an 8-month-old put on the floor may bend over, get hands on the floor, and shift the body's weight forward. There begins the story of locomotion and exploration of a wider world, told in our next chapter.

7

✦ ✧ ✦ ✧ ✦

What Infants Learn About

Locomotion and the Spatial Layout

Locomotion is a biologically basic function, and if that can be accounted for then the problem of human space perception may appear in a new light. The question is, then, how an animal gets about by vision. How does it react to the solid surfaces of the environment without collision whenever there is enough light to see them by? What indicates to the animal that it is moving or not moving with reference to them? What kind of optical stimulation indicates approach to an object? And how does the animal achieve contact without collision? What governs the aiming and steering of locomotion?

J.J. GIBSON (1958, P. 183)

While posture has traditionally been thought of as a static state, I adopt the approach here that posture is dynamic, and emerges from both muscular forces and the extant forces acting on the body to initiate, maintain, change, or halt a movement.

E.C. GOLDFIELD (1995, P. 185)

Perhaps the most exciting change that goes on over the first year of life is the development of locomotion. As infants begin to move around the world on their own power, parents watch proudly, offer encouragement and erect protective barriers. But the real excitement belongs to infants themselves. Babies manifest a remarkable urge to go someplace even before mobility becomes a reality, rocking and squirming in an effort to move ahead. This highly motivated activity seems at first to have no particular goal except to keep moving, but as skill is attained, goals become more specific, more numerous, and more diverse. This chapter tracks the way locomotion develops, from simple change of position, to crawling, and finally to walking on two legs, a feat of balance accomplished by few creatures. It goes on to show how locomotion comes to serve strategically the achievement of multiple goals, coping with all kinds of surfaces of support, steering around barriers and through gaps, taking the shortest routes when choices are possible. Finally, we consider the knowledge acquired by mobile exploration of the layout: where things are or might be, the permanence of the geographical world, and the establishment of "I"—the moveable self that can cruise the layout while retaining its own kind of continuity.

Active Orientation to the Environment

We pointed out in chapters 4 and 6 that posture is never static but is rather an active process of orientation to the environment. This is the case from the start, long before a baby is ready to go somewhere. Actions occur against a background of posture, which maintains stability for turning the head, moving a limb, or sitting up. Development of locomotion is preceded by emergence of partial action systems, themselves requiring postural preparation and adjustment. Turning the head and moving the eyes to gaze at a target or to follow an ongoing event appears early, as we saw in considering communication: the baby orients body and head so as to focus on the caretaker and maintains stability while actively gesturing with the head and with facial musculature. Holding the head and shoulders upright so as to gaze about, the body prone with arms extended on the surface of support, is a typical posture that appears around 4 months. Infants are progressing in taking in events and layout features of the surround, actively looking about. Sitting alone comes somewhat later, making strong demands for balance, especially when an object is to be held or reached for at the same time. Leaning forward to lengthen the reach is precarious and may result in loss of balance and a tumble. This overreach itself is often a precursor of crawling, since babies typically extend an arm to the floor and find themselves in a near crawling position.

How do infants actively maintain their posture so as to hold up the head, sit erect, and so on? An essential condition for these balancing acts is the use of flow patterns in the optic array. When an organism moves, the optic array surrounding it flows, as J.J. Gibson showed many years ago (1955). As the body moves forward, the array streams past radially from a motionless center that specifies the direction of movement. But if the head or body tilts away from the upright, there are perturbations in the array that specify the nature of the unstable equilibrium—which way the head or body is falling. Visually perceptible information that can be used to correct posture is produced in the resulting flow and is used for maintaining stability from a very early age (Lee & Aronson, 1974). Infants as young as 7 months detect optical flow specifying sway and use it to make postural corrections (B. Bertenthal and Bai, 1989). Even newborns may be sensitive to optical flow that will eventually affect their control of posture (Jouen & Lepecq, 1989). (See Goldfield, 1995, chap. 8, for an excellent discussion of early postural control.) Locomotion makes still greater demands on active use of perceptual and action systems informed by optical flow.

Modes of Locomotion and Their Development

Crawling

As Goldfield (1995) points out, crawling, the earliest form of human locomotion, has two important characteristics: it is intentional (goal-directed and motivated), and it is regulated by information from the perceptual systems about the state of the environment as regards the crawler's actions and their consequences. We have discussed the importance of optical flow produced by movement of the head, shoulders, and trunk, and the resulting information for maintaining stable posture when looking around or sitting. But moving forward over the ground entails intervals of actual loss of support, when one or another supporting limb is lifted from the surface to reach ahead on the path.

According to Goldfield, there are three capabilities underlying prone locomotion in infancy. They are orienting, using the information from optical flow to maintain balance while lifting a part of the body off the surface; propulsion, using limbs to push against the support surface; and steering, using hands and arms to direct body movement. In the beginning stages of crawling, Goldfield (1995) noted remarkable variability in modes of progressing, even in the same infant during one period of observation. It is as if the baby tries everything its action systems will allow, before settling down to some favored pattern of progression. This variability apparently reflects active exploration. Goldfield suggests that infants who show the greatest variability in modes of progression are also likely to be earliest to crawl, having selected a workable means from an extended array of attempts.

Infants often begin with belly crawling and progress to a hand-and-knee pattern with chest and abdomen raised off the ground. The latter achievement permits greater speed but is obviously riskier as regards stability, since equilibrium must be maintained while an arm or a leg (or both) are raised off the ground and the abdomen no longer provides support. The baby in a sense falls forward, with a hand reaching to the ground surface (fig. 7.1). Infants must maintain their balance and steer at the same time, perhaps making differential use of optical flow specifying "straight ahead" contrasted with flow specifying sway or wavering (E.J. Gibson & Schmuckler, 1989). It is likely, in fact, that experience in crawling effectively promotes the use of peripheral flow patterns in maintaining postural stability (Higgens, Campos, & Kermoian, 1993). Crawling offers needed opportunities for exploring the optical flow patterns and observing the consequences of adjustments to them before the really tricky activity of balancing on two legs begins. But the trick isn't the same: different action synergies must be controlled, and the flow patterns varying with them are observed from different loci and heights.

The age at which crawling begins varies widely over children, ranging in a longitudinal study by Adolph (1995) from 4.77 to 9.73 months. Age of begin-

FIGURE 7.1. Infant making an early attempt at locomotion. When progression occasionally resulted, it was sometimes forward and sometimes backward. Attempts were characterized by great variability and evident pleasure when any propulsion resulted. Photo courtesy of Maren Patterson.

ning walking is also highly variable, ranging in the same study from 9.27 to 14.89 months. Older studies of the development of locomotion in infants emphasized maturation as the essential reason for change and typically referred to "stages" following one another in a regular pattern (A. Gesell, 1946; McGraw, 1945). More recent work shows the importance of variability of an infant's own activity for effecting changes in pattern, along with selection of patterns that yield efficiency of moving forward, combined with maintenance of stability. Season of birth has even been shown to be associated with variation in the age of onset of crawling for babies born into a temperate climate (Benson, 1993). Seasonal variation in temperature, amount of clothing required for warmth, and number of daylight hours are among the factors that conceivably could promote greater or lesser sheer amount and variability of activity by young infants. A longitudinal study by Freedland and Bertenthal (1994) focused on the transition from belly crawling or no forward movement to hands-and-knees crawling. The change in pattern appeared to be a function of many factors,. Variability in pattern of action and timing of movements was marked in individuals and between them. Hands-and-knees crawlers, however, eventually settle on a diagonal pattern of gait, with diagonally opposite limbs (arm and leg) moving together. This pattern yields greater stability and also efficiency in progressing, moving the baby forward while providing support and maintaining balance, a highly functional outcome. Why, then do babies move on to upright walking?

Walking

Why did early hominids stand up? Why did walking evolve as a favored method of locomotion when posture and gait are more stable on four legs? It is generally accepted that evolution of bipedalism, even more than brain size, is the key trait that separated homo sapiens from other species. The ability to carry food when foraging, so as to bring it to the young of the species, is one advantage that contributed evolutionary pressure to select this trait. Whatever the reason, human infants, no matter how adept at getting around on all fours, are eager to stand upright, and they typically "cruise" on two legs, while holding on to furniture, for example, well before they can balance alone in an upright stance. The elevated point of view permits wider scans of the surround and may itself be motivating, but blind babies stand and walk too, eventually (Fraiberg, 1977; Bigelow, 1992), so it is likely that many other factors underlie the change.

As babies stand while holding on, they begin gradually to allow periods of lesser stability, using their ankle joints and knees to help control sway. From this partial instability, systematic shifts of weight eventually occur, emerging finally as the anticipated gait pattern characteristic of mature walking. Changing body proportions as well as developing mechanisms for maintenance of balance play a role in this species-evolved activity.

Recent intensive study of the development of infant walking makes clear that neither the traditional maturationist view nor the notion that babies simply "learn" to walk is correct (Thelen, 1984; Thelen & Smith, 1994). There are many precursors to walking. Among the most interesting are the so-called "stepping movements" of newborn infants. These movements disappear after about 2 months, but Thelen and Fisher (1983) discovered that they are actually almost identical in pattern to kicking movements that appear about that time and continue for several months. Stepping movements occurred when older infants of 7 months were held upright on a treadmill. The two legs maintained an alternating gait pattern and were organized as a functional unit. But this pattern does not reoccur, without the treadmill, until infants become able to progress on two legs, with support. This activity only becomes possible as weight distribution and muscular strength in the legs and lower torso develop appropriately and balance is achieved. In addition, dynamic properties emerge from the physical construction of the body's movement system, contributing to the eventual organization of the many factors that prepare for the onset of locomotion. Development of walking is sensitive to both internal organic and external environmental events, and its appearance in any particular child is context-dependent to a notable degree.

We see that walking does not emerge out of the blue, as a finished product. All the earlier postural achievements—lifting the head and shoulders from a prone position, followed by sitting, crawling, standing with support, and "cruising" or walking with support, in turn antedate independent bipedal movement. Furthermore, when independent walking first emerges, a baby moves with feet well apart, arms partially extended, and with a lurching gait as the body's weight is shifted forward. The walk of a beginner varies from that of mature walkers in many ways, as we know from several major studies (Thelen, 1984). There is little or no heel strike, some joint and ankle rotations are stiff or absent, stance may be unstable, stride length is shorter, and there is a wider base of support, to name a few.

There are three sources of information for postural stability: visual, from optical flow generated when moving; vestibular, from organs in the inner ear; and mechanical, from muscle activations in the ankles and thighs (information produced by contacts with the support surface). These sources must be organized functionally so as to give specific information for stability, but also so as to be flexible when external conditions change. It is clear that many characteristics of the novice walker (mechanisms of postural control, body proportions, muscle strength, and ability to adapt to environmental conditions) require a long period of refinement before the gait, adaptability, and control of mature walkers are attained.

A clever method of demonstrating the progression of skill as novice walkers practice (which they do, enthusiastically) was devised by Adolph, (1996). Felt tabs were fastened on the heels and toes of an infant's shoes, the tabs inked, and a long stretch of butcher's paper provided as a path for the baby to traverse from the experimenter to a waiting parent. A trail of footprints resulted, leaving traces that could be measured for length of stride, length of step, step width, and tendency to rotation. With days of walking experience, all of these improve from a first clumsy gait to a smooth more economical one (see fig. 7.2).

Is Locomotion "Learned"?

A major lesson from this text should be that in some sense everything behavioral is learned, action and cognition alike. At the same time, to ask whether a behavioral achievement is learned or not is unprofitable, since it is clear that a great many factors interact to produce any given behavior. Formal properties of getting around the world emerge from continuous dynamic organization and reorganization of genetic, environmental, and biological factors characteristic of the species. Genetic factors peculiar to the species surely contribute to the development of bipedal locomotion—to the anatomy of the body, to perceptual mechanisms that monitor uprightness in relation to gravity and other external conditions, and to action systems that operate dynamically to make possible a functional gait and propulsion of weight forward. At the same time, all these factors mature in a context and are influenced by environmental conditions and by the perceiver-performer's intention to perform the task and practice it until skill is attained. This all amounts to achievement of an affordance, that is, mov-

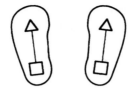

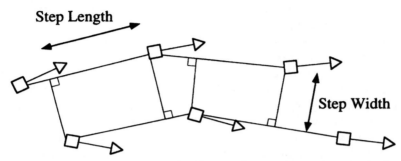

FIGURE 7.2. Footprint measures of walking proficiency. From "Learning in the Development of Infant Locomotion," by K.E. Adolph, 1997, *Monographs of the Society for Research in Child Development, 62* (3, Serial No. 251), p. 56. Copyright © 1997 by the Society for Research in Child Development, Inc. Reprinted with permission.

ing the body into an environment that provides support, a clear path, and a place or an object to be attained by the movements. Learning is indeed occurring.

What, then, is learned? In general, children learn how to cope with the various affordances offered by their environment, as their own body's proportions, strength, and capacity for balance are changing. Infants learn about properties of themselves as they learn about affordances of the environment such as traversable properties of surfaces and negotiable paths. In a nutshell, they learn to control locomotion for the task of achieving a goal. The next section considers what is learned with reference to more specific environmental properties that support locomotion.

Information for Locomotion: Surfaces of Support

Do infants know, by the time they are ready to move off under their own power, that a substantial surface must be available, directly under them, that is strong enough and large enough to support their own body's size and weight? Baillargeon, Needham, and DeVos (1992) found that infants under 6.5 months of age, when watching a box make contact with a surface, seemed to perceive that *any* amount of contact between the box and the platform on which it rested was sufficient to ensure the box's stability. Older infants apparently expected a more complete surface of contact to ensure stability. How do infants come to detect a solid surface of support that will hold their bodies while resting and even moving?

The Ground

Locomotion is only possible upon a surface that can support the weight of the moving creature. A very flimsy surface, even the surface of a pond, may support a bug, but a terrestrial mammal requires a surface that is substantial, rigid, continuous, flat, and reasonably smooth. The surface must be identified as traversable, with potential paths extending ahead, before one sets out to locomote over it, and there are properties that specify traversability of a surface available to creatures with adequate perceptual systems. These include an optically specified textured array and multimodally specified solidity. Human infants must learn to detect the presence of a traversable surface before moving onto it. Exploring a potential ground for locomotion includes scanning it for optical evidence of sufficient stability, extension, texture, and so on, and testing it haptically for its frictional properties and weight-bearing potential. To afford locomotion, these properties must be scaled to the infant's own size and weight, as well. Although babies sit or rest in a prone posture on surfaces before locomotion begins, it may be that self-guided movement over a surface is a preliminary requirement for detecting information that specifies good traversability.

Experiments were conducted with crawling and newly walking infants on a platform with changeable surfaces to investigate the development of infants' perception of traversability (E.J. Gibson, Riccio, Schmuckler, Stoffregen, Rosenberg, & Taormina, 1987). The testing situation was a walkway (see fig. 7.3) constructed to permit change of surfaces varying in visible and substantial properties. The frame of the walkway was raised off the ground, with side frames holding protective netting. A firm, padded starting platform was placed at one end, backed by curtains that served to conceal an experimenter. Parents stood opposite the infants at an open end, waiting to receive the infant. Subjects were crawling infants and young walkers. Various surfaces were contrasted to determine whether the infants would explore them for traversability and proceed to the coaxing parent or would refuse to embark.

A rigid surface was constructed of sturdy plywood, covered with a textured, opaque fabric of a white-and-brown cross-hatched pattern. The fabric was stretched tautly over the plywood and felt hard to the touch. A nonrigid surface constructed of a waterbed covered with the same patterned fabric was pliable. It oscillated gently, presenting a wavy appearance, and felt "squishy" when touched. The infant was placed on the starting platform in a sitting position by the parent, who then quickly moved to the open end, smiling silently at the infant. A trial, lasting up to 2 minutes, was videotaped and later coded for latency to embark (move off the starting platform), time spent in visual and haptic

FIGURE 7.3. Model of the walkway. The baby's mother stands at the open end; an experimenter stands behind the closed curtains at the entrance. Surfaces beyond the starting platform (SP) may be changed for testing. From "Detection of the Traversability of Surfaces by Crawling and Walking Infants," by E.J. Gibson, G. Riccio, M.A. Schmuckler, T.A. Stoffregen, D. Rosenberg, and J. Taormina, 1987, *Journal of Experimental Psychology: Human Perception and Performance, 13*, p. 534. Copyright © 1987 by the American Psychological Association, Inc. Reprinted with permission.

exploration, and "displacement" behavior (evasive activity such as looking away, playing with nets, etc.).

The rigid surface, as might be expected, was embarked on sooner, was explored less, and generated less evasive activity than the pliable one. Nearly all the infants crossed the rigid surface to the parent within the allotted 2 minutes. But overall behavior of the walkers and the crawlers differed. The walkers spent more time in haptic exploration of the waterbed, fewer crossed it, and all those who did crawled across, whereas more than a quarter of them rose and walked across the rigid surface. In a second experiment, the two surfaces were placed side by side, the parent standing in the middle, permitting an infant to "choose sides." Walkers chose the rigid surface by a large majority, and the few who chose the waterbed crawled over it. Crawlers showed no preference. The walkers explored the waterbed to a greater extent, discovered its poor affordance for upright walking, and only crossed it, if at all, on all fours.

Visual exploration (extended scanning) was a factor in these experiments.

What might constitute optical information for presence of a surface that will support locomotion? A further experiment with the walkway contrasted two surfaces equally firm to the touch, one covered with the same patterned fabric as before, the other covered with matte black velveteen that exhibited no inhomogeneity whatsoever to an adult eye. When the surfaces were presented singly, they were crossed by crawlers and walkers alike, although latency to embark was considerably longer for the black surface. Just as many walkers walked on the black surface as on the patterned one. When the two surfaces were presented so as to force a choice, both crawlers and walkers chose the patterned surface significantly more often. Lack of optical information for a firm surface leads to wariness, even when available haptic information specifies supportability. The experiments contrasting the waterbed with a rigid surface showed greater haptic exploration by walkers than by crawlers. Longer active experience with surfaces leads to increased exploration for their affordances for locomotion.

Drop-offs

What if there is no information for a surface of support? No adult human deliberately walks off into a void. A blind person taps ahead with a cane. We do indeed avoid a drop-off. Must we learn the requirement for specification of some surface before self-directed locomotion is safe? Walk, Gibson, and Tighe (1957) asked this question when they had at their disposal a small colony of rats reared in total darkness. They constructed a so-called "visual cliff" to test the rats (see chap. 3 for details). Both dark-reared animals and their light-reared litter mates showed a very strong preference for descending on the shallow side, rather than onto the evident "cliff," and did not cross back and forth.

Experiments with some other animals tested at an early age, including baby chicks and very young goats (both precocial animals), showed a similar preference (E.J. Gibson & Walk, 1960; Walk & Gibson, 1961). Experiments with cats were not so clear. Kittens reared in the dark and tested soon after their eyes opened wandered awkwardly about the apparatus in either direction, occasionally bumping their noses against a wall but, after a day or two in the light, avoided the cliff. If learning via reinforcing a performance were at stake, the kittens should have learned that the transparent glass floor supported them, despite the appearance of a drop. But learning to guide self-initiated locomotion on an optically specified surface that can be both felt and seen as traversal occurs may be the result of a different kind of learning. Less precocial animals like kittens and human infants need practice. Many human infants have been tested with the cliff. Walk and Gibson (1961) in their original research with crawling infants concluded that infants detected the depth at an edge as soon as they could crawl.

There are several kinds of information for depth at an edge. Stereopsis will come first to mind, perhaps, but it is not functional in human infants for at least 4 months after birth. Information from movement, such as motion parallax, is available earlier and is undoubtedly used in detecting sizes of things (see chap. 6). Accretion and deletion of texture at an edge is excellent information for comparing depths of surfaces and appears to be functional, as indicated by reaching preferences, by 5 to 7 months (Granrud, Yonas, Smith, Arterberry, Glicksman, & Sorknes, 1984). However, perceiving what the layout affords is geared to action and to a task (going somewhere, in this case), and detecting the information that specifies the affordance may well require experience. This is a positive kind of learning, not conditioning of a fear. Detecting an adequately specified surface that will support self-controlled locomotion and learning to guide locomotion over it are major tasks. More recent research suggests that experience in guiding the body over a well-specified surface plays a role in perceiving the affordance of a surface for action.

Self-produced movement, while guiding locomotion visually, emerged as a critical factor in research with kittens by Held and Hein (1963). In one experiment with a "kitten carousel," dark-reared kittens were given experience walking about, one guiding its own action and the other, yoked to its partner, pulled about passively over the same territory in a small gondola. Afterward, both "active" and "passive" kittens were tested on the visual cliff. All the active kittens avoided the deep side, whereas all the passive kittens failed to. This finding strengthens the notion that guided action combining visual and kinesthetic information from the action systems involved is essential for the kind of affordance that is being learned.

Campos, Langer, and Krowitz (1970) and Campos and Langer (1971) found that heart rate of 2- and 3.5-month-old infants decelerated on the deep side of the cliff but not on the shallow side, leading them to conclude that human infants detect information for depth by this age but show no fear, which would be indicated presumably by accelerated heart rate. A comparison of younger and older infants suggested that heart rates of 9-month-old infants accelerated when they were on the deep side. A 9-month-old group of infants who had been crawling for 2 months avoided the deep side of the cliff but crossed, crawling to their mothers, on the shallow side (Campos, Hiatt, Ramsay, Henderson, & Svedja, 1978). Campos and colleagues (1978) concluded that emergence of fear of heights accounts for these differences, but their results also indicate the importance of previous locomotor experience for avoiding the cliff.

Several other studies have presented evidence that length of crawling experience predicts cliff avoidance (see, e.g., Bertenthal & Campos, 1990). Learning about surfaces while crawling is evidently an important factor. These studies have varied considerably in circumstances of cliff presentation, age of infants, and significance of the differences obtained. But it seems pertinent to point out that virtually none of them observed *exploratory* behavior. This could be a serious oversight, because exploratory activity, active searching for information, is the essence of perceptual learning. If perception of the affordance of a surface is dependent on experience, then perceptual learning by way of exploratory activity must be involved. This activity would most certainly include detection of information from multiple perceptual systems (visual, tactual, and muscle-joint). If experienced crawlers are better or faster learners about surface properties, it may be because pickup of multimodal information is better coordinated for them. Multimodal information is important for learning about object properties (Eppler, 1995) and probably also for exploring surfaces for their traversable properties. Such exploration may be more extensive and more effective on a new surface for more skilled crawlers (Eppler, Adolph, Gibson, Lax, & Shahinfar, 1992).

It seems clear that the facts are not yet all in for understanding the role of experience in avoidance of a drop-off. There is reason to think that exploratory activity is more effective in discovery of affordances in more experienced infants, because of the need for detection of multimodal information and its meaning for action. An experiment on multimodal visual-tactual exploration of surface properties was conducted by E.J. Gibson and Schmuckler (1989) with precrawlers and crawlers. Infants were presented simultaneously with videotapes of a hand pushing on either a net or a firm Plexiglas surface with a net stretched underneath it, while their own hands (unseen) rested on one or the other of the two surfaces. The question was whether the infants would identify the surface being felt and look preferentially at the one specifying it visually. Crawlers exhibited a preference for watching the haptically specified surface, but precrawlers did not. Research that focuses on the role and quality of exploratory activity as new surfaces are presented to prelocomotor and locomotor infants will help resolve many questions.

A further point needs to be clarified with regard to the visual cliff. Considerable research in recent years has sought to trace the development of fear of heights in young children (Campos et al., 1978; Bertenthal & Campos, 1990). In this research the visual cliff is often used as a device for testing such a fear. That fear of heights is not innate and may begin to be apparent after an infant has had some experience with self-guided locomotion is quite likely. This issue should not be confused, however, with the one under discussion here—that is, how human infants detect the affordance of a surface for locomotion. That it is a matter for perceptual learning; experience exploring surfaces appears to be a requisite, but fear as a mediator is highly unlikely. This conclusion is supported by the finding that infants with Down's syndrome avoid the deep side of the visual cliff but do not exhibit heart rate acceleration when placed directly on it (Cichetti and Sroufe, 1978). There are many kinds of surfaces to be differentiated by a mobile infant, and the motive for doing so arises from the infant's own need to use the resources offered by the surroundings for such a task as moving through them.

Locomotion on Slopes

An experimental situation that gives us valuable information about development of locomotion in potentially risky environments is a descent paradigm in which

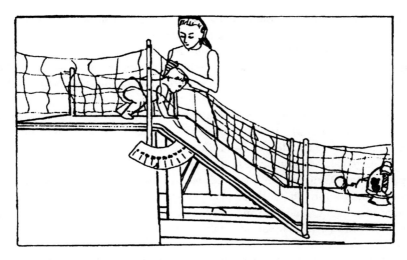

FIGURE 7.4. Walkway with adjustable slope. Infants began at one end of the walkway and traversed the sloping middle section while an experimenter monitored their safety. From "Learning in the Development of Infant Locomotion," by K.E. Adolph, 1997, *Monographs of the Society for Research in Child Development, 62* (3, Serial No. 251), p. 42. Copyright © 1997 by the Society for Research in Child Development, Inc. Reprinted with permission.

a path's degree of slope can be varied. This paradigm was used by Adolph (1995, 1997) for studies with crawling and walking infants. A novice crawler or walker will be at risk proceeding on a slope beyond some threshold where control of stability is lost. Adolph's investigations show that infants have much to learn about coping with slopes. Her equipment featured a reversible walkway with an adjustable slope between a starting platform at one end and a receiving platform at the other (see fig. 7.4). The procedure was to place the baby on the starting platform, with a parent at the receiving end offering a Cheerio. Either end could serve as the starting platform, so the baby could be confronted with either an ascent or a descent, at inclinations varying from 0° to 40°. The infant's exploratory activity before ascending or descending was observed and videotaped, as was the method of ascent or descent (or refusal). Of particular interest were the infants' ability to assess their capability for climbing or descending the slope and the observable changes as the method and skill of locomotion develop.

Adolph began her research by observing walkers' behavior on the slopes. Her method permitted her to assess both actual ability to ascend or descend and willingness to try (by no means necessarily the same). On the average, the toddlers' judgments were appropriately scaled to their ability to walk on the slopes, so that they walked on the safe ones and refused to walk on the riskier ones. The infants were more willing to try steeper ascents than steeper descents, ascent being actually less risky. Better perceivers, that is, those whose prospective judgments of risk were more accurate, explored the hills more effectively by looking, touching, and trying out different positions for descent, such as backing or sliding. They were evidently seeking to determine whether the hill *afforded* descent for them and by what means the descent could be accomplished, if not by walking.

A comparison of walkers with crawlers on slopes proved particularly interesting (Adolph et al., 1993a). Unlike the average toddler in the study just cited, a majority of crawlers showed little wariness of the downhill slopes and often plunged ahead on inclines that were too steep, having to be rescued by an experimenter. Obviously, an infant has much to learn about traversing sloping terrains. As Adolph put it, "What good perceivers do is gauge their abilities online, from moment to moment and task to task. They know how to explore, when to explore, and what information to take from it" (1995, p. 749). But this knowledge must be acquired.

How it is acquired was the question Adolph (1997) asked in a longitudinal study observing the same group of infants from precrawling status until they became competent walkers. Their behavior on slopes was assessed at intervals of 3 weeks, and their parents kept diaries of locomotor activity at home, including such incidents as falls. Babies were tested in their first week of crawling, and testing ended at about 16 months. A control group of infants came during their first week of crawling, the tenth week of crawling, and during their first week of walking, so that the effect of repeated testing on the slopes could be determined.

Infants' ability to crawl or walk successfully downhill (crawling or walking boundary) changed at every session, increasing with expertise of crawling, decreasing when an infant shifted from belly crawling to hands and knees, and decreasing again when the infant shifted from crawling to walking. All babies had trouble walking down slopes when they began walking. Although their boundaries tended to increase with experience, the boundary did not always mirror the baby's perception of what was possible; many babies, even as walkers, overestimated their ability on occasion and had to be rescued. Although perceptual judgment of whether or not to descend had improved over weeks of crawling, this knowledge did not transfer from crawling to walking. There were in fact two learning curves for perceptual judgments of safe descent, one for crawling, followed by a second one after onset of walking. Learning to perceive the limits of their ability was no faster for walking than for crawling.

Learning involved acquiring expertise in preliminary exploration, including looking, touching, and trying out alternative means of descent. Hills no doubt looked different from a standing rather than a prone position, and problems of controlling posture were entirely different. The very few babies who did "transfer," not overestimating boundaries when they began to walk, were late walkers and seemed to carry with them a wary attitude. Learning to cope with slopes requires experience in using all possible information for postural control in relation to the surface the inclination presents, essentially learning to perceive what a particular slope affords for a particular perceiver-actor at the present moment.

Besides learning how steep a slope was safe for walking, these babies learned to use secondary means of descending—a sitting slide, backing prone, and so on. Such means were tried out as part of their exploratory activities, and their consequences perceived. Alternative means discovered earlier by a crawler were seldom transferred automatically to the baby's repertoire when walking began. Viewing the scene from a new position yielded different information, and maintaining equilibrium was a different problem. It is interesting that experience on these slopes in the laboratory was not a critical factor in learning. Babies in the control group showed the same improving pattern of boundary changes when crawling and decrement when they began to walk as did the babies observed every 3 weeks. Neither did falls outside the laboratory accelerate learning. What is essential to the learning experience appears to be practice in maintaining posture in ongoing activity plus learning to gauge consequences of exploratory activity in a new situation.

The sheer joy, for new crawlers or walkers, of striking out on one's own, is impressive to a watching adult. But mobility is a means that makes many new affordances attainable, and an infant soon appears to be heading somewhere: toward a parent, for a toy, and even, after a while, for an object that is for the moment occluded. Steering around obstacles, through openings that admit passage, as well as choosing a path that offers safe "footing" become important. What is the information for steering?

Going Somewhere

Guiding Locomotion

Locomotion is action, but with many qualifications. The manner of locomotion (crawling, walking, running) depends on environmental supports: is the terrain firm, even, extending well ahead, or is it slippery, uneven, uphill, downhill, possibly dropping off entirely? Furthermore, when we move our bodies we are going somewhere, to some destination that may even be invisible for the time being. Locomotion is "prospective," requiring constant decisions. Choosing the path that affords reaching the destination is crucial, as an adult driving or riding in a vehicle knows, and so is it for an infant, even in the early stages of locomotion. The kind of layout the terrain presents is important, as we have been stressing, and so is the goal, the mover's destination. The journey's end, for a novice crawler or walker, may be rather undefined, but as less effort is required to maintain balance and to cope with problematic conditions of getting ahead, goals can become more specific.

Obstacles and Apertures

Obstacles ahead of one "loom larger" as they are approached and thus can be perceived prospectively. Such a situation was dramatized in the so-called looming experiments. These experiments present information for "imminent collision," as J.J. Gibson put it—accelerated optical expansion of some object in the field of view. Even a shadow expanding provides such information, as demonstrated by Schiff (1965). He produced such an expansion pattern with a shadow cast on a large screen. The looming shadow was presented to subjects of several species (monkeys, kittens, chicks, crabs), all of which exhibited some form of avoidance behavior. Similar experiments with human infants (Bower, Broughton, & Moore, 1971; Ball & Tronick, 1971; Nanez, 1988; Petterson, Yonas, & Fisch, 1980) found that infants as young as 2 or 3 months, presented with a looming object, show avoidance behavior such as head retraction or blinking, especially when texture is present to provide further information for depth. These experiments projected an object or its shadow toward the stationary perceiver; but accelerated optical magnification of a contour or structure also occurs as an expanding flow pattern when the observer moves toward a barrier or obstacle of any kind. Information is thus provided for imminent collision unless the observer slows down. Background structure is progressively *covered* as the observer approaches.

On the other hand, an opening or aperture that can be passed through reveals magnification of a *vista,* so that background structure is progressively *uncovered* during the approach. One (the obstacle) must be avoided so as to prevent collision, whereas the other (the opening) invites passing through. The information for these opposite outcomes is available to anyone engaged in locomotion through the environment, and it is detectable at an early age, although its usefulness for guiding locomotion may not as yet be known. Carroll and Gibson (E.J. Gibson, 1991) performed an experiment patterned on the looming paradigm, contrasting the two types of information for infants of 3 months. Babies sat in an infant seat opposite one of two panels that approached them at a constant speed. The moveable panels were located in front of a textured background and began their journey there. One of these panels was solid, covering only a small portion of the background. The other covered the whole background, except for an opening the same size as the solid panel, through which the textured background could be seen. As the solid panel traveled toward the baby, less and less of the background was visible. But as the opening in the larger panel approached, more and more of the background vista became visible. In one case the display simulated approach to an obstacle, while in the other it simulated approach to an aperture affording passage. Measures of head pressure against the back of the infant seat indicated that babies pulled back their heads as the solid panel approached but did not do so as the panel with the aperture approached and opened up a widening vista. Schmuckler and Li (1998) repeated the experiment with a different measure, eye blinks, and found that obstacles elicited more eye blinks (looming responses) than did apertures.

Discrimination of these two events shows that babies are equipped perceptually to use the differentiating information, but how and when to use it in guiding locomotion that is self-instigated and self-propelled is another matter. Rules for visual steering need to be discovered in the course of action. The perceiver-actor's speed, size, and agility must be factored in. Steering depends not only on avoiding obstacles and heading toward openings that permit passage; heading toward the goal and maintaining *stability* are equally essential. Again, the optical flow patterns produced by one's own movement provide useful information. The center of the radial flow pattern during forward movement is the direction of movement, specifying where one is heading. Up-and-down motion in the periphery of the layout specifies how well one is maintaining balance during locomotion. Putting all the information together requires exploration of one's own dynamic capacities during active locomotion.

Detouring around a depression or hole in the ground requires a certain amount of foresight and attentive visual exploratory activity. In an experiment by E.J. Gibson and Schmuckler (1989), toddlers detoured around an apparent hole in the floor, but only a minority of crawlers did so. When an upright obstacle is placed in the path, so that postural adjustments are required to pass around it, novice walkers may well find it difficult to steer around the obstruction and still maintain their equilibrium. Gibson and Schmuckler compared the effect of imposed optical flow on young walkers as they attempted to move through a cluttered versus an uncluttered environment. They walked along a 12-foot hallway affording a clear path in one condition, whereas obstructions (orange traffic pylons) were irregularly placed on the path in the other condition. The hallway was movable (resting on wheels) so that it could be moved slightly (creating exaggerated flow patterns) while the children were walking to a parent at one end. There were three groups of children, with varying lengths of walking experience (3, 20, and 30 months). Room movement, producing an imposed optical flow, resulted in greater postural perturbation when the path was cluttered with obstacles, with the greatest effect on the least experienced walkers and least effect for the most experienced walkers. The less experienced walkers staggered and sometimes fell when attempting to negotiate the cluttered path. The effort of maintaining postural equilibrium while steering around things requires practice coordinating locomotion in a real-world environment.

Round-about Behavior

In the real world, locomotion typically has a goal. Unlike the experimental situation just described, the goal may be temporarily hidden, the scene may present more than one path, or one path may be more economical than another. The actor must not only steer around a barrier but foresee a route to the goal. Again, actual experience in locomotion seems to be a prerequisite to successful performance. The path to be traversed must be coordinated with locomotor activity as a means to the goal, which must be located relative to both actor and barriers. There are three parts in the equation, so to speak: the perceiver-actor, the barrier or obstacle, and the destination. The latter two must be related to each other as well as to the perceiver's path of movement in getting from one place to another by a particular mode of activity.

A very instructive experiment by Lockman (1984) compared performance of infants when they either reached or crawled around a barrier to retrieve an object that they had just watched the experimenter place behind the barrier. The infants (8 to 9 months old) were already both reaching and crawling at the first testing session, and they were tested again at intervals of 3 to 4 weeks. They were presented with two types of barrier, as well, either an opaque one or a transparent one of the same size and placement. In the case of the opaque barrier, most of the infants succeeded in the reaching task 6 weeks or so before they succeeded in making the crawling detour. The transparent reaching task was solved later than the opaque task, and again the crawling detour was slower. The locomotor performance of detouring seemingly had to be achieved on its own. Achievement of success in the earlier maturing activity did not transfer to the later maturing one. This specificity to the mode of action is similar to the lack of transfer from crawling to walking on slopes. Generalization of layout knowledge, which we will return to, is not automatic at first, reminding us that learning about an affordance includes the way the body is used to achieve it in a given task.

Learning about barriers was easier when the barrier visibly occluded background and had obvious contours that could be seen around. In this case, slight head movements informed the perceiver visually that background was being occluded, whereas only touching was informative for the transparent barrier. Exploratory touching when the hands are occupied in crawling may require some experience until good crawling skill is achieved.

A different view of what changes developmentally, the so-called information-processing view, might have predicted that successful detour behavior, such as reaching or crawling around a barrier to retrieve a toy, would depend on developing ability to "represent" the toy when it is no longer in sight. But Lockman included in his research an experiment on "object permanence," a Piagetian term for expecting that an object will continue to exist even when one has watched it disappear from view. The same infants were tested, sitting on the floor, with three opaque covers before them. They watched the experimenter hide a toy under one of them, in successively different locations, and were allowed to retrieve it. This task was performed successfully by all the infants at least as soon (or before) both detour tasks. Presumably the infants were capable of remembering where the object was, before they were able to regain it by appropriate action.

The notion that the layout, in very early development, is not perceived as a single organized entity like a map, irrespective of what is done in it, is supported further by research of Hofstader and Reznick (1996). In their experiments, locating a covered object by gaze direction was compared with reaching for it. Looking around to locate things develops earlier, as we have seen, than reaching for and grasping them. In a simple delayed-reaction procedure, infants of 7, 9, and 11 months watched a toy being hidden in one of two wells on a surface in front of them. An occluder was then raised for 3 seconds. Next, the infants could either look toward the hiding place and reach out to obtain the toy or, in other trials where a transparent barrier prevented a reach, only look toward the correct hiding place. The toy was made available (retrieved by either the infant or the experimenter) if the gaze or the reach was correct. Gaze direction was more often accurate than reach at all three ages, with reaches becoming more accurate as age increased. When the baby looked and reached in the same trial, gaze was frequently correct even when reach was not. Errors were apt to be perseverative (a repetition of the last response made), and such errors occurred more often in the case of reaching. We conclude that looking correctly toward an occluded goal precedes reaching correctly, and reaching correctly precedes direct crawling to it. Comparable results were obtained by Ahmed and Ruffman (1996), who demonstrated correct visual search despite still inaccurate manual search.

Flexibility of exploratory activity in selecting an open path to a goal was studied by McKenzie and Bigelow (1986) in a detour situation with three age groups: 10, 12, and 14 months. The infants were presented with a simple detour path, with the baby's mother at first visible and then seated behind a barrier. The barrier required a detour to either the left or the right to reach the mother. The infants were given an aerial view of the arrangement before they were placed at the starting point. After four trials, the barrier was relocated so that the open route was at the other side of the space. No infant was as yet walking in the youngest group, a third were walking in the 12-month-old group, and most of them walked in the 14-month-old group. Although nearly all succeeded in reaching their mothers in the first four trials, the older ones chose more efficient routes. When the screens were relocated, the oldest age group again chose more efficient paths around the barrier.

Together, these experiments suggest that exploring the layout occurs with each mode of activity as one follows another developmentally, and that moving toward a goal, whatever the arrangement of barriers and visibility of the goal object, becomes more efficient and more flexible. These achievements have profound consequences, laying the groundwork for knowledge about the world.

Exploring the Layout: The Consequences for Knowledge

Independent locomotion is important for learning about the layout of the world, about oneself, and about other people and social situations (Benson & Uzgiris, 1985; B.I. Bertenthal, Campos, & Barrett, 1984; B.I. Bertenthal & Campos, 1990). Gustafson (1984) compared three groups of infants between 8 and 10 months of age in terms of their exploratory activity in a free laboratory situation. Two groups were prelocomotor, but the infants in one group were moving about in mechanical walkers. Babies in the third group had achieved independent loco-motion by means of crawling. Gustafson provided them with access to toys and other people and observed them for interest shown and time spent in social ac-tivities and object manipulation. The mobile infants—both those in walkers and those who could crawl independently—explored on their own and attended to more features of the environment, giving them quite different experiences from the nonlocomoting infants. Infants who can move about are no longer confined to near space and can autonomously explore more distant vistas, thus expand-ing their functional world. Their frame of reference can gradually become a more distal one. Freedom to move on one's own provides a fantastic opportu-nity to learn about what the world affords. The point may be obvious, but we need to consider the nature of the information given by motions of things and by movement of ourselves. What is the information, how is it obtained, and what exactly does it tell a developing infant?

Disappearance, Reappearance, and the Persistence of Surfaces

One of the first tasks awaiting newborn infants is learning about the layout of the world around them. People come and go; the baby is picked up and moved from crib to changing table, held, and put down. The scene changes, but some aspects of it remain constant. Gravity was an effective force even in the womb, and sounds could be heard, varying in intensity depending on nearness. Scan-ning the layout to explore with the visual system is new. Newborn infants have poor visual acuity for picking up details of static objects, but optical changes produced by movement are informative and can be discerned. This ability is very useful because it permits differentiation of permanent features of the en-vironment from shifting or temporary ones. The ground, the sky (or ceiling, per-haps), and a horizon between them are unchanging features of the world that persist even when people go away, or the baby is moved.

Information about where things are is relative, always, to the persisting, constant features of the world. It is also relative to the baby. When the baby is moved, optical flow of the entire surround results, nearer things at a faster rate, farther things more slowly, in an orderly way known as motion perspective that results in information for relative locations of things. If an object moves, on the other hand, it moves separately against the background. This difference pro-vides an immediate source of information for the baby as unique and separate from other objects and from the surroundings (see chap. 6).

When objects move, they provide another source of information for arrange-ment of the layout, by covering and uncovering whatever is behind them. The moving edge of the object gradually deletes part of the background scene, and the area being uncovered gradually accretes in visual substance. These orderly results of movement of an object provide excellent detectable information for where things are in relation to one another. The baby has a lot of looking to do, but perceptual learning about the environment is possible long before infants can move on their own, and it most certainly happens. There is information for what is permanent in the layout, for what changes, for what is nearer to the viewer or to something else. Surfaces like the ground are seen to persist; as objects move across a background scene, things are seen to appear and disappear as they are uncovered and covered. Babies can even supply some of this information by raising a hand and observing the consequence for what is now visible. They can also move their heads and watch the optical motion that results.

Self-produced movements, first of the head and eyes, then of the arms and hands in reaching for things, and finally of the limbs in locomotion, are of critical importance for gaining knowledge of the layout and object location. An object moving behind something and then emerging is a spectacle that babies witness frequently before locomotion, and expectation of the consequences may be set up, as a result. Haith and his colleagues (Haith, Wentworth, & Canfield, 1993) have demonstrated anticipatory visual gaze direction in experiments with 3.5-month-old infants. Von Hofsten (1983) found that by the time infants are able to reach for stationary objects, they can also catch moving objects, predicting their path and aiming ahead (see chap. 6). Baillargeon (1993) has reported a number of experiments investigating infants' expectation of the reappearance of a temporarily occluded object after watching it being covered, extending a method devised earlier by Bower (1967, 1972). The method uses visual attention (gaze and tracking) to show that infants of 2 to 5 months expect reappearance of an object passing behind a screen.

Baillargeon's interest in "occlusion events," as she calls them, has been to examine infants' development of "physical knowledge." We share her concern with the role of events in revealing structure of the layout and the dynamics of movement of objects in relation to other objects. Her research has centered on infants' detection of objects passing behind a screen and emerging (or being procured by an experimenter's hand) after apparently moving through barriers while covered. What is observed and measured is the infant's looking behavior. Longer looks at the outcome of one of two events being compared are interpreted as indicators of surprise at the object's presence or availability, or some feature of it. These experiments have produced evidence for infant knowledge of structure and location of things in the layout through observing the dynamics of occlusion as objects move in relation to other objects that impose barriers.

We present one example of a Baillargeon experiment (see Baillargeon, 1994, for this and others). The infants (4.5 to 6.5 months) were first habituated to a screen rotating through a 180° arc, "in the manner of a drawbridge" (see fig. 7.5). Habituation was followed by one of two events. One was a "possible" event: a box was placed behind the screen; the screen then rotated but stopped when it encountered the box. The other was an "impossible" event: the screen rotated 180°, through the space occupied by the box, as though the box were not present. Even the 4.5—month-old infants looked longer at the impossible event.

Habituation Event

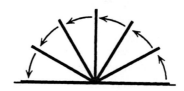

Test Event
Possible Event

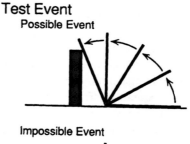

FIGURE 7.5. A "possible" and an "impossible" event (screen rotating through, an arc and stopping at, or apparently rotating through an obstacle). Infants looked longer at the "impossible" event. From "How Do Infants Learn about the Physical World?" by R. Baillargeon, 1994, *Current Directions in Psychological Science, 3,* p. 138. Copyright © 1994 by the American Psychological Society. Reprinted with permission.

Impossible Event

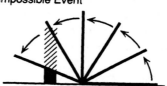

This experiment has been replicated by Baillargeon with many elaborations in the size of the barrier, the manner of occlusion, and even the substance of the obstacle. As conditions are elaborated, younger infants are less able to predict violations of possible spatial encounters, but it is quite clear that infants can discover, by visual exploration, some very important aspects of location of things, when dynamic information in the form of an event is provided. Searching for things to be accessed by reaching and grasping is a later development, and as we now know, knowledge gained with one action system does not automatically transfer to another. We next consider why this may be so.

Finding Hidden Things

If babies know that something they have seen covered up or occluded by another object is still physically there, why are they not immediately able to reach out and retrieve it? This story begins with Piaget (1954), who thought that babies over the first 2 years gradually develop a concept of "object permanence," passing through various stages of prereasoning, and maturing around 2 years. The world as originally perceived by infants, he thought, consists of fleeting images, fragmented and evanescent; only after long development aided by activity can children conceive of an object as solid, occupying a place, and enduring despite disappearance behind or under something else. The baby only perceives the object as permanent, Piaget thought, after a *concept* of the object as an enduring thing has been attained; no concept, no object—at least if it's not in plain view.

Piaget's experiments all used manual search tasks. These experiments (and many replicating them) found that infants do not consistently retrieve an object correctly after watching it hidden in one of two locations before them, until they are 8 or 9 months old. They are especially prone to make an error (the so-called A-not-B error) of reaching to the spot where the object was last hidden, even when they have just seen it hidden in another spot. But we have now reviewed evidence that babies are aware of the existence of occluded objects at a much earlier age and are able to access this knowledge by visually scanning the layout and gazing attentively for longer or shorter periods.

One resolution of this puzzle is that an infant must achieve control of a response system, such as reaching and manipulation, before knowledge can be appropriately related to a goal. It is also true that exploratory use of the emerging response system leads to knowledge. We have seen in the preceding chapter that skilled exploratory use of the manipulatory system is extremely effective in yielding knowledge about objects. It should be—and is—equally true that exploratory locomotion is particularly effective in yielding knowledge about the spatial layout and the position of oneself in relation to surrounding objects, including hidden ones (B.I. Berthenthal & Campos, 1990; Gibson & Spelke, 1983).

Locomotor ability has been shown in a number of experiments to predict success in search tasks such as Piaget's. Horobin and Acredolo (1986) investigated search behavior using a Piagetian object-permanence task, seeking to relate accuracy of search to the mobility of crawling infants and also to their visual attentiveness (described by "keeping an eye on" the movement and place of disappearance of a hidden object). A foam table constructed with hiding wells was placed just out of reach of the sitting infant, who watched the experimenter hide a small toy. After 3 seconds, the table was pushed within reach of the infant. After the infant had watched and retrieved the object several times at the first location (A), the experimenter hid the object at a second location (B). The direction of the infant's visual attention during the delay and during search behavior was coded, and information was obtained from parents as to how long their infants had been able to sustain a sitting posture, and how long they had been capable of independent locomotion. Neither age nor duration of unsupported sitting predicted correct performance on the B trials, but duration of independent mobility did. Visual attentiveness also predicted correct search. Looking back toward A (the earlier correct location) on a B trial was associated with a perseverative error, but keeping an eye on the B hiding place augured success. Visual exploratory activity, following movements informative about location of objects in relation to oneself, aided retrieval of hidden objects. Furthermore, mobility and visual attentiveness were positively related to each other.

Mobility was again found to predict correct search in an object-permanence task employed by Kermoian and Campos (1988). Their infants were all 8.5 months of age and were divided into three groups varying in locomotor history. One group was as yet prelocomotor, with no mobility experience; one group (also prelocomotor) had walker-assisted practice for a period of 2 to 17 weeks before the search test; and a third group had been creeping on hands and knees for a period of 1 to 14 weeks. Both the walker-assisted group and the group of infants who were independently creeping performed better on the search tasks than did the prelocomotor infants. The duration of locomotor experience was a significant predictor of search success. Infants with 9 or more weeks of experience (either creeping or in walkers) were better at the search tasks. A supplementary study compared search performance of hands-and-knees crawlers and walker-assisted babies with babies who crawled on their bellies (the abdomen not lifted from the floor). The belly crawlers were poorer at spatial search than both other groups, performing at the level of prelocomotor infants. These results imply that locomotion with a good view of the layout being explored is markedly facilitating. Guiding action while visually exploring the layout promotes ability to locate things in a permanent spatial layout.

Layout of a room or an accustomed terrain remains permanent in most respects as the observer moves around. Objects that are out of sight are often occluded by features of the space like furniture, as well as by landscape markers that do not change. But furnishings in a larger space can be moved, relative to the permanent overall layout. Keeping track of where things are in relation to shifts of other objects makes guidance toward a goal more difficult and demands a higher order of exploratory skills, both visual and locomotor. Generalization of these skills to new situations and tasks may not be automatic. Bai and Bertenthal (1992) examined the role of locomotor status in a search task that involved a change in the egocentric relation of the hidden object to the infant (whether it was now on the right or the left), although the hiding place on a table remained constant. Infants (31 to 34 weeks old) watched the object being hidden in one of two wells on the table; then either the infant or the table was rotated, so that the correct hiding place as viewed originally by the infant was now right-left reversed. The researchers found that search performance interacted with mobility status. Creeping infants with longer durations of locomotor experience showed superior search performance in the infant-displacement condition, but *not* when the table was displaced. Search accuracy of the other infants (prelocomotor or inefficient, less-experienced crawlers) was inferior and did not differ for the two conditions. A similar task had been given to infants in two previous experiments, with opposed results. Bremner (1978) reported better search following rotation of the infant, rather than the table; Goldfield and Dickerson (1981) reported the opposite result. But neither study had introduced the infants' locomotor status as a variable.

Bai and Bertenthal (1992) also observed infants' visual attention to the target, as had Horobin and Acredolo (1986). However, they found no relation between time of looking at the target cup and locomotor status, nor any interaction of visual attention with displacement condition. Visual tracking did nevertheless predict search performance in both infant-displacement and table-displacement conditions. The contributions of locomotor efficiency and visual attention were apparently independent in this task. These results extend the evidence of importance of mobility and locomotor experience in a task where egocentric localization poses a risk. But visual attention appears to be a pretty consistent predictor, however the disruption of the egocentric view is accomplished. Visual attention has been available longer as an exploratory strategy than locomotion, which may explain its more general usefulness at this early age. The task given the infant in this procedure is complicated by the disruption of the infant's point of view. We now consider points of view and the kind of information they provide for perception of the spatial layout.

Geographical Space and "Points of View"

Piaget liked to emphasize that infants view the world egocentrically, detecting the relations of things only as they appear from their own location at the moment. This opinion helped explain the prevalence of perseverative errors, but we have seen that such errors are closely tied to an infant's task, for example having to reach for something rather than indicating its location by gaze direction or by looking time. The restriction of a point of view—how things look from where I stand—is indeed a fact, however. The term "allocentric" has been coined to denote an objective, unbiased view of the layout of the world as opposed to an egocentric one. How things look from *here*, where I sit, is not the same as the arrangement of things as they look to *you*, or as they are geographically organized. Infants do have to learn something about this, and independent locomotion that allows them to adopt changing views of the layout has much to do with acquiring the knowledge that the layout remains invariant no matter where one is presently located.

Piagetian theory of how the layout is viewed by very young children, ultimately developing to an adult notion of geographical space ("Euclidean Space" in Piagetian terminology), is presented in detail in *The Child's Conception of Space* (Piaget & Inhelder, 1956). Briefly, infants' views are thought to be dominated by their own perspective, as in, for example, "we know very well that the child's outlook is at first completely egocentric and tends to change appearances which are in fact purely relative to his perception and activity, into false or spurious absolutes" (Piaget & Inhelder, 1956, p. 209). The child must "coordinate perspectives" as seen from many different angles to eventually achieve an objective concept of the layout. A now famous research task, "The Three Mountains," was employed to study developmental progression in coordinating views. A small toy landscape containing three differently sized and shaped mountains was displayed with a doll facing the display from one angle or another. A child was asked to indicate, by selecting from an array of photographs, what the doll could see. Awareness of changes in the appearance of the scene with changes of point of view was inferred from children's responses. The various aspects would eventually be integrated through an "act of intelligence" to achieve true coordination, presumed to be accomplished by 6 to 7 years. "Thus the perspective system which the child builds up . . . is not perceptual but conceptual in character" (Piaget & Inhelder, 1956, p. 245).

Our concern is not with such a conceptual system, which may or may not be attained in later childhood, but with childrens' opportunities to learn about the layout as their exploratory systems expand their horizons, long before knowledge can be tapped with questions and answers. We question whether the assumption of total egocentricity about the layout is correct, because babies are active obtainers of information, moving their heads and using exploratory systems, as they become available, to pick up information about the layout. The notion of static views that must be integrated seems wrong from the start.

Knowledge of the layout is not innate, however, and active use of the perceptual systems to acquire it can be severely retarded when perceptual exploratory activity is curtailed. Consider, briefly, the deprivation in this respect for children blind from birth (Fraiberg, 1977). Although these children are normal with respect to limb movement and development and with respect to hearing, they cannot visually explore the world, missing entirely the optical information available about object relations and the layout relative to themselves. Reaching and locomotion, both normally visually guided and motivated, are necessarily more difficult to achieve and slow in coming. Although language mostly progresses on schedule, Fraiberg found in a longitudinal study of a group of blind children that they were delayed in accomplishing correct usage of "*I*" and "*you*." Some invariant information that specifies *oneself* versus the *other one* was unavailable to them. This information may well be the station point in the visible layout where the speaker is located. *I* am *here*, and *you* are *there* (E.J. Gibson, 1991, pp. 5–22 ff.) The terms refer always to the speaker's station point. If the meaning of "I" is defined by the speaker's station point, a blind child may well be handicapped by lack of the opportunity to observe changing points of view as he or she begins to move around and change station points. Loveland (1984) investigated the possibility that understanding spatial points of view is a prerequisite to learning about locational invariance relative to the speaker. She followed a group of prelinguistic children for many months, assessing knowledge of the spatial layout with tasks of hiding and recovering toys, showing pictures to others, and so on, assessing also progression in their comprehension of "*I*" and "*you*." Understanding spatial points of view and their interchangeability was supported as a prerequisite for understanding the two pronouns. Deprivation of deaf children is in great contrast to the blind, since sign and gestural language are produced in a gesturally outlined physical space and make use of locational contrasts for communicative purposes (Emmorey & Reilly, 1995).

Although blind infants have the capacity to reach out and to move themselves as early as do other children (Fraiberg, 1977), their reaching out and mobility is curtailed by inability to explore visually and prospectively the external affordances of objects and layout. As locomotor ability advances exploration and ability to search for objects, so a delay in locomotion in blind children is accompanied by a delay in successful search for objects. Fraiberg (1977) suggested that developmental causal relationships may be different in the two cases, with attainment of "object permanence" preceding progression to upright locomotion for blind children and helping to provide incentives for walking by supporting their expectation of a permanent layout. For them, the advent of reaching out to a sounding object signaled the dawning of "object permanence" and thus in turn promoted locomotion. Visually perceived incentives for locomotion demanded a substitute mediator, the knowledge that objects exist externally in the spatial layout and can be reached for. Tactual and auditory discovery of objects' location in space would necessarily precede locomotion.

A.E. Bigelow (1992) investigated this hypothesis with three blind children. They were seen at home over an extended period. Locomotor development, reaching, and search were regularly observed. Locomotion (crawling) began at approximately the same time as reaching out for sounding objects at chest level. But walking was much delayed, and reaching out for sounding objects above or below chest level preceded it. Walking did not begin until 32, 17, and 36 months for these three children. These findings underline the importance of visual detection of a surface of support for locomotion and the advantage of interacting with objects while moving and exploring the layout from various perspectives. Ability to perceive the affordances for self-initiated action, especially locomotion, makes possible an easy progression of discovery of the layout of the world.

Perceiving the layout as permanent and objectively existing underlies perception of geographical space, as opposed to an egocentric perspective. Experiments on what is termed "position constancy" illustrate this change. Infants have to learn that when they move to a new location, the layout of objects and paths from one object to another stays the same. The position of an object remains constant, while bearing a new directional relation to the mover. It may be that gaining mobility helps to shift infants' frame of reference from an egocentric to an objective spatial reference system. But viewing the world is never a matter of looking at a static picture. By moving only the head back and forth an infant can easily observe the invariant relation of objects in the near layout to one another. But maintaining invariance of the perceived layout after a bodily rotation is generally thought to require detection of bodily information for the rotation itself and monitoring of the relation of the self to features of the environment.

Many experimenters have sought to unravel the developmental history of position constancy (see McKenzie, 1987, for a summary). These experiments are typically conducted in a homogeneous circular enclosure, with reference points inserted (or not) by the experimenter so as to control and vary systematically the information available for self-localization. In addition to any external reference points, infants would be, presumably, sensitive to vestibular and possibly other somatic information from their own body as their position moved. Keeping track of such information may be a rather sophisticated achievement, but it is one that is available to many other animals. Position with respect to gravity, for example, is relevant and used even by the young of most mammalian species. External referents provided in the experiments are most often visual, occasionally auditory.

An experiment by Rieser (1979) used a circular experimental chamber, without normal doors or windows as reference points. The 6-month-old infants were placed so as to face four round small windows that might or might not contain displays. All the infants learned to anticipate a display appearing in one of these windows (a human face or a puppet). A light flashed and a bell sounded, after which the display came on as a reinforcement for the infant's turning to gaze at the window containing the display. The training was continued until a criterion of correct responding was met. After meeting the criterion, all the infants were rotated 90° around the line of sight, so they no longer looked straight ahead at the bank of windows. Test trials were then given, with no display in the windows. The experiment included six conditions, each presenting different reference information. Condition 1 presented no extra information other than that provided by the infant's bodily movement following training. Condition 2 had a bright pattern surrounding all the windows, not distinguishing any one. In condition 3, (gravity condition) the infants were tilted to the left during training. The display appeared above and to the right of their line of sight. They were rotated 90° after training, so that they leaned to the right during testing. The other three conditions varied in visual patterning of the windows, so there was some distinctive visual pattern for reference. At testing, gazes toward the window bearing the same spatial relation to the infant as during training were labeled "egocentric"; gazes at the window where the display had actually *appeared* during training were labeled "geocentric." Other gazes were labeled irrelevant. The majority of the test gazes were egocentric for all groups except group 3, the group that had been tilted with respect to gravity. These latter infants also showed some tendency to egocentric response in later tests. The author concluded that at 6 months, infants are not yet able to update their spatial positions as they are moved with respect to a target. But the direction of gravity did effectively influence their responses and served as a partial referent.

We cite two recent examples of research on this problem: one with prelocomotor infants and one with older, newly locomoting infants. In the first, infants from 4 to 8 months were observed for their ability to locate an invisible target after a change in their direction of gaze (Tyler & McKenzie, 1990). The authors were concerned with development of their ability to use information arising from movement of the body, in the absence of constant external signposts or landmarks. In one condition, the infants were trained to anticipate a "peekaboo" in a fixed location with no other reference points. The peekaboo was preceded by a signal. The baby sat on the mother's lap, and the mother rotated her chair from trial to trial just before the peekaboo, so that the baby witnessed the event from three different locations in a training routine. On a following test trial, the baby was moved to a fourth novel viewing position. This sequence was called "association" training. In a second condition, the babies had a comparable changing rotational pattern, but the peekaboo event followed only *after* babies turned their heads to anticipate the correct fixed location. This routine was called "instrumental" training. The baby was tested from the novel position after this training. In the first ("association") condition, the 6- and 8-month-old infants were able to anticipate the peekaboo event correctly from the novel position, but in the second ("instrumental") condition, none of the infants anticipated correctly. Apparently, training that specifically reinforced a head turn inhibited the infants from attending to vestibular stimulation so as to monitor their own position with reference to the concomitant peekaboo event. So in one task, babies exhibited position constancy from 6 months onward, but in the other they did not.

In a further experiment with 8-month-olds, a landmark was provided for half the infants—a red-and-white arrow suspended above the target spot—thus giving the babies a constant referent. Two training conditions were included, as before, half with the arrow and half without in each condition. The babies who received "association" training looked expectantly to the peekaboo site at the test trial, both when the visible referent was present and when it was not. But the instrumentally trained babies looked correctly more often than chance only when the referent was present. The instrumentally trained babies needed the visual referent to maintain position constancy, evidently unable to monitor their location to the target on the basis of vestibular information alone. Their instrumental training without the landmark evidently led them to learn three distinct turning responses for the three directions of turning, rather than to use vestibular information alone to detect relocation with respect to the layout. It is of marked interest that the so called "association" infants could do so. It is also notable that they were indicating the target position by gaze alone, the looking system that is first available for exploring the spatial layout. We have seen that use of the manipulatory or the locomotor system does not necessarily follow immediately for successful object-location finding.

Consider now a position constancy experiment with 1-year-olds in a locomotor search task (E.W. Bushnell, McKenzie, Lawrence, & Connell, 1995). The infants watched as an experimenter hid a toy under a cushion in a large circular enclosure. The floor of the enclosure was entirely covered with cushions, identical in size and color except for "landmark" conditions. In a landmark condition, the baby saw a toy placed under a distinctively colored cushion. In near-landmark conditions, the toy was placed under a cushion next to a distinctively colored cushion or between two distinctively colored cushions. In a no-land-mark condition, infants saw the toy being hidden under one of many homogenously colored cushions. The infants (some crawling, some walking) were able to retrieve the toy quite successfully in the landmark condition, but search was far less successful with a "near" landmark, even poorer than with no landmark at all. It would seem that these mobile infants could locate a hidden object given a direct landmark, and even without one they could search better than chance would predict by relating the location of the hidden object solely with reference to themselves. But using position relative to other distinctive objects that were not direct referents was confusing in this unfamiliar situation.

On the whole, research to date on development of knowledge about the spatial layout suggests that infants begin by attending to the changing perspective structure, which they can explore actively by turning the head and trunk to look; that they then progress to ability to use a direct landmark as locomotor ability emerges; and that considerably more locomotor experience is needed before information about other-object relations in an invariant layout is useful in finding hidden things. Transfer from one exploratory system to another (from looking to reaching to moving the body toward a goal) is not automatic in searching the layout. Constraints on one particular search task are not necessarily those on another, and they thus can affect predictability of outcomes about developmental progress toward general knowledge of a constant spatial layout.

What babies do learn that has general usefulness is how to find their way around their own homes or familiar day-care centers to places of interest like the kitchen, where Mother is, or the play corner that holds toys. There are those psychologists who would claim that the baby has constructed a "cognitive map," a term invented by Tolman (1948), whose research was concerned with rats finding their way around a maze. But this metaphor of a static representation to be consulted for guidance can hardly apply to these infants, who will not be able to use even the simplest pictorial representation of a space for finding their way, locating a toy, or even themselves in a real place, for several years to come. They learn something far more functional: the affordances of corners to go round, doors to go through, and enticing glimpses, sounds, and odors to head for, anticipating a goal. "Going somewhere" implies prospectivity, a highly significant characteristic of human behavior. Paths or routes offer anticipatory affordances for a good place to head for. It is highly instructive to observe infants traveling around in a familiar place, spontaneously and actively learning about it.

Current research procedures do not seem fruitful in advancing our wisdom about how flexibility of locomotion in a general, inclusive, geographically objective layout is attained. The currently popular account that the infant progresses from an egocentric view to one containing external landmarks to one with routes and finally to a concept of objective, geographical space still lacks totally persuasive evidence, nor does it include a detailed and convincing theory of how the progression comes about. Development of action systems and learning how to control and use them in relation to surrounding environmental supports and goals plays an important role, we may be sure. The hand-arm system provides a means for reaching, holding, and manipulating objects, and for exploring near space. The locomotor system provides a means for getting to goals too far for arms to reach, and for exploring all sides of the layout. Exercise of these systems yields rich information about the nature of the layout: its permanence, its directions (extending all around as we turn 360°), and most of all, its affordances. Learning to *control* one's own movement synergies (including eyes, arms, hands, trunk, and above all, posture) in relation to what objects and places afford is the road to knowledge about the spatial layout. Knowledge of geographical space and attainment of flexibility in use of routes remains a problem. Adults vary in their way-finding abilities, but we all learn that the layout is permanent, however we change our places in it.

Where We Stand: Retrospect and Prospect

We have just examined in some detail the three most important tasks of an infant's first year. We began in chapter 5 with communication—learning the affordances of other peoples' gestures, facial expressions, vocalizations, actions and intentions directed toward oneself, and learning to respond to them adaptively. It is nice to think of this as how a baby is becoming a person! In chapter 6 we considered learning to control the arm-hand-trunk and finger system to use the affordances of objects—toys, simple tools, anything that can be handled and manipulated. This task includes learning to use the haptic system to feel properties of objects, such as their weight and shape, their roughness or smoothness, and also learning when objects are attainable and what one can do with them. In this chapter, we have studied the progress of locomotion, learning to control the whole body so as to move around the layout, extending vastly the ability to use the affordances and resources of the world. In all of these tasks, babies are learning at the same time about themselves as persons, agents, and actors with certain dimensions, capabilities, and intentions.

In the next chapter, we will move on to a more general topic, asking how learning occurs as babies progress through all three modes of development during the first year. How can we understand change? What principles underlie and help to explain it?

8

✦ ✧ ✦ ✧ ✦

The Learning Process in Infancy

Facts and Theory

What Is Learned in Perceptual Learning: The Facts

This chapter presents a theoretical approach to perceptual learning as it functions in development. The first question for any learning theory is *what is learned*. For what phenomena, cognitive accomplishments, or behavioral changes does this theory offer an explanation? One general, fairly abstract answer for perceptual learning is that infants learn to perceive *affordances:* that is, to perceive what the events, objects, and layout of the environment offer that relates to and may be controlled by the infant, a relation that can be referred to as an organism-environment fit. Learning about affordances is learning *meanings* for what can be perceived.

Perceptual learning is also the way developing organisms discover *invariants* of events, things, and the layout of the world. Invariants characterize the total event. In reaching out for an object, the arm moves away from the body, approaching closer and closer to the object, closing in as it begins to make contact. Momentary segments of this event, like still shots from a film, do not characterize the event at all and could vary in a number of ways without changing what is invariant about the event. The event can be characterized as a whole and is meaningful to infants long before they can describe it linguistically. The invariant aspect is particularly impressive in this case, because it can be felt (specified by proprioceptive information) at the same time that it is seen (specified by visual information). This is multimodal information specifying the common aim and direction of the act.

There is also invariant information for objects and places that makes them meaningful and distinguishable from others. We may refer to such invariant information as *distinctive features* of the object or place. These features have a permanence that the event lacks. Even when they are stationary, they may be observed. But discovering them involves movement, for we can only detect invariance (permanence, in this case) over change, such as moving ourselves and viewing from different angles. Babies view their cribs and feel them from many angles; what they see may vary in superficial appearances such as covers or disarray. But cribs are always of a certain size, hardness of surface, and surrounding edges, and the same events take place in them over and over. They are objects (and places) with permanent, meaningful features that are constant over superficial changes.

We describe now a number of cases of perceptual learning from the experimental literature. Some of these were referred to in greater detail in earlier chapters. The cases progress from the earliest perceptual learning we know about to more elaborately organized sequences in older infants, when tasks with nested subunits (embedded information) become part of what is perceived and acted upon. In every case, information is picked up that comes to specify events, things, and layout that afford something meaningful.

A Case of Prenatal Learning

Does birth determine the moment when learning can begin? There is no reason to suppose so, unless one holds a brief for a learning theory that demands external "reinforcement." A fetus is capable of learning, as research with animals has shown (Smotherman & Robinson, 1996). We have already noted evidence that learning happens in human fetuses as well (see chap. 5). In a well-substantiated case, exposure of a fetus to repeated events of the mother speaking aloud was investigated by DeCasper and Fifer (1980). Shortly after birth (less than 4 days), the infant could differentiate the mother's voice from that of another person, even from another woman of similar age and vocal characteristics (language, vocal range, etc.). The speech event, although presented before birth, was heard and attended to, could be discriminated later by the newborn infant, and was preferred over other voices and alternative content.

An even stronger test of specific prenatal learning is the study discussed in chapter 5 in which a story was read aloud by the mother each day for the last 6 weeks of her pregnancy. Newborns showed a preference for the story they had heard over another story, even when both stories were read at the test by a woman other than the mother. The babies generalized to a nonmaternal voice on the basis of some content information, perhaps intonation contours or other structural segmental characteristics of that story (A. DeCasper & Spence, 1986).

What had the newborns learned? They seem to have differentiated and extracted pattern and order (*invariant* features of the mother's voice and structure of the story) in a repeated event that contrasted with other sounds of the uterine environment, such as heartbeat and digestive noises. We will return to the notion of order later when considering principles that characterize a theory of perceptual learning. Listening to speech and differentiating structure such as its suprasegmental or segmental features at the earliest possible age (as soon as the auditory system is sufficiently functional) may play a major role in learning to segment the speech stream after birth and in developing a preference for the sounds of one's native language.

Learning About Oneself

In chapter 3, we referred to an experiment by A.L.H. van der Meer, van der Weel, and Lee (1995), who provided infants 2 to 4 weeks old with light weights attached to both wrists. Strings were attached to the weights and wrists so that the weighted string pulled the hand down. The babies lay with the head turned to one side, a position that allowed a view of only one arm and hand. Lifting the *visible* hand became significantly more frequent than lifting the nonvisible hand. The more weight added, the less the nonvisible hand moved. Controls (see chap. 3) showed that the baby was counteracting the external force applied to the wrist, in order to keep a hand in view.

Is this a case of early learning? It would seem that the babies' normal spontaneous activity becomes controlled in such a way that they have an opportunity to discover properties of their own self, contributed multimodally by proprioceptive and visual information. The sight of the moving hand also presents an optical frame of reference for the dimensions of the world in relation to the infants themselves. The babies learn spontaneously about their own action capabilities, the results of the action, and how a part of their own bodies compares with dimensions of their world. This remarkable experiment suggests that infants have a way of learning to *control* action intentionally and thus to gain information about their own capabilities and the visible world around them. At the same time, raising the hand *occludes* whatever part of the room was in the infants' view. But as the hand drops, the background is again visible. This covering and uncovering provides information about *continuity* of things in the world. They don't go away when they are briefly out of sight. Perhaps it is the beginning of learning about "object permanence." A baby's own spontaneous activity offers remarkable opportunities for perceptual learning about both the self and the world. It is, in a sense, exploratory activity.

Learning to Control an Event

The last example showed infants learning to control an action of their own (hand lifting) that provides information about the dimensions and powers of their own bodies. There is evidence from other experiments that young infants can also learn to control an external event. Several paradigms of so-called instrumental learning were described in chapter 3. One of these will suffice here to show that what is learned very early includes control of an event in the external scene, that the baby is learning to use an opportunity offered by the

FIGURE 8.1. A 3.5-month-old infant exhibiting thrusts of the
left leg to control a twirling mobile. Note the look of pleasure
on the infant's face. Photo courtesy of C.K. Rovee-Collier.

world—learning about an *affordance*. Recall the example of an infant learning
to kick a leg attached by a cord to a mobile hanging above the crib (Rovee &
Rovee, 1969; C.K. Rovee-Collier & Gekoski, 1979). When the kicks had the consequence of making the mobile twirl, the action was quickly repeated by infants
as young as 2 months of age (fig. 8.1). The babies had received "reinforcement"
(movement of the twirling mobile contingent upon their own kicks), which resulted in an increased rate of kicking. But when the string was detached from
the babies' ankle, their kick rate rapidly dropped, despite noncontingent movement of the mobile supplied by the experimenter. *Control* of the interesting sight
by spontaneous, self-produced movement was clearly the significant consequence for this learning. The infants learned to control an environmental change
through an action of their own. An affordance was perceived and realized in

this case as the babies discovered that their own exploratory activity led to the consequence of producing the change.

Learning to Perceive a Unitary Object

Babies may perceive unitary "things" as soon as they perceive at all. The priority of unity in perception is emphasized in the case of perceiving an object as a unit even when a portion of it is occluded by something in front of it (as happened when the babies with wrist weights lifted their hands in the case discussed earlier). Imagine a hand rising to push back a bit of hair, partly shielding the owner's face. Without ever considering it, we continue to perceive that face as a face and as a whole face. A bit of the hand viewed when covered by strands of hair is still perceived as a whole hand. The economy and environmental order given by this perceived unity is as obvious as it is useful. Do babies have to learn to perceive wholeness despite partial occlusion?

P.J. Kellman and Spelke (1983) investigated this question with 4-month-old infants (see chap. 6 for details). The babies' looking (length of fixations) was habituated to a display consisting of an object moving behind a central occluding bar. In subsequent preference tests, the babies looked longer at an object presented in two pieces (a gap displayed where the occluder had been), suggesting that the rod moving behind the occluding bar had been perceived as a unit. However, it seems from a more recent experiment that perceptual learning about unity and coherence may go on in early months. Slater and colleagues (1990), using a similar method, investigated perception of a partly occluded object with babies 2 days old. Their results, unlike those of Kellman and Spelke, suggested that the infants perceived two pieces behind the occluder rather than one unbroken object, since they exhibited a novelty preference for the unbroken object in dishabituation tests.

How can we explain this change in what is perceived between birth and 4 months? The results illustrate a critical principle of selectivity that operates in learning—*selection for order and economy*. The moving pieces of rod are at the same depth behind the occluder, and they move together—indeed, they move as a unit. Shared motion ("common fate," in Gestalt psychology) embodies economy and literally *specifies* unity in the world—a powerful perceptual discovery. It seems likely that infants are helped to detect this information by making several other perceptual differentiations: the difference in depth between the rod and the occluder; the alignment and the synchrony of motion of the two sections of the rod; the difference between optical motions produced by a moving object as contrasted with those produced by self-movement; and perhaps the difference between the kind of optical motion produced by movement of rigid objects and nonrigid, elastic, or animate ones. Infants have many opportunities (including self-produced ones) for observing these differences.

We now know that at 4 months, an infant has good depth discrimination, evidently has no trouble detecting alignment and synchrony (this can be done even at 2 months), differentiates self- from object-produced optical motion (Kellman et al. 1987), and differentiates rigid from nonrigid motion (E.J. Gibson et al., 1979; E.J. Gibson & Walker, 1984). The conditions for detecting that synchronous, aligned motion of parts specifies unity of a rigid object are fully available. The reduction of information thus achieved (decrease of uncertainty) is impressive. The world is divided up, to be sure—but in an orderly way that provides for functional interaction of an active organism with unitary, persisting objects in the environment.

Learning What Happens Next in an Observed Event

We have presented examples of very young infants learning to control a simple event with their own actions. They learn to perform an action, such as kicking, and to expect consequences that ensue as a result of it. What about learning to expect an event that happens with regularity following some prior event, when the sequence of events is *not* controlled by the infant's own actions? Learning an expectation of this kind is important partly because it may underlie the concept of causality, which is only attained much later. Haith and his colleagues (Haith, Hazan, & Goodman, 1988) presented infants 3.5 months of age with events that were regularly preceded by another observable event. The sequence of events did not depend on the infant's activity, but the eye and head movements of the baby were monitored. The infants quickly learned to expect a picture slide to appear on the right when it was preceded by one on the left, and they turned their eyes toward the correct spot in anticipation. They could in fact learn to anticipate more complex sequences (Canfield & Haith, 1991).

It is interesting that this event sequence is anticipated even though it is not controlled by the infant, because older experiments that attempted classical conditioning with young infants usually were unsuccessful. In a classical conditioning experiment, a signal is given, followed a few seconds later by some other "stimulus" that presumably excites a reflex response. The best-known example of classical conditioning is the case of Pavlov's dogs. When given a signal, such as a tone or a buzzer, followed shortly by a drop of acid in the mouth, which caused salivation, the dogs learned to anticipate the drop of acid and began salivating at the sound of the tone or buzzer. Another procedure used very often in this country was foot withdrawal from an electric shock preceded by a tone or buzzer. With such a procedure, animals (dogs, sheep, goats, etc.) learned to anticipate the shock by foot withdrawal or other actions (E.J. Gibson, 1952). Such "conditioning" was presumed to be a primitive kind of associative learning. Consequently, attempts were made to demonstrate it in newborn humans.

A study by Wickens and Wickens (1940) elicited foot withdrawal in newborn infants by applying a mild electric shock. A buzzer preceded the shock on repeated sessions over 3 days. A control group was presented with the shock, but no buzzer was sounded. Foot withdrawal to a buzzer occurred in a final test in *both* groups, apparently unrelated to the potential signaling property. Other experiments were equally inconclusive or unsuccessful. Sameroff (1971) commented regarding these unsuccessful attempts that newborns had yet to differentiate modalities before two of them could be "integrated at higher levels" in classical conditioning. Perhaps the response was poorly chosen since it was not spontaneous and the consequence was aversive. Whatever the reason, we now know that newborns learn readily to control their own spontaneous actions such as looking, sucking, or kicking, when they are followed by consequences that bring useful information or culminate in an event like feeding (see chap. 3). Before 3 months, a repeated condition will lead to exploratory activity in anticipation of a predictable event (recall the babies with wrist weights). The infants learn the *predictability* relation between the two events, whether self-controlled or not, and without any externally applied reinforcement. What is important is exploratory activity such as looking around. Infants spontaneously seek information about order of events in the world, a necessary accompaniment of prospectivity, which is inherent in learning an affordance relationship.

Learning to Participate in a Communicative Event

An example of both discovering and controlling order in the neonatal period concerns a social, communicative event (see chap. 5). As we have discussed, newborn infants are familiar with their mother's voice, prefer it to another female's, and can acquire some familiarity with an oft-repeated speech sample. Two or two and a half months later, the infant may be taking a role in a social event, known as turn taking, that incorporates such information. The event is a kind of "conversation" marked by control and anticipation of subgoals in the total event (see chap. 5 for details). The mother addresses the infant with smiling gestures in a rather high-pitched heavily intoned speech form known as "motherese" (Fernald, 1985), stopping after a short message as if to wait for her baby's answer. And typically, the baby does respond, smiling and making sounds within the vocal repertoire, perhaps attempting to control the mother's behavior as she waits for her companion to finish. The baby is responsive and in turn anticipates a response from the mother (Murray & Trevarthen, (1985).

   This behavior exhibits the event characteristics of a task (see chap. 3). There is intention, prospectivity (anticipation of information and consequences to follow), and ends or subgoals marking segments of the task. Infants at this age have yet to learn their native language, but they are learning to perceive its sounds and they are certainly picking up pitch and intonation signaling an event with expected consequences. Some of the action is performed by the infant as the agent and some is observed happening in another person, but the event as a whole is ordered in an anticipated pattern. It becomes a complex event, segmented into subunits, with expectations and subgoals embedded within it. Expectation of order and anticipation of consequences clearly underlie this learning. Furthermore, this is an opportunity for an infant to begin learning about intention and agency in another person.

Learning to Differentiate Multimodally Specified Events

Perceiving multimodally specified objects and events occurs very early, certainly in the neonatal period. It is likely that multimodal information specifying the same object or event is perceived as meaningful well before differentiation of modal information is achieved (A.S. Walker-Andrews & Gibson, 1986; A.S. Walker-Andrews, 1997). Perception of segregation and unity of an event is essential, and temporally coordinated multimodal information facilitates its detection.

We illustrate with an experiment on attention in infants approaching the first half-year. L.E. Bahrick, Walker, and Neisser (1981) asked whether infants could attend to the progress of one event when two events were going on at once, "bombarding" them with information. The infants watched videotaped performances on a TV screen, one videotaped event superimposed on another. The events were topically different. One was a hand-clapping sequence, the other a "slinky" toy being manipulated noisily by a pair of gloved hands. As the baby watched the screen, the sound track that accompanied just one of the events was played. The question was whether the sound track enabled the listener to attend to the appropriate videotaped event, effectively segregating the two, and in this way decreasing the information attended to by creating order from the jumbled presentation. To answer the question, a variation of the habituation procedure was chosen. Infants were habituated to the superimposed scenes on the screen, accompanied by the sound track specifying one of them. Then the two events were presented separately and silently on screens placed side by side. If an infant now looked preferentially at the nonspecified event (the one that had not been accompanied by its sound track), it would indicate that the baby had indeed succeeded in segregating and attending to one event (the one heard as well as seen) to the exclusion of the other. Such indeed was the result, showing differentiation of the two events.

A second, very different example of learning to differentiate multimodal information stresses the role of recalibration with growth, and reorganization of multimodal information for specifying the locus of an external event. An elegant experiment by Ashmead, Davis, Whalen, and Odom (1991) measured free-field localization of sound sources by infants ranging in age from 20 to 48 weeks. The test required the infants to turn their heads to the correct side following sounds that varied in the extent of the "audible angle" (time difference in arrival at the two ears). The minimum audible angle was calculated for infants in three age groups (20, 24, and 48 weeks). A significant age effect for discrimination was found, showing gains up to 48 weeks in the minimum angle responded to by a correct turn, with a high rate of change between 20 and 24 weeks (a gain of 5.5° in only 4 weeks).

A second experiment presented sounds over earphones, rather than externally from loudspeakers, creating an unnatural listening situation. The purpose of this experiment was to measure isolated sensitivity to interaural time differences (discrimination of difference magnitudes). Directional responses of the infants were also obtained. Three age groups were tested (16, 20, and 28 weeks). There were no significant age differences, and threshold sensitivity was greater than would be expected from the results of the free-field localization study. It follows that sensitivity to the interaural time differences as such did not account for the age differences found in the first experiment, where the audible angle of shift in location in a free field showed a significant developmental change.

Interpretation of this developmental change rests on the fact that free-field localization of external sounds is generally accompanied by other information such as visual (viewing the sounding object) and kinesthetic (activities involved in reaching, turning the head, leaning forward, and handling the object). The earphone lateralization task isolated the interaural information from vision, posture, or head movement. The authors suggest that the age discrepancy between the two studies is "attributable to the need for integration across sound localization cues" (p. 1124).

We suggest that *differentiation* is a better description of the process than integration. As an infant views the surrounding layout and begins to reach for and eventually grasp objects located in it, proprioceptive information and sounds made by any attractive object would be part of the complex of multimodal information potentially specifying the location of the object. Perception would at first involve all the information (interaural time differences and visual, kinesthetic, and vestibular information). But perceptual learning would eventually differentiate the embedded interaural difference. Infants around 20 weeks of age are just at the start of their reaching, leaning toward, and touching engagement with objects. The resulting information about where these things are must result in newly focused attention to invariant, separable aspects of the information for location of things in the layout. A perceptual system may possess capacities that are constrained by development of other systems' differentiation as potential informers about affordances of environmental events. Activities like manipulation and locomotion play their own role as potential information for orientation of oneself and other objects in the layout. Interaural time differences were already present and discriminable, but not until 5 or 6 months of age were they differentiated as information uniquely specifying the location of a sound source, while coordinated with exploratory movements of head and trunk. We know that auditory information, alone, can be used at this age to locate an object (Clifton, 1998).

Learning Distinctive Features of Things

It was once thought that newborn infants saw, at best, a mélange of light, dark, and colors in a chaotic arrangement. We now know that although vision has a long course of development, neonates detect very fine differences on certain visual dimensions; their eyes move in the proper direction to fix on and follow a moving target appearing in their field of view; their view of the world is three-dimensional; and they perceive things as objectlike, not a kaleidoscope of spots differing in brightness. But we also know that neonatal visual perception of objects is without fine detail, and that detecting some of the distinctive features that define objects as visually unique awaits maturation of the visual system. There is evidence that neonates do not attend to elements of visual patterns within an outline or a larger framework unless the elements are moving (Maurer & Young, 1983; Bushnell, 1979), a phenomenon sometimes referred to as the "externality effect."

Differentiation and recognition of the human face have been studied by many researchers. The questions posed differ, but all involve an important affordance relation. The face of another human affords the prospect of comfort, communication, and companionship. Are faces responded to, originally, as a class, generalized with one another and detected by some very simple, critical, and universal information? Is one face, for instance, the mother's, recognized as particular, apart from others (see chap. 5)? Does the developmental course of face perception proceed from vague and rather general to specific differentiation of individual faces? Consider a set of experiments on neonatal recognition of a facelike pattern. Goren, Sarty, and Wu (1975) presented newborn infants with cartoon faces (ovals cut out of cardboard) moving around in a path within the infants' field of view. One oval was a schematic face, with eyes, nose, and mouth arranged in an appropriate pattern. Two others were scrambled arrangements of these "features," and the fourth was blank. The infants were said to track the path of the cartoon bearing the facelike pattern preferentially, their eye movements following its path. This experiment was replicated by M.H. Johnson, Dziurawiec, Ellis, and Morton (1991), who also found that infants in the first hour of life visually track the cartoon with the appropriate configuration of features preferentially. However, Morton and Johnson (1991) found, in a follow-up experiment, that preferential tracking of the cartoon faces tended to decline during the second month. They suggested a two-process developmental theory of face perception: an original phase in which newborns attend to a schematic facelike arrangement of mock "features," followed later by a lengthy process of learning about the characteristics of individual faces.

Other research (Pascalis, de Schonen, Morton, Dernelle, & Fabre-Grenet, 1995) suggests that by 4 months, infants recognize their mother's face, even when a scarf covers her outer head contour. By this age, the baby may have the need and the opportunity to make finer, modally specific differentiations, although the affordance of a maternal person, specified by multimodal information, is obviously learned much earlier, with maternal voice, feel and, odor all part of the complex from which visual appearance is differentiated. It has been suggested that even very young infants recognize the mother's face, without any accompanying multimodal information (see chap. 5).

As infants progress in handling objects and discover uses for them, they learn to identify them by distinguishing features. Learning to identify objects is an important task in the latter half of their first year. At some point this process is assisted by adults, who tend to label objects for their babies. This practice may actually be useful even before the baby understands the words. Not only does the word emphasize the uniqueness of the object, it may also play a role in building concepts. Labels nearly always apply to a class of objects, and even when they don't, they refer to the same object in many different places and events. A parent says, "Here's the *cat*," or "Pat the *cat*," and so on, under many different circumstances. Furthermore, when another cat appears, the baby will hear the same word. This parental procedure undoubtedly helps infants classify objects and discover something about abstractions—that some features are shared and that these differentiate a set of objects from other kinds of objects.

Another spur to concept formation rests in the differentiation process, as infants are exposed to a variety of members of a class, such as toy stuffed animals. They are all distinguished from other objects by their features of wooliness, warmth, size, and use (such as a bedfellow). But one is singled out by more frequent exposure, possessing a name and a "cute" appearance, for example, and as this one becomes specified for the baby by more individualistic features, the common features may be generalized to form a class. Similar features define a class, but particularly distinguishing ones are singled out for the individual member. This process may begin with mothers, indeed, and eventually lead to a concept of women of a certain age, general similarity in tone of voice, and so on, as the specification of the own mother's appearance becomes more finely drawn. The two processes, both based on differentiation, complement one another while describing two types of learning, identification of a particular object and more general specification of a class of objects, with similar but not the same affordance. Learning based on a formal set of visually specified distinctive features comes into its own when preschoolers of 4 or 5 begin to differentiate letters of an alphabet from one another, a much later accomplishment (A.D. Pick, 1965).

Learning to Use an Object or an Act as Means

Learning that an act can be a strategy for achieving an affordance or that an object can be a tool for acquiring a goal object sounds like a simple accomplishment. We even thought once that Köhler's apes were exhibiting fairly simple behavior as they groped for a distant banana with a stick or moved a box under a dangling banana that was too high to reach. But extending one's body artificially to make it "fit' with a potential affordance, or engaging in an activity that does not itself achieve the affordance but makes such an attainment possible, is a huge step in development of behavior and in perceiving prospective events. It means not only perceiving oneself as an agent of control, but also perceiving an object (a tool, not oneself) as a potential controller of another object—a kind of causal relationship between objects. To quote Piaget: "The subject begins to discover that a spatial context exists between cause and effect and so any object at all can be a source of activity (and not only his own body)" (1952, p. 212).

In chapter 3, we stressed that the course of behavior, far from being a chain of reflexes or random bouts of reaction to stimuli, is continuous and segmented, with nested segments or subroutines an important part of accomplishing a task. Nested segments of action within the total task may involve use of objects as means to obtain a goal, or use of strategies like locomotion around an obstacle or tiptoeing over a dubious spot to reach a goal. Even traversing a path to transport something to another place is a kind of means and does not occur for some time after locomotion is possible. As we pointed out earlier, locomotion itself (moving on one's own power) is highly motivating in the beginning and is practiced over and over, not necessarily in the service of going to any particular place. The same thing is true of carrying an object. When infants can walk steadily on two legs, their arms are free to transport something. Babies do this happily, simply for the sake of carrying the object. Carrying a red golf ball down a walkway, changing it for another, and carrying it back is a pleasing activity to a new walker (Gibson & Schmuckler, 1989). When children finally attain a behavior such as taking a block or a toy to a box to add to a collection, they are performing a triply nested activity—picking up the block, walking across the room to the collection receptacle (carrying the toy), and adding the toy to the collection in the receptacle.

Learning a simple means, such as pulling a surface on which rests a toy that is too far away to reach with the arm alone, is an often cited example of a nested act or subroutine (Piaget, 1952, p. 285; Willats & Rosie, 1988). A one-step task (one subordinate routine), such as pulling a cloth that supports the toy, is accomplished by most infants around 8 or 9 months, but a two- or three-step task takes longer. Once the subroutine is discovered, it can be *differentiated* from the total task of getting the toy and may be transferred eventually to new tasks or generalized to obtain a new object. (See Piaget [1952, p. 228 ff.] for his classic discussion of this process.)

Pushing a pivoting table or "lazy Susan" to obtain an out-of-reach lure was a task used by Piaget (1952, p. 284) and later by Koslowski and Bruner (1972). The pivoting table affords *exploration* on its own since it will move in two directions. When it must be pushed away to bring the toy within reach, moving of the tabletop becomes hard to differentiate as a subordinate task and as a means to gain the distant toy. Differentiating an activity that was learned in its own right, and then perceiving it as a path leading to a further end, is a real landmark of development. The test is whether the activity can be generalized to a new situation (new place, new toy). The process may not be too different from earlier learning where some external constraint makes special demands for appropriate exploratory behavior and the perception of a new relation. Exploration is a key factor in learning here too, but on a new level, nested within a larger task.

Learning means to an end includes learning to use an *act* as a strategy, as well as to use an object as an instrumental intermediary. A new activity or a new way of using existing facilities may be a strategy that serves as a means to an end.

Thelen (1994) reported learning of an unusual activity that served as a means to optimize a highly satisfying achievement by infants only 3 months old. The infants were given the opportunity to control a mobile above them by a string attached to the mobile and to one of the infant's ankles (Rovee and Rovee, 1969). Babies typically kick so as to activate the mobile, moving both legs in an alternating motion, but eventually differentiating the contingent movement of the attached leg alone (C.K. Rovee-Collier, Morongiello, Aron, & Kuperschmidt, 1978). Thelen looped the infant's legs together with an elastic around the ankles. The legs could still be moved individually, but moving them together activated the mobile much more vigorously. As Thelen put it, the elastic "made simultaneous kicking much more effective for vigorous activation of the mobile because full excursions otherwise required stretching the elastic" (1994, p. 281). All the babies increased their kick rate when a leg was attached to the mobile (that is, learned the contingency), but only those who learned simultaneous action of both legs, an unusual strategy, achieved vigorous movement of the mobile.

A very basic constraint on behavior becomes important when infants begin locomotion on their own. Locomotion—crawling and eventually walking—requires a surface of support, normally a flat, firm, solid, extended area that supports the weight of the mover. When surfaces lack these attributes (present a drop-off or are slippery or sloping, for example) locomotion is at risk. In chapter 7, we cited research with a risky sloping surface, one precarious for both walking and crawling (Adolph et al., 1993a). Adolph (1997) investigated crawlers' and toddlers' locomotion on slopes of 0° to 36° in both crawlers and toddlers. Beginners at either form of locomotion frequently attempted to descend too steep slopes and had to be rescued by the experimenter. The infants eventually learned to descend safely, having explored many means of coping with the constraints imposed by the inclined surface, such as backing feet first or sitting and sliding. Strategies other than walking upright were learned through exploratory activity and discovery of a safe alternative means. This is a kind of causal knowledge: learning about the consequences of dynamic strategies of movement in relation to different environmental supports and affordances. Learning about the causal nature of a means, however, does not happen instantly. Adolph found that crawlers who had learned to contend with slopes by appropriate strategies did not transfer those strategies when confronted with a similar situation as walkers. They had learned a strategy for performance within a specific situation as crawlers, not an immediately generalizable relation. Babies first learn expectations, and these may underlie later discovery of more general causal relations.

Learning about Causal Relations in Observed Events

Learning to make use of an object or a strategy as a means to an end is not the same as learning about observed relations between objects in a performance that is not self-initiated and does not involve one's own actions. Actions and their consequences or events that follow them are often entirely external to oneself, but they are witnessed frequently, even early in life. Perceiving *control* of an outcome in an event external to oneself seems to be a more sophisticated achievement than discovering control of an outcome initiated by oneself. In other words, control is first discovered in oneself, perhaps in as simple an act as moving the hands and watching the consequences of the act, such as occlusion of portions of the background environmental scene (A.L.H. van der Meer, et al., 1995). Observing control in an external event might occur as an infant watches another person control a simple situation, perhaps by means of hand movements not unlike the infant's own. The role of controller or agent is eventually generalized, but probably begins in the discovery of control in oneself.

When an inanimate object appears to control a change or a movement of another object, we are apt to speak of a *causal* effect, a dynamic change in which one object is the mover and the other the moved. Michotte's research on perception of causality is the classic example of research on one object influencing movement of another. Perceiving causality in an impact event has been studied in infants. The dynamic relation of one object causing an ensuing event is not perceived as early as simply what will happen next, although the "launching" experiment devised by Michotte (1963) was interpreted by him and by others working with 6-month-old infants as a case of directly perceiving a causal relation (Leslie & Keeble, 1987). The relation involves more than one event; a causal event is embedded in a larger event implicating two objects. In a typical procedure, one object, the "mover" is seen moving toward another stationary object (the "moved") and colliding with it, sending it off on a course of movement ("launching" it). E.J. Gibson (1984) suggested that what is actually perceived in the event is not causality as such, but an affordance of the lead object as a launcher, the initiator or agent of a dynamic event (a collision). The abstract concept of causality undoubtedly requires much wider experience and perhaps the acquisition of speech. Five-year-old children do observe a causal relation in a launching experiment and can distinguish events that conserve momentum from nonconserving events (Kaiser & Profitt, 1984). In fact, the conservation of momentum rather than contiguity or precedence was their essential criterion for causality.

An experiment performed by Oakes and Cohen (1990) with 6- and 10-month-old infants found a developmental difference in perception of a typical launching event. In a videotaped episode, a toy rolled across a surface and either struck or did not strike a second toy that then moved over the surface. Three slightly different episodes were used: (1) a direct launching event in which the second object moved off at once when impact occurred; (2) a delayed launching in which the second object did not move immediately upon impact; and (3) a no-collision event in which the first object stopped before impact, but the second moved on in any case. An infant was shown all the events, using a habituation-of-looking-time procedure. If an infant had perceived a causal relation during habituation to episode 1, it was expected that looking time would be

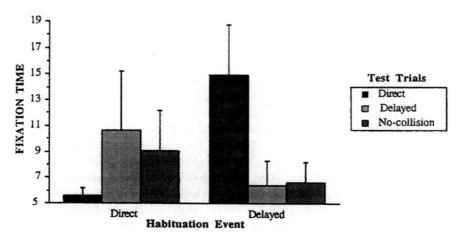

FIGURE 8.2. Comparison of looking time to causal and noncausal events in 10-month-old infants. From "Infant Causal Perception," by L.M. Oakes and L.B. Cohen, 1995, in C.K. Rovee-Collier and L.P. Lipsitt (Eds.), *Advances in Infancy Research* (Vol. 9, p. 23), Norwood, NJ: Ablex. Copyright © 1995 by the Ablex Publishing Corporation. Reprinted with permission.

greater for novel events that did not exhibit the causal relation. The 6-month-olds did not show dishabituation to the novel launching events, thus not differentiating them from the episode that presented a causal relation. However, 10-month-old infants dishabituated to both noncausal events. When the habituated event was the delayed launching, appropriate dishabituation again occurred at 10 months, with the causal episode looked at longer during the dishabituation procedure (see fig. 8.2). The experiment was repeated with 7-month-old infants, using two differently colored balls as the mover object and the moved (Oakes, 1994). These infants differentiated the causal and noncausal events.

It would seem that in the typical launching experiment, there is development between 6 and 10 months, with apparent causal perception demonstrable around 7 months or later. Oakes and Cohen (1995, p. 49) hold that infants must "use available information to infer that objects may have acted as causal agents." It seems more likely to us that the infants have been learning to differentiate an episode into subevents in which objects have different roles: one object is a controller, *agent,* or mover, and the other is the moved object, the *recipient* of action or force. The infants' day-to-day experience at this time, when they have just achieved fairly good manipulative skills of their own, may allow them to differentiate this relation external to themselves. A true concept of causality may yet be far ahead.

The interpretation of early perception of causality as that of perceiving the affordance of the mover or agent is supported by the results of another experiment of Cohen and Oakes (1993). In this experiment, the object presented as agent in a causal type of event was replaced, after habituation, with a new object. Infants of 10 or 12 months of age noticed this change and dishabituated. But a change in the *recipient* in the same event did *not* result in dishabituation. Infants apparently can learn by 10 months when a particular object has the affordance of exerting momentum or force on another so as to produce a dynamic result. Oakes and Cohen (1995) interpret the perception of causal relations in their various experiments as due to an inference of causality on the basis of "cues" such as spatial and temporal contiguity. But in that case, the inference made by the infants must refer to some concept of causality that they already possess. It seems far more likely that infants of 10 months have succeeded in differentiating subevents within the total event of one object striking another and launching it into movement, and in so doing perceive the affordance of the mover—its impetus and effect on a dynamic event, not unlike one they can themselves control if they push an object (as they can, by 7 months). Thus, as perception develops along with action, it *contributes* to a developing concept of causality, rather than *deriving* from it, as an "inference" theory (see chap. 1) would assume. Perceptual learning has priority.

What Happens in Perceptual Learning: The Theory

Differentiation

Perceptual learning is not properly described as association or as an addition of any kind, as a response to a stimulus, or as a "representation" of "input." Information is present in the environmental context (the medium available to the perceiver) that potentially *specifies* objects and events in the world (J.J. Gibson, 1966, 1979). An active perceiver has the tasks of extracting the information that specifies relevant events and, especially, of detecting information that specifies an *affordance* of the environment relevant to the perceiver's species, needs, and powers. Learning to detect the information that specifies such a relationship is perceptual learning. Attempts at acting on such information contribute further information, serving to increase the specificity of what is detected. This ongoing process underlines once again the importance of treating perception over time. Information about the world is obtained in a continuous flow by an active perceiver. Cycles of perceiving follow one another, often in an exploratory fashion. Invariance over transformations can only be detected over time. It is only the information that remains invariant over activity that is reliable and valid. Perception indeed has a "temporal dimension" as A. Michotte, J.J. Gibson, and others told us long ago.

   Perceptual differentiation can be characterized as a narrowing down from a vast manifold of information to the minimal, optimal information that specifies the affordance of an event, object, or layout. As the information is extracted, useless information is discarded—quite the opposite of a process that acquires or connects or amasses something. The process is one of *selection*, not addition.

We emphasize again that by no means all the information needed to specify an affordance resides in the environment. The dimensions and capabilities of the would-be user are equally pertinent. The potential user must detect information about his or her own effectiveness in order to perceive the relation between the two aspects that together specify the affordance. It is no wonder that perceptual learning is going on almost continuously in the daily life of a young, growing, alert baby, long before learning by verbal instruction is possible. As the relevant information is narrowed down, the relevant activity is refined and the relation more sharply defined.

To summarize, perceptual learning of young organisms generally shows increasing specificity within a task frame. This specificity may involve selecting from the environmental information that initiates the action, individuating and refining the action pattern that occurs, or specifying the affordance relation as a whole. Both specification of information and individuation of action pattern are illustrated in Rovee-Collier's experiments with young infants controlling a mobile. The surroundings in which the baby's control is exercised appear to become specific with learning, down to decorative features of the mobile itself or even the crib lining surrounding the baby (Hayne & Rovee-Collier, 1995). The action of kicking increases in specificity too, differentiating activity of the leg attached to the mobile from the more diffuse kicking of both legs, the usual spontaneous activity at the start.

An example of differentiating the affordance relation as a whole is a young infant watching a caretaker's face and learning that smiling brings smiles, cooing brings talk and socializing responses, while wailing brings the comfort of touching and handling—all very relevant to a baby's varying needs. These events involve perceptual learning of relations, which have functions much as organs do, serving to maintain the individual organism's survival in its characteristic environment. The function itself is learned about as the consequences of actions are observed.

It is not only such early affordance relation that clearly demonstrate perceptual learning as differentiation. Infants in the second half of the first year achieve individuation within perception-action patterns of both object manipulation and locomotion. In the case of object manipulation, for example, infants learn between 6 and 8 months of age to use different types of manual behavior to explore object properties. Fingering explores texture, hand-to-hand transfer and rotation explore shape, and squeezing and banging explore substance. Rigid objects are more likely to be banged and flexible ones pressed or squeezed. The differentiation of behavior and the perceived-object properties go hand in hand (Lockman and McHale, 1989; Palmer, 1989; Bushnell and Boudreau, 1993). Role differentiation of hand use in playing with toys begins to develop at about 7 months, and from 9 months on it is ever more influenced by features of the toy being played with (Kimmerle, Mick, & Michel, 1995).

Differentiation of the affordances of various emotional expressions goes on during the second half of the first year. Infants respond first to multimodal expression of emotions of others, when facial, vocal, and contextual aspects provide a highly redundant presentation; earliest perception of the affordances of different emotional expressions is probably based on redundant, multimodal information. But perception of the affordance of particular emotions may eventually be specified by visual or vocal information alone. "Infants may first recognize the affective expressions of others as part of a unified multimodal event having a unique communicative affordance" (A.S. Walker-Andrews, 1997, p. 47). Later they learn to differentiate visual and auditory modes of specification, detecting invariants that specify the same emotional meaning (A.S. Walker-Andrews, 1988; Soken & Pick, 1992, 1999).

Differentiation goes on at many levels, increasing with development as the environment broadens and the dimensions and capacities of the perceiver-actor's body are extended. The tasks themselves become both more specific and more complex in organization, notably in the second half of the first year. Achievement of a primary affordance, the function of the task overall, is accomplished with greater complexity as subunits that involve use of varied means begin to be nested within the task as a whole. The means for accomplishing a task is learned as an affordance itself, but it can later develop into a subunit embedded in the larger and longer task structure. Note the example of infants learning to move a pivoting table surface, so as to reach a toy resting on it. This behavior is a simple example of tool use, which will increase as the child's manipulatory capacities progress to skillful handling of objects such as spoons (Smitsman, 1997). Ontogenetically and theoretically, the same concepts help us understand the 3-month-old extending a leg to pull a string attached to the mobile and the 22-month-old scooping a spoon into a container. But the action synergies available for wielding the tool and the knowledge about acquiring control of an external consequence have increased vastly during the months between. Manipulation of objects with the hands has been extended to an array of possible operations, and knowledge of a variety of objects and their different properties has been acquired, making possible control of a much greater world of events.

The organization of a task is further differentiated into embedded structures as babies learn that some events necessarily precede others, both for their own actions and for external events that they only observe. Learning about causal relations such as one object controlling the movement of another in the "launching" experiment falls in this category. Specificity is increased by the requirement that an event of a particular kind must precede another. This relation may be learned first in infants' own discovery of a means to an expected end, along with the discovery that they themselves can control such an event. A concept of causality will develop later as more instances of causal event structure are encountered.

Exploratory Activity

If perceptual learning is preeminently a process of differentiation, then selection from an array of information and potential behaviors must be possible. Such a varied array of information is in fact underwritten by nature for the young of many creatures, including human infants, who are highly motivated to use their perceptual systems and action repertory to explore themselves and their surroundings. The layout and the events going on in it are specified by information in an ambient array of energy surrounding an organism (J.J. Gibson, 1979). This array must be searched by the appropriate perceptual systems in order to extract the invariant information that specifies what may be useful to the organism. Infants are naturally exploratory creatures, reaching out with all the means they have to make contact with their surroundings. Motor synergies useful for exploration can be observed even in the fetus—movement of limbs, torso, head, and fingers. We know that listening goes on even then. All these means of exploration, with the addition of looking, are readily observable in newborns. These exploratory behaviors will be ready for active probing of the world and the information it offers, some at birth and some later when control of the required muscle synergies becomes available.

Exploratory activity is far more than a mere motor process accompanied by registration of input from the existing layout. It is itself an event, a perception-action sequence that has consequences. Exploring brings about new information of two kinds: information about changes in the world that the action produces and, at the same time, information about what the active perceiver is doing. Pickup of information about affordances may seem to be relatively undirected groping in the newborn. But anyone who has observed an alert newborn is struck by the active gaze, auditory awareness, and limb and head movements.

Is exploratory activity a misnomer at this stage? Is the behavior totally haphazard, or is it guided at least minimally? We emphasized in chapter 3 that behavior is neither a chain of reflexes nor totally random activity. It can be roughly segmented into what are conveniently called "tasks." In the earliest days these tasks are pretty much biologically assigned: eat, sleep, wail when uncomfortable. But that is not all; there is also the task of seeking information about and making contact with the surroundings—layout, objects, and people. This task is biologically guaranteed by the very properties and propensities of the human organism, by its perceptual systems and its motor synergies (Goldfield, 1995). More specific tasks are soon differentiated from the general propensity for attentiveness and movement: listening for footsteps, turning the head when possible to see what is there, making vocal and mouthing movements, and differentiating these movements as soon as possible into ones that result in communicative and feeding consequences.

The motivation to explore is so strong in infants that the propensity to search for new information can be harnessed in a standard research method, known as "habituation" (see Chapter 3). The same information is presented over and over, followed by an opportunity to choose between that and new information. Infants (even newborns) reliably prefer to explore the novel presentation (Fagan, 1974; Richards, 1997; and others).

All of the action systems and the more particular tasks that evolve from them are prospective with respect to some affordance for which resources exist. They are not reflexes or changes in elementary movements; they involve larger systems of coordinated acts. Perceiving the resources and discovering how or whether available action systems can be used to exploit them is learning about affordances. Activity that starts as exploratory may become performatory as an affordance is discovered, making possible control of acting on the environment.

The examples of perceptual learning in the first part of this chapter provide varied instances of the role of exploratory activity in learning. Learning control of an event requires self-generated actions that are orchestrated in preparation for an anticipated event, narrowing down to economical and appropriate actions. Kicking the legs is a spontaneous activity. When a baby lies in its crib looking up at a mobile that spins when a leg is kicked, the kicking action is repeated with variations. As the perceptual consequence of spinning the mobile is observed, the actions become increasingly pared down and efficient. Exploratory looking at, scanning, and visually examining the ongoing scene is perhaps the most ubiquitous form of exploratory activity and characterizes nearly all the examples cited. Its consequences are an ongoing source of information about order, uniqueness, and invariance in potentially changing conditions.

Exploratory activity is not confined to simple actions like looking, kicking, reaching, and listening. It occurs at higher levels as well as infants become able to differentiate subunits of tasks. A simple activity like pulling on a cloth can become a means of bringing an object resting on it within grasping distance, but that strategy is preceded by many exploratory efforts. Developing the ability to explore *means* is also illustrated nicely in the task of negotiating a sloping surface by sliding or backing down. The broader the range of exploratory behaviors, the better. Caruso (1993), in research with 11- and 12-month-old infants, found a significant correlation between a wide range of exploratory behaviors and success in the task of retrieving a toy from behind a Plexiglas barrier. Ability to engage in greater diversity of exploratory actions predicts greater success in problem solving.

Exploratory activity guarantees variation in the exposure of the baby to information about what is going on external to it as well as about what is happening simultaneously in its own body, a kind of variation equally essential for learning. Also essential is a selection process that enables detection of affordance relations and ensures differentiation and increasing specificity of both information and action. Perceiving is again the key process.

Observation of Consequences

Human perceptual systems are not designed for momentary exposure to stimulation, but for prolonged bouts that include cycles of perception and action, as we discussed earlier. Thus an opportunity is provided for observation of the play-by-play cycles of whatever activity is being performed by the organism and what follows as a consequence. An affordance-related consequence (or an irrelevant one) can be observed as infants probe with self-initiated exploratory actions. When some kind of contact is achieved, the contact will be perceived, and its usefulness in providing further information or some satisfying outcome such as food, comfort, or simply self-initiated control of an event can be observed. Such observation leads to evaluation and selection, guided by two principles, the affordance fit and economy.

Selection Processes

Since the essence of perceptual learning is to learn about affordances, it stands to reason that selection will be determined by the fit between an infant's actions and the ensuing consequence of making contact with the resource offered (or perhaps removing the perceiver from contact if the affordance is of a negative type). This is another way of saying that the information specifying the affordance and the behavior that ensues must be adaptive for the organism-environment relation.

To illustrate from the cases described, mouthing and vocalizing that bring a return of smiles and vocalizing from a partner provide a good fit. In the case of control of the mobile, a sturdy thrust of a leg tied to the mobile provides a whirling mobile and even more—the information, as the act and its consequence are observed, that the performer is herself initiating the action and controlling the resulting event. Achieving control has a strong motivational accompaniment.

Other examples abound of selection for *affordance fit*. Simply learning to grasp an object in view and then carry it to the mouth for further exploration provides information for a good organism-environment fit, an important lesson because babies have to learn what is within reaching distance, how long their arms are, and how large an object they can grasp, transport, and mouth. Attempts at locomotion, either in a creeping or in a walking mode, can bring the baby closer to objects in the surrounding space. Just getting over the supporting surface underneath leads to perception of a good fit: if the surface is extensive, flat and rigid, it affords locomotion. Discovery of the motor synergies that accomplish this feat divulges a relation that an infant learns to control increasingly well. All these cases are obviously serving functions that are of biological value to the organism. Perception of an affordance fit has to be a major principle of selection and learning.

Many psychologists are satisfied that learning is explained only when it can be ascribed to processes at a nonbehavioral, neural level. In the past, they often hypothesized association at a neural level. More recently, some psychologists have found evidence for selective processes that eliminate excessive neural connections that already exist (Greenough, Black, & Wallace, 1987). Such a sculpting process may occur, but it does not go far in enriching our understanding of the part that learning takes in development. We need to focus first on processes that can be described and validated at a perceptual-behavioral level—such as exploratory activity and selection of perception-action relations that have functionally acceptable consequences for obtaining some environmental resource and furthering the task in hand.

Seeking an affordance fit is not the only principle of selection. Perception-action cycles involved in achievement of an affordance are refined and differentiated as more opportunities for practice and discovery of alternative means become possible. Economy of action and reduction of perceptual information stand out as principles of selection for increasing *specificity.* Economy is implemented sometimes by the discovery of order and sometimes by the discovery of simpler means that improve the effectiveness of the behavior.

Reducing information that specifies the affordance of an event is illustrated in many of the examples presented earlier. Perceiving an object as a unit is a perfect case of detecting order and thus of reducing information in what some early writers assumed otherwise to be perceptual chaos. Earlier in the chapter we discussed perception of an object as a unit in very young infants—an object like the occluded rod that "all moves together when it moves." Another wonderful example of the usefulness of detecting unity is the perception of intermodal redundancy. Such redundancy occurs naturally in every behavioral event, for there is always both proprioceptive and external information for whatever is going on. Perceiving the unity of intermodal experience of an event has been shown to be present by 3 to 4 months of age. Very likely, it is present even earlier (A.S. Walker-Andrews, 1997).

Bahrick has given us many examples of detection of amodal invariants by infants aged about 3.5 months. In one experiment (Bahrick, 1992) auditory-visual information about an object's properties that occurred naturally together (always redundant) was contrasted with arbitrarily paired auditory-visual information as 3.5-month-old infants looked and listened. The infants were habituated to two types of event (natural or arbitrary pairings) and then tested with a slightly changed event. For example, a large metal object was raised and dropped against a wooden surface or a group of small metal objects was dropped on the surface, the look and sound of the two events being easily differentiated. Other pairings of properties were artificial—for example, combining the sound and color of a particular object or objects. The events were always presented on a video screen with soundtrack. After repeated pairings resulted in habituation, a test condition was presented in which sight and sound were combined in a novel relation. The infant's looking time at the changed event was recorded. Results demonstrated that changing the composition of natural pairings, such as a large object and its sound versus several small objects and their sound, produced dishabituation, whereas changing the color that had occurred with a sound was not noticed. Invariant relations, such as the size of a metal object and the noise it makes when dropped, are perceived as a unitary phenomenon and perturbing the relation is noticed, whereas color and an artificially associated sound are not an invariant combination in the world and a change in one or the other is unremarkable. Natural invariant relations occurring over time seem to be detected as a unit, not associated by frequent pairing.

The tied relation of the sight of part of one's own body, a limb or a hand, performing an action and the accompanying proprioceptive information provide a particularly striking invariant relation (information for unity) that is crucial for learning about control of external events. We have experimental evidence that quite young babies detect this invariant. L.E. Bahrick and Watson (1985) performed an experiment with 5.5-month-old infants in which the babies could view either a video display in front of them showing their own legs kicking simultaneously or a different display placed beside the first that showed either another infant's legs kicking or their own at an earlier moment. The question was whether they would show awareness of the contemporaneous movements of their own legs, as detected by simultaneous correlated visual and kinesthetic information. They did, in fact, demonstrate sensitivity to this invariant information by looking preferentially at the discordant view of either another infant's legs or their own kicking at some previous moment. These results were confirmed independently by Morgan and Rochat (1995), with 3.5-month-old infants.

Morgan and Rochat (1995) extended the results further by showing that the infants not only detected the invariance but changed their preference from the discordant to the concordant view when an object within leg reach could be kicked at or targeted. Thus the infants not only detected the invariant relation, but used it adaptively, when control was extended to possible contact with an external object (another example of the operation of the principle of selection for an affordance fit). Kicking at an object and making contact with it has a different affordance than does merely exercising one's legs. The experiment illustrates nicely both principles of selection. The babies detect the order and information for unity between their own felt and seen activity, and after habituation they choose the novel performance to explore when no further environmental affordance is offered. But when there is a potential target that *affords contact* (if properly aimed at), they prefer to attend to the activity that profits by guidance and control.

Economical pickup and use of information can be described as a kind of minimum principle, as well as a demonstration of development toward specificity. Treating redundant information as a unit, both in perceiving an object as a unit and in detecting multimodal information for an event, seems to be the way perception develops, perhaps without a need for extensive learning in recurrent everyday events. Selection of invariant, minimal information also operates as a principle later in development to guide what is learned when incorporation of means and selection of information in more complex situations occurs. Selection of the minimal information that works for operating a tool, for dancing, for learning a language, or for reading and writing always characterizes successful learning.

Learning distinctive features of objects such as faces or letters of the alphabet or trees is an obvious part of progress in learning about a new domain. The learner seeks the minimal information that differentiates one classmate from another, a maple leaf from an oak, or an *A* from an *X*. Reducing the information is not just a lazy man's way of operating—it occurs typically in skilled performance of a sport or in a professional skill like surgery. Detecting unity, order, and redundancy are all ways of reducing uncertainty and of achieving specificity and economy.

The propensity to find order in the perception of events is elegantly illustrated in experiments on point-light displays (see chapter 5). This method, created by Johansson (1973), portrays a performing actor walking or climbing stairs or even two actors dancing together. The actors are filmed in darkness with only a few lights or luminous patches on their heads and major joints. The activities and the actors are easily recognized and differentiated as long as the display is moving. A static display of any part of the film is perceived as a random collection of spots. It is noteworthy that the actor can only be identified as such within the ongoing event context, again demonstrating that invariant information must be detected in a temporally extended array. Infants as young as 3 months of age appear to extract structure from these displays (B.I. Bertenthal, Profitt, & Cutting, 1984). The human perceptual system tends naturally toward pickup of invariant, uniquely specifying information, and it develops toward still more efficient use of minimal information (Profitt & Kaiser, 1995). This propensity to use minimal information is shared with other creatures, for it has been shown (Blake, 1993) that cats can discriminate the natural biological motion of another cat from such foils as scrambled dots and scrambled phases of motion when presented with only 14 light points depicting the event.

Even education can make use of such demonstrations of specificity and economy. They been used in training a novice in a sport (Abernethy, 1993). It is possible to instruct a tennis player with presentations of an expert wielding a racket in a point-light display on a video screen. The viewer is helped to detect invariant information in the event for performing optimal actions and to apply the minimally critical information in the display.

Detection of order and selection for it is so entrenched in human cognition that their occurrence is often referred to as an urge, a primary drive. Our early ancestors found constellations in a starry sky and gave them names that we still refer to. Everyday citizens seek order in strings of numbers and invent systems for remembering them. Search for order is a hallmark of science, culminating in physicists' search for order in particles and in galaxies. One newspaper science writer declared, "So strong is the hunger for pattern that we see it even when it isn't there." This search for order and the selection of invariants that reduce uncertainty are already evident in the perceptual learning of infants.

Conclusion

What is learned, generally speaking, is to perceive the affordances offered by the environment. Learning what the environment affords for an individual (and by an individual) in any given case confers *meaning* on information that is detected and related to what can be effected. Learning to perceive an affordance is learning to perceive meaning. Perceptual learning is not an association of elementary processes nor is it a construction from elements of any kind nor is it the formation of a representation. It is a process of differentiation resulting in specification of information for an affordance, a relation of an animal and its environment.

Processes leading to differentiation are spontaneous exploratory activity, observation of this activity's consequences, and the process of selection. Two principles determine what is selected for learning. We refer to one as the *affordance fit*, meaning the adaptability of a perception-action cycle for the organism-environment relation. The other is *economy*, meaning selection of the minimal information that specifies the affordance for the organism. These principles are in harmony with the thesis of the ecological approach, that perception must be understood in terms of the reciprocal relation of an organism and its environment, a relation that has evolved adaptively in the species and that develops adaptively in a creature in its own niche.

9

◆ ◇ ◆ ◇ ◆

Hallmarks of Human Behavior

Characterizing Behavior

Behavior has distinctive properties observable in neither physiological processes nor in any ultimate reduction to a lower level. Because behavior has such properties, we need a science of psychology that studies behavior in its own right. These properties are not just elements of action. They become apparent only when we have observed enough behavior to detect the persistent properties that reappear over time, in many guises and exemplars. We shall refer to these properties as "hallmarks of human behavior," recognizing that they apply to the behavior of all of humankind, and perhaps of other animals as well. They make behavior special. It would take far more knowledge than psychologists now possess to program them in robots (if that could be done at all). They become apparent in the behavior of very young infants, and they develop over the years as tasks differentiate and become lengthier, and exposure to new and different environments brings opportunities for wider experience and generalization.

We have been dealing with behavior in detail, in terms of the development of interactions with other people, with objects, and with getting around in the world. The key concept that we have stressed in understanding this behavior is *affordance*. Learning about the affordances of the world and how to use them was the subject of the preceding chapter. It is the major task of infancy. Now we take a look at the emerging properties that behavior exhibits as a person uses these affordances in adaptive ways typical of our species. Four properties that stand out as descriptive of behavior at its own level are agency, prospectivity, the search for order in the world, and flexibility. It is these properties that a psychologist must take account of, document with appropriate evidence, and chart developmentally. They are the province of psychology, and of no other science.

Agency

"Agency" is the self in control, the quality of intentionality in behavior. Infants learn at a remarkably early age that their actions have an effect on the environment, that some events going on around them are amenable to their control, and that they can in fact regulate their own actions. The term "self" has a long and varied history in psychology, with many terms indicating different approaches to understanding it, such as "ego" or "will." William James addressed the concept in his own way, arguing that "we are not automata" (James, 1879). In recent times, Neisser has argued that there are five kinds of self-knowledge, one of them being an "ecological self" that originates in infants' early encounters with their environment, a self that is perceived (Neisser, 1988, 1993).

We agree that the "self" is rooted in perception, and that there is information for a self that makes it possible to learn about this important ingredient of an affordance at a very early age. We prefer to refer, as functionalists, to the ability to learn *control* of one's own activity and of external events. This is what we mean by "agency." Actors learn that they are agents, in the course of learning control (E.J. Gibson, 1993, 1994, 1995). Infants literally perceive that a change in the world and in their relation to it can be produced by their own activity. This is one aspect of learning an affordance, and there are frequent occasions for it. As we have noted, J.J. Gibson said that to perceive the world is to coperceive oneself. Perceiving changes in the external world, as one uses the perceptual systems to explore it, simultaneously provides information about the perceiver. Both an action and its consequences provide information about what the perceiver has done. From early days, infants are thus enabled to learn that they are agents—that their actions can control changes in the world, in themselves, and in the actions of other people. Now we review some evidence for this wonderful accomplishment.

A group of tiny preterm infants only a few days old, housed in the intensive care unit of a hospital, exhibited a remarkable ability to learn to regulate their own internal systems (Barnard & Bee, 1983). One group of infants automatically received 15 minutes of rocking and simulated heartbeat sounds each hour. A second group, called the "self-activating subjects," received the stimulation only when they had been inactive for 90 seconds, also just once an hour. When these two groups were compared with control infants (no stimulation), both showed better orienting responses and fewer abnormal reflexes. The self-activating group showed the most benefit in quieting behavior, indicating that they were able to learn the temporal patterning and detect the contingent relation to their own internal state, thus learning to control superfluous activity. They were able to discern something about their own inner state (suppression of activity), relate it to something happening in the world, and learn to act on that knowledge. The ability of very young infants to profit by procedures that permit them some spontaneous control of events is illustrated, likewise, by the so-called "infant control" method of conducting habituation experiments (see chap. 3). The display for habituation is presented to infants until they look away from it for as long as 2 seconds, when it is withdrawn. The display is re-presented at regular intervals until a criterion of habituation is reached, as the infants shorten their looking time on their own. Economy of exploratory looking at a novel display is greatly enhanced by this procedure, and so is the effectiveness of the method.

We refer once again to an experimental procedure now familiar from earlier discussions, that of contingent reinforcement (so-called) of a voluntary and spontaneous action, kicking a leg or pulling an arm attached to an overhead mobile. The action has the consequence of making the mobile turn, and infants as young as 2 months quickly learn to kick the attached leg or pull an arm, attaining an efficient control of an interesting scene (C.K. Rovee-Collier & Gekoski, 1979). Comparison groups presented with the mobile without an attachment that permits them to control it are not equally attentive and do not develop the differentiated behavior. When the action is made ineffective after an infant has learned to control the mobile, a marked behavioral change is exhibited. Infants' response rates rise very high, and crying and fussing ensue, whereas most infants smile and coo when their actions are effective (C.K. Rovee-Collier & Capatides, 1979). In a similar procedure in which a string attached to an infant's arm was pulled to activate the mobile, Alessandri, Sullivan, and Lewis (1990) noted that deactivation produced "frustration-like responses toward a thwarted goal" as the infants pulled harder than ever. The thwarted infants wore angry facial expressions (fig. 9.1).

The motivating effect of securing control over an external happening such as a whirling mobile or the presentation of a slide of a happy face was first demonstrated by Watson (1972) and since that time has been noted by many others. Referring to infants' active kicking to turn a mobile, Rovee-Collier and Gekoski said that "the control which the infants gained over the consequences of their own actions seems to have been the reward, rather than the specific consequences" (1979, p. 197). Lewis, Sullivan, and Brooks-Gunn (1985) monitored affective behavior and expressions of a group of infants given a similar task. A ribbon attached to a cuff on the infant's arm activated a microswitch, so that pulling the arm triggered presentation of a colored slide of a smiling face accompanied by a song. A second group of infants were given the same "show" as the experimental group, but not as a result of the contingent arm-pulling. The noncontingent babies lost interest (50% had "dropped out" 10 minutes into the presentation). They fussed more, and smiled less. Active control of an expected environmental change produces positive affect and is its own reward.

It thus appears evident that learned control can be achieved over internal regulating processes and over external events in young infants. Infants also

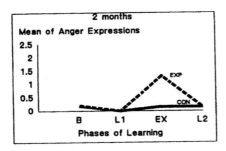
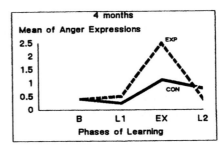
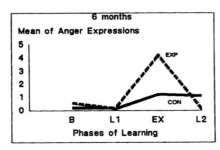
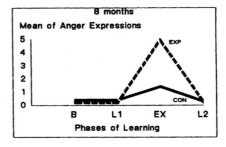

FIGURE 9.1. Frustration following deactivation of a controlled mobile. B = Baseline; L1 = Learning 1; EX = Extinction; LZ = Learning 2 From "Violation of Expectancy, Loss of Control, and Anger Expressions in Young Infants," by M. Lewis, S.M. Alessandri, and M.W. Sullivan, 1990, *Developmental Psychology, 26*, p. 749. Copyright © 1990 by the American Psychological Association, Inc. Reprinted with permission.

achieve control fairly early over social events. Most people are persuaded of the occurrence of this kind of control by anecdotes describing the effectiveness of crying, smiling, and cooing for obtaining the attention and services of caretakers. There is fortunately research, as well, to demonstrate that infants are in fact involved in managing interactions with adults by 6 months or so. Mosier and Rogoff (1994) examined infants' instrumental use of their mothers between 6 and 13 months. The experiments featured episodes in which the mother held an attractive toy that involved some manipulation just beyond her infant's present ability. The mother could hand a toy to the baby, operate it for the infant to watch, then hand it over for exploration, retrieve it from the floor, and so on. Tapes of infants' behavior were coded, noting verbalization, pointing, gaze initiation, and gestures that revealed intent to use an agent. Coders agreed that infants deliberately used their mothers to achieve a goal in 36% of the episodes at 6 months, rapidly increasing up to 78% of the episodes at 13 months, when conventional means of communication (especially by gestures) became fairly common.

The occurrence of communication between infants and a caregiver was discussed in chapter 5. The turn-taking, conversational-like behavior has received considerable attention, a number of researchers remarking on the pattern of vocalization and silent pauses that seems to be learned and to characterize the exchange (see, for example, K. Bloom, 1977). In this kind of exchange, the infant and the partner take turns in the role of agent and recipient. The distinction between these two roles, in which the infant eventually learns that agency may characterize the behavior of another person, presumably develops over the first year. We do not know exactly when a child comes to perceive what an object or event affords for another person. An experiment by Golinkoff (1975) with infants 14 to 18 months of age suggests that these infants were able to distinguish the roles of agent and recipient in a simple event involving two persons. One person, the agent, pushed another person, the recipient, across a small stage. The filmed event was shown to the infants for repeated watching and eventual habituation. Following habituation, infants were presented with another film in which the actors' roles were reversed. Duration of fixation of this event was compared with a film in which the direction of the action was reversed, but not the roles of the actors. Results indicated that the infants did detect the change in agent and recipient. It would seem that behaving as an agent and instigating an action was perceived and, in this case, attributed to another person.

This finding raises the question whether babies are cognizant of their own actions as an agent. Research suggests strongly that they are. L.E. Bahrick and Watson (1985) investigated the self-perception of 5-month-old infants, by asking specifically whether or not they were sensitive to the bimodal information (visual and proprioceptive) available to them as they kicked their legs and watched them simultaneously on a television screen (see chap. 8). The infants were presented with views of their own legs kicking, and also with views of another infant's legs, similarly clothed and situated. Direct view of their own bodies was occluded. The question was, did the infants recognize their own ongoing action pattern and distinguish it from the action of the other infant by showing a preference for looking at one display or the other? They did indeed show a preference for watching the noncontingent display. In another condition, they were presented with the current on-line video display of their own legs contrasted with a display of their own kicking taped at an earlier moment. Again, there was preferential visual exploration of the noncontingent display. This preference could only have been possible if they detected the invariant intermodal relationship between the visual and the proprioceptive (kinesthetic) information about their ongoing action, information for self-control.

We refer again, in considering the development of self-control, to experiments by Morgan and Rochat (1995) and Rochat and Morgan (1998). They compared looking preferences when infants watched their legs on videotape kicking in an object-free context with preferences when infants were given an object target at which to kick. In the free context, a microphone produced a sound whenever either leg was moved off the floor. In the object context, the microphone was placed on the object, and sounded only when a leg made contact with the target object. For each context, the infants were presented with two video displays of their own legs. In the "noncongruent" display, the view of the legs was reversed, left to right. In the "congruent" display, their right leg was on the right, and their left leg was on the left. When infants were presented with a choice between a congruent and a noncongruent view, results differed for the two contexts. In the object-free context, the infants preferred to watch the non-congruent view, as if exploring the unusual visual-proprioceptive results of their movements. But when a target object was present and a sound produced when it was contacted, infants preferred the congruent view, reversing the findings. We conclude that these infants perceived when they were controlling an action that produced an externally visible and audible consequence; they knew that they themselves, as agents, made the object sound by means of a well-aimed kick and guided the limb in accordance with the perceived affordance of the object.

Agency is sometimes referred to as "intentionality," a term that implies a contrast between actions performed involuntarily and those that are in some sense planned. This implication of an expected outcome links the behavioral property of control with another important property, prospectivity.

Prospectivity

"Prospectivity" refers to the forward-looking character of behavior. Psychologists have used many terms to describe this characteristic, such as purposive, foresightful, goal-directed, intentional, or anticipatory. Some have framed a theory around it, for example, Tolman (1932); others have admitted it reluctantly and tried to fit it into a theory, for example, C.L. Hull (1943); but there it is, plain to see. We have adopted the term "prospectivity" following Lee (1976) and von Hofsten (1993), both of whom have performed important research revealing this characteristic in actions of adults and infants. The concept of *affordance*, central to our approach to development, implies prospectivity of behavior; to perceive an affordance means to perceive some potential environmental resource and a means of action that will lead to attainment of it. Indeed, J.J. Gibson remarked that "what the philosopher called foresight I call the perception of an affordance" (1979, p. 232). Controlling behavior, which we have just discussed as the hallmark of agency, also implies prospectivity. Perceiving that one is in control implies expectations of the consequence of one's own action.

There is a wealth of evidence for prospectivity in its own right. Prospectivity pervades behavior, cognitive and observable activity alike. Behavior extends over time, any moment of it relative to preceding and succeeding events; as Eddington (1927) put it, "The great thing about time is that it goes on." Even remembering extends into the future. "Prospective memory" is a popular topic for research, including memory for such planned incidents as taking prescribed medicines, or keeping appointments. We make preparations for even the most basic behavior, such as reaching for something.

There has been a substantial amount of research on reaching in infants; recently much of it has dwelled on the anticipatory nature of the movements (see chap. 6). Before reaching even begins, posture must be prepared for it by putting the infant :л a stable position to lift and move a limb. During a reach, the abdominal and trunk muscles must be activated and begin firing before the arm can be elevated (von Hofsten, 1993). If an object is to be grasped, there must be preparatory opening of the hand and orientation to the position and size of the object. The hand even starts to close in anticipatory response to encountering the object (von Hofsten & Rönnqvist, 1988).

Particularly convincing evidence of prospectivity in infants' reaching was presented by von Hofsten (1980) in his study of reaching for a moving target (see chap. 6). If a target object is moving, the would-be catcher must anticipate where it will be by the time the arm can arrive at its location. Von Hofsten studied five infants longitudinally at intervals of 3 weeks, beginning at 18 weeks. The infants' reaches were subjected to an extensive quantitative analysis of their spatiotemporal properties. The target object was an orange-and-gold wobbling toy duck's head mounted on a metal rod that rotated in a horizontal circular path in front of the infant, at nose height and about 11 to 16 cm in front of the infant's eyes. It could be moved at three speeds (3.4, 15, or 30 cm per sec), and it stopped moving when it was grasped. Typically, the infants tried to grasp the object immediately when first presented with it in a motionless trial.

According to von Hofsten, "most reaches were aimed approximately at the meeting point with the object" (p. 381), so predictability was good. Even at the youngest age, the infants were aiming quite well. Developmental changes were concentrated in increasing motor skill, as the infants acquired greater economy of movement with experience (see fig. 9.2). Von Hofsten (1983) repeated his observations with a group of infants aged about 34 weeks and measured timing as well as aim of the reach. His earlier findings were confirmed, and timing of the reach found to be very precise.

As we have also discussed, infants' reaching is predictive even when they are trying to catch an object moving in the dark (see chap. 6). In one experiment (Robin, Berthier, & Clifton, 1996), infants of 5 and 7.5 months were presented with a moving target covered with fluorescent paint, which could be seen moving in an arc in a completely dark surround. They reached successfully for the moving object in both the light and the dark, aiming ahead of the current visible position of the object.

Exploratory activity of perceptual systems is often anticipatory. Exploration has, indeed, the adaptive function of preparing the way for performatory action. Even when exploration is not specifically predictive, its function is prospective. An example is found in a study of gaze control in which von Hofsten and Rosander (1996) demonstrated predictive tracking of moving visual objects in 3-month-old infants.

Lee's emphasis on the prospectiveness of behavior stems from his discovery of a constant (Tau) that specifies the ratio of the distance of an obstructing surface to the rate of approach to the surface. Lee has shown that this constant

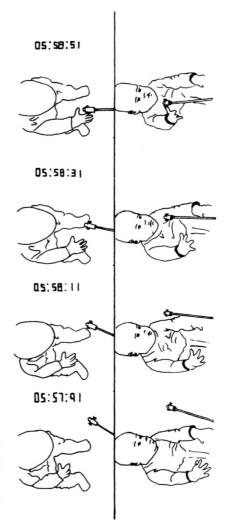

05:58:51

05:58:31

05:58:11

FIGURE 9.2. The performance of a well-
aimed reach for a moving target at 21
weeks of age. The frame bottom-left is the
start of the reach. The interval between
frames is 0.2 sec. From "Predictive
Reaching for Moving Objects by Human
Infants," by C. von Hofsten, 1980, *Journal
of Experimental Child Psychology, 30,* p.
377. Copyright © 1980 by the Academic
Press, Inc. Reprinted with permission.

05:57:91

is optically specified in many situations, such as driving a vehicle (Lee, 1976),
and that this information is used in the direct perception of impending contact
by at least one animal (the gannet), as well as by humans (Lee and Reddish,
1981). While no experimenter wants to precipitate actual collisions for a baby,
it has been possible to study the ability to detect useful information that serves
for avoiding contact with an approaching obstacle in experiments on "looming"
(see chap. 7). Avoidance of collision with a solid surface ahead or with an obstacle advancing toward one is an important affordance. Even prelocomotor infants have been shown to detect information for it, using indicators such as

blinking, head retraction, or raising the hands, all anticipatory of a collision (Bower et al., 1970; Ball & Tronick, 1971; Carroll & Gibson, 1981).

We noted the prevalence of infants' expectations of consequences (what leads to what) in predictable sequences of events in the preceding chapter, particularly in the research of Haith (1993; Haith, Wentworth, & Canfield, 1993). Expectations in infancy are not normally aversive; rather, the opposite, such as expectations of being fed or picked up and comforted when a caretaker approaches. Documentation of infants' expectations of a pleasurable affordance, as contrasted with an aversive one, was obtained by N.D. Rader (1997). She familiarized infants with teethers that could be grasped and brought to the mouth for sucking. Some had been dipped in sugar water and tasted sweet, whereas others had an unpleasant taste. Infants quickly learned which teethers afforded a pleasant taste, and they guided their behavior accordingly when given an opportunity to make a selection.

As knowledge of affordances is gained, the possibility of perceiving "means-end" segments of activity as ways of attaining affordances increases. Intentional behavior in a segmented, two- or three-step task is a big attainment in later infancy, advancing prospectivity to the level of "planning ahead." Learning to use an object as a means or a tool toward a further end is an important step toward "planning ahead." It implies essentially that the object has a secondary affordance that gives the actor the capability of attaining some other affordance. This is prospectivity embedded in a longer task. We discussed nested segments of action in a task in chapter 3 and again in chapter 8, where we described learning to use an act as a strategy, or an object as a tool. Pulling a cloth on which rests a toy, too far away to reach is an example, as is removing an occluder to obtain a hidden or partially hidden toy. Adolph's experiments on traversal of a slope found that infants discovered strategies to reach a waiting parent, such as turning around and sliding backward on their stomachs, when the slope was too steep to proceed directly on two feet (Adolph 1997).

Learning a new means for realizing an affordance also implies retrospectivity of behavior. Behavior goes on over time, learning occurs, and knowledge about affordances changes. Using means and strategies learned in earlier experiences is often referred to as an instance of memory (or remembering something, to put it in more active terms). In recent years, cognitive psychologists have differentiated many classes or subtypes of memory, such as "explicit" and "implicit." Explicit memory refers to recall of events (episodic or autobiographical). It is usually studied by tapping verbally accessible experience in children who have acquired language. "Implicit" memory includes perceptual and motor skills that are not usually verbalized and also the kind of learning that we have been discussing. We have seen that infants remember some features of speech that they heard even before birth.

We do not need to talk about memory, however, to discuss perceptual learning, and it may be misleading to do so, because perceiving, acting, and learning to perceive are all highly dynamic processes, whereas the term "memory" suggests something static and inactive. Perceiving and acting are retrospective in the sense that dynamic processes are spread over time and reflect preceding behavior as well as point to prospective behavior. Retrospectivity is, in a sense, the other side of prospectivity. A "retrospective exhibit" of a painter's work, for example, shows the evolution of the work, where the artist *was going*. Perceiving where one *is going* is the essence of prospectivity. Later on, perhaps, one can reflect on it retrospectively. This is not an activity that is equally descriptive of development, however, and factors that influence prospective activity are not the same as those that influence retrospecitve activity.

Looking back at where one was going does, nevertheless, point to another hallmark of human behavior: the pervasive search for pattern and order in external events and even in our own lives, especially as we interact with the world. We look for order and for invariance in changing events over time.

Seeking and Using Order

The search for order, regularity, and pattern is evident in the most ordinary human behavior. Even very young infants express surprise at violations of regularity (Baillargeon, 1993). Order is quickly noticed, giving rise to expectations of "what follows what" predictably. Search for regularities in language is particularly apparent in development. Before 9 months, infants in an English-speaking environment begin to detect the strong-weak stress patterns predominant in speech in that language (Jusczyk, 1997, p. 90 ff.). Taking advantage of this order will help them differentiate utterances (e.g., segment words) in the ongoing speech flow of different speakers.

We search for invariance over change. Nature presents us with diversity, and variation is essential for evolution. But the affordances of the environment must have some permanence to be useful to animals, and what is invariant, despite transformations in moment-to-moment stimulation, must be perceived. Only invariant information specifies an object or a place or a critical aspect of an event. Properties of objects like shape, size, and substance give rise to varying information with movements of either object or observer, but orderly relations specify those properties. J.J. Gibson spoke of "invariance over transformation" as the major problem for understanding perception. Perception experiments investigating this issue are referred to as "constancy" experiments (see chap. 6). In a sense, perceiving always involves learning, because it requires extracting the invariants that specify the affordance or the critical feature. Certainly, discovering invariant relations that specify an affordance is the epitome of perceptual learning.

A bonus of the search for order and invariance is the extent to which discovery of invariant relations yields *economy*. Animals are, some would say, deluged with information via multiple perceptual systems. But detection of order and invariance reduces the information at the same time that it specifies affordances and therefore meanings. An apt example of this economy of specification is the point-light experiment described earlier. A few points of light on body joints are sufficient for specifying a person walking, two persons dancing, a cat, and so on, as long as there is movement to display the invariants over appropriate transformations. A static display of the lights looks simply random. If they are rearranged (e.g., upside down), the display may resemble nothing but a swarm of bees, even when in motion.

The Gestalt psychologists emphasized *organization* and frequently pointed out its economy. Only one of the Gestalt laws, however, acknowledged the value of movement—the law of "common fate," which specifies that an object is a unit if it all moves together when it moves. In many experiments, this principle has been shown to operate for young infants (see chap. 6). Perceiving an object as a unit is an example of invariance and economy in perception.

The search for and function of order and invariance has been illustrated frequently in the foregoing chapters. Discovery of order or invariance serves as a selective mechanism for perceptual learning. We stressed the role of spontaneous exploratory activity in providing variation in exposure to the environment, because it is the changing, moving exposure that makes possible the discovery of whatever critical relation specifies the invariant. Search for order can be a conscious motive in solving a puzzle or seeking a way through a problem or a novel layout, but in everyday situations it seems that the organism is simply prepared to operate this way and needs no incentive or conscious direction to do so. The search for order is, indeed, a hallmark of human behavior.

Flexibility

Finding the relation that remains invariant over change and that specifies a potential affordance does not mean that either perception or action is rigid and unchangeable as situations change. On the contrary, perception is an active, exploratory process that continues as one makes use of knowledge of affordances and invariant relations that specify them. Perception adjusts to new situations and to changing bodily conditions such as growth, improved motor skill, or a sprained ankle. The system is continually adjusting to presented conditions; daily life requires the flexibility to perceive and use whatever affordances are necessary for the tasks at hand. Stereotypy of reaction is perilous. Evolution profits from diversity, and so does daily behavior.

Flexibility raises major questions for psychological inquiry and needs thoughtful consideration. In recent years, the prominence of such concepts as "modularity of mind" (Fodor, 1983) and "domain specificity" (Karmiloff-Smith, 1992), implying genetically constrained segregation and encapsulation of certain cognitive operations with respect to others, has raised the spectre of inflexibility and stereotypy in behavior. Not even confirmed S-R behaviorists accepted that. Human and animal behavior admitted some flexibility, some set of alternatives, some generalizability from one task or situation to another, even for theories often labeled as the most inflexible. Nevertheless it has come to be rather widely accepted that some behaviors are "informationally encapsulated" and "task specific." "Core abilities" are said to be domain specific, for example, language and spatial orientation (Hermer & Spelke, 1996; Karmiloff-Smith, 1992). If this be the case in infancy, as goes the claim, how does flexibility of behavior develop? Hermer and Spelke (1996) and Karmiloff-Smith (1992) recognize the problem but do not solve it for us, save for Karmiloff-Smith's offering of the phrase "conceptual redescription" as development advances. Network theories of elaboration and broadening of connections (relations?) may be more promising, but we have yet to see.

We go back in the history of psychology a bit to make clear the importance of acknowledging flexibility as a hallmark of human behavior. Early in the 20th century, psychologists had been made aware of the so-called "reflex arc," and Pavlov made scientific history with his experiments on the conditioned reflex. A stern kind of radical behaviorism was introduced in the United States making use of these concepts, promoting stimulus-response association and the chaining of S-R elements as the foundations of a mechanistic learning theory. This theory led logically to a view of behavior as very stereotyped. Karl Lashley (1942), a great neuropsychologist of the time, protested that behavioral functions were not set patterns of special groups of muscles firing but were flexible, so that if one group of muscles used habitually was rendered ineffectual, other groups not specifically trained could perform equivalently. A famous illustration that Lashley used to make the point involved the writing of two blindfolded individuals with their right and left hands, writing mirror reversed, and writing by holding a brush with the teeth; figure 9.3 shows the functional equivalence for these individuals. The same point has been made more recently and elaborately by Bernstein (1967). The most sophisticated of behaviorists, Clark Hull, was obliged to admit the flexibility of behavior even in rats running in a maze; when a habitual path through the maze was blocked, they were able to reach the goal box by an alternate route. Hull solved the problem of "behavioral equivalence" with his elaborate hypothesis of a learned "habit-family hierarchy" that accounted for transfer in this situation (Hull, 1934a,b). He had already accepted the concept of a goal, thus admitting the prospectivity of behavior.

If even rats exhibit flexibility in using equivalent maze routes, we can expect flexibility in human infants. Piaget (1954) observed transfer from one arm to another in his 2-month-old son Laurent. Laurent was making a toy doll dance by pulling on a ribbon attached to his right wrist at one end and to the doll on the other. When the ribbon was shifted to Laurent's left wrist, he tugged at the doll with that one. C.K. Rovee-Collier and colleagues (1978) found similar bilateral transfer in 3-month-old infants who had been trained to kick to produce movement of a mobile. During training, the cord activating the mobile was tied to the baby's right leg. Later, when the contingency was reversed and the cord tied to the left leg, there was a "rapid and complete shift in leg dominance."

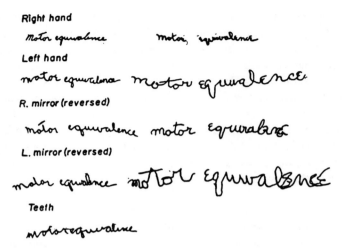

FIGURE 9.3. Flexible transfer of writing skill. Originally from "The Problem of Cerebral Organization in Vision," by K.S. Lashley, 1942, in H. Klüver (Ed.), *Biological Symposia* (Vol. 7, p. 318), Lancaster, PA: Jaques Cattell Press. Copyright © by. R.R. Bowker Company. Used with permission of R.R. Bowker.

Shifting to equivalent motor systems does not by itself guarantee flexibility in learning about affordances, however. The information about the environment is equally important in the affordance relation. For an infant to perceive a once-learned affordance in a changed situation, similar invariant information for the affordance must be present and detected. We look briefly at some experiments on transfer of training in a modified context.

Transfer to a changed context was examined by Rovee and Fagan (1976) in the task of pulling on a string to turn an overhead mobile, the same task cited for bilateral transfer. Three-month-old infants were given 9 minutes of practice on 3 consecutive days with an identical mobile. The infants' kicking rate grew high on the first day and rose even higher on the following days. On the fourth day, half the infants were given a novel mobile. Their kick rate was significantly lower than that of the infants given the familiar mobile. Infants given a new mobile maintained a high rate of attention, nevertheless, as indicated by gazing at the mobile, and their kick rate subsequently increased to the previous rate. They apparently noticed the difference and slowed down, but they watched the mobile and eventually resumed their previous activity. A later experiment (Fagen, Morongiello, Rovee-Collier, & Gekoski, 1984) found that infants trained with a series of different mobiles generalized to new ones. In everyday life, small changes are more likely to occur from one occasion to another and are less likely to be as set off from usual happenings.

The experiment in which infants were trained with varied mobiles is reminiscent of research on the phenomenon called "learning to learn." This phrase was coined by Harlow (1959), who gave a series of simple discrimination problems to monkeys. A monkey was slow in mastering the first problem but became very fast at solving similar ones after solving several problems. A monkey presented with an array of three objects, two alike and one different, had to select the odd item. Sets of objects were changed on every trial. The monkey formed a "learning set," Harlow thought. Younger monkeys were slower to form these sets. Harlow said, "One of the most striking facts already disclosed is the large temporal separation between the development of effective individual-problem learning and the development of learning sets for the same kind of problem" (p. 504).

Educators were quick to apply Harlow's concepts. An example is the very extensive research program of House and Zeaman (1963), who gave series of discrimination problems to retarded children. There was interproblem improvement. The problems were all of a kind, as were Harlow's. After a series of oddity problems were presented with objects physically present, children did not show transfer to oddity problems presented verbally by questioning them. Performances of individual children could not be predicted from one method of presentation to the other (House, 1964). Generalization over problems was specific to the training situation, which always involved the same strategy.

Transfer of learning on a more varied set of problems was studied longitudinally by Ling (1944) with a group of infants aged 6 to 12 months. Two solid geometrical figures were presented on a board, one fastened to the board, the other detachable and sweetened. The babies learned to discriminate five pairs of forms, then various transformations of the forms, then reversals of them, and so on. Learning was more and more rapid as the program continued. The children grew older, of course, but a control group of comparable age gave evidence that the improvement with practice was real. What generalized? From Ling's descriptions, it seems to have been exploratory strategies: "their visual regard was of an anticipatory, 'critical,' and sustained type," and "their manipulative activities were more varied" (p. 56). Strategies of exploration seem to be transferable and may contribute to flexibility of behavior; a training situation, to be successful, must encourage exploration. These babies learned economy and perhaps flexibility in their search, and they learned to hunt for the minimal distinctive information.

It seems likely that flexibility of behavior is best studied not in the context of transfer of particular acts or elements of behaviors, but rather in terms of broader strategies of exploratory search and knowledge of when to use any skills already possessed. Two recent developmental studies of infants learning to cope with spatial problems support this view. The longitudinal research by Adolph (1997) on infants learning to traverse slopes is very instructive. In chapter 7, we described her findings that when the infants first made the transition from crawling to walking, they did not immediately perceive the affordance of the slope for walking or use the alternative means of descending they had discovered while crawling. Walking was a whole new ball game: the children had to learn anew what slopes they could safely traverse with their new mode of locomotion, and when to use alternative means of descent. Adolph's study also made it clear, however, that there is transfer of skill even without practice in the same task. Recall that a control group of infants was tested only at the endpoints of the developing skills, without exposure to the sloping surfaces every few weeks. When tested as experienced walkers, these babies, like those observed at frequent intervals, coped appropriately with the slopes, walking safely down or descending steeper slopes by other means. The control-group babies' experience in becoming skilled walkers in normal daily circumstances provided something transferable to the unusual slopes encountered in the laboratory.

What explains this generalization to the particular situation? Flexibility, which is is guaranteed by the functional nature of behavior, is segmented into tasks, functional units, and these into nested subunits that constitute a repertoire of subskills or strategies. As mobility develops with experience and practice, a repertoire of strategies, subskills, and attentional skills is learned. These are differentiated in experience once the new skill or mode of locomotion (e.g., standing upright and walking) has emerged and is practiced. As small differences in the affordance of the ground surface and the path (obstacles, barriers, gaps) are encountered, new subskills (e.g., alertness in watching for information about surface properties, slower steps on slopes, bending the knees or torso, using arms protectively, etc.) are learned. The toddlers are also learning about their own body-scale in relation to the surroundings, and they are becoming aware of the limitations posed by biomechanical constraints. When a novel task is presented, the experience gained is available prospectively for functional adjustments as the task progresses. Perhaps something analogous happens as adults gain experience driving vehicles and encounter novel highway and traffic conditions.

A second experiment is also instructive about the general effectiveness of experience in walking. Schmuckler (1997) observed barrier crossing in 12- to 30-month-old toddlers, presenting them with barriers of varying height to step over. Successful crossing of increasingly higher barriers naturally increases with age and body scale (e.g., height and leg length). Of particular interest is the finding that the threshold for successful crossing is predicted by experience (length of walking practice) in each age group studied. In fact, the effect of experience on increasing general locomotor control may be greater than that of body size in the early growth of skill. Schmuckler's findings also suggest a developmental trend toward improving perceptual judgments of possible as opposed to impossible barriers, which would indicate increasing differentiation in perceiving affordances for locomotion in a cluttered layout.

Other examples of the development of flexibility come from studies of route finding and "roundabout" behavior. Lewin (1946) gave the term "roundabout" to the behavior of very young children who were able to detour around a direct route to reach a goal that was visible ahead but blocked by a barrier. A child of 1 year, placed in a U-shaped enclosure with a visible but not directly accessible goal ahead, seemed unable to turn away from the goal and travel round the barrier. For somewhat older children, the barrier presented no problem: they walked around it. Lewin thought that the "space" the child inhabited was "differentiated" during the intervening time. This interpretation may in a sense be true, since mobility increases constantly from the age of 1 year, giving children the freedom and the means to explore new or changed places. Flexibility in selecting a route becomes greater.

Detour behavior in children between 10 and 14 months was studied by McKenzie and Bigelow (1986) and discussed in chapter 7. Children first crawled or walked across a free path to their mothers to obtain a toy. Then a barrier was placed across the path between the child and the mother, who first stood and displayed the toy, then sat down so that she was no longer visible. An aerial view of the arrangement was provided to the child by the experimenter, and then the child was allowed to proceed. After four trials the barrier was relocated. The older children showed flexible detour behavior and chose a new and more efficient path. The younger children did manage to go around the barrier to find their mothers, but they took a less efficient path. The problem for them was modification of the behavior they had just found successful. Again, we see greater specificity in what was learned in the younger group, with increasing flexibility as exploratory activity and developing control provide the older group with more ability to use locomotor skills appropriately in varying layouts.

Research with somewhat older children reported by H. Pick (1993) yielded similar findings. Children of 16, 20, and 24 months of age were taken on a short walk around a room with four exits, leaving their parent at one of the doors. After being guided around the room, the children were taken to the center and asked to return to their parent. Nearly all the youngest children—even those who had been guided three-quarters of the way around the room—returned to the door they had entered, by reversing the exact route they had taken. The older children (all of them at 24 months) were able to take a shortcut and return by the most economical route. Transfer of way finding from maps and from verbal directions would become possible later, greatly extending flexibility.

Increasing ability to communicate obviously extends flexibility of behavior enormously; indeed, it continues to do so far into adult life, for human communication is very creative. All animals communicate, using diverse means—chemical, tactile, visual, auditory—depending on the species. Some species communicate via more than one system, as do humans. Human systems of communication can be exceedingly complex and varied. We hear of children who invent secret languages, for example, and we expect all children in our society to learn to read printed words and mathematical symbols and to use sophisticated systems via telephones and computers. We deal here with only the beginning of this impressive array of systems.

Communication begins almost at the very start of life. A prospective mother feels her baby moving about, and in later pregnancy, the fetus hears the mother's voice and knows it well enough to distinguish it from other speakers after birth (see chap. 5). Early communication with a parent begins with facial gestures, cries, and coos. Mothers commonly talk to their infants as they bathe them, feed them, and pick them up. What they say is often in response to some action or vocalization of the infant, very likely at first inadvertent, but babies catch on very soon, noting the contingency between their own action and some response from the partner; and so communication begins in a responsive environment, taking place by any available means. In chapter 5 we presented evidence for early communication between partners, often in a turn-taking pattern. During the first year, communicative activity develops impressively, progressing to joint attention with a caretaker as objects begin to be noticed and handled; to attention to others' facial expressions in risky situations; then to attention to the characteristic sounds of the language that is spoken by the community, zeroing in on the commonly expressed sounds and accents in rapid perceptual learning. And of course, vocabulary begins to be acquired as toys and people are named and actions are labeled when a baby points or makes expressive gestures.

We call attention to just how creative communication can become in extending the flexibility of behavior to writing systems and codes. Flexibility is indeed a hallmark of behavior. Perhaps the most important point to emphasize is the intertwining of communicative creativity with the other hallmarks of human behavior. Flexibility of behavior is increased dramatically when language can be resorted to as an alternative means; prospectivity is extended by the ability to make verbal plans with others (or just for oneself); agency is enriched beyond mere control of one's own acts by an expanding sense of self, as communication teaches an infant about agency in others and how to recognize affordances for oneself in relation to others.

Summary

We have described four distinctive hallmarks of human behavior. They characterize the behavior of various other animals also, to some extent, but they are the essence of human behavior. Neurological explanations or descriptions of them may one day be possible, but as students of human behavior we cannot wait for that and, in any case, they are not reducible to a neurological level of explanation. They are not elements or units of any kind, nor are they localized in any way, but rather they characterize action and cognition broadly over time in an environment in which they evolved and in which they are enhanced as development proceeds.

Agency comes first. That we have control over our own behavior is remarkable in contrast to other inhabitants of the physical universe—to planets, for example. Learning to control behavior is a critical part of development, a potential that is gradually realized as individuals learn about the affordances of the world and how they can be used.

Prospectivity of behavior—its forward-looking character—is observable soon after birth, but again we see impressive developmental change in the ability to plan ahead and subordinate lesser goals to future expectations. Differentiation of what is perceived, as more events and layouts are experienced, goes far toward encouraging this development.

Perceiving *order* begins early too. Very young infants prefer a symmetrical, properly arranged face image over a representation with scrambled features. That is a far cry, still, from a 10-year-old's ability to locate the North Star in the heavens. The "hunger for order," as one newspaper feature writer observed, is so great in humans that people seek order even in a random set of elements, like dots. The usefulness of order in perceptual and cognitive economy is obvious and makes evolutionary sense, because order exists in the world all around us and in our bodies. We need to detect it and use it.

The case of *flexibility* is particularly interesting developmentally. Tiny babies exhibit variability, and their behavior is spontaneous, not stereotyped or reflex. But true flexibility suggests accommodating to new circumstances with alternatives that not only are not random but are appropriate to the task. Flexibility in this sense implies learning from experience, easy command of action possibilities, and a repertory of exploratory activities and eventually strategies. Surely transfer of potential strategies from tasks already within one's experience, and from affordances already familiar and useful, can be expected. Encapsulated modular structures within closed domains would not favor such intertask relations. If such domain specificity exists originally, a means of emerging from it must be part of development. At present, modular theories offer us no way out of the dilemma.

Perceptual development is a process of differentiation, and perceptual learning accounts for accessibility of sophisticated strategies for using affordances, both familiar and novel. It is a discovery process in which exploration and affordance-fit play key roles. All the hallmarks of human behavior are inherent in this process, developing as experience broadens means and strategies of exploration. Many people report feeling threatened by a computerized system such as "Deep Blue", the chess program that can tie a game with a human expert. The computerized chess expert, Deep Blue, simulates prospective planning of moves ahead, takes control of the game, detects order in the human competitor's moves and has the flexibility (apparently) to change plans appropriately. No wonder it looks human and appears to threaten our status in the universe. But it is a simulation, a remarkably astute one, created by human intelligence. Deep Blue is incapable of perceptual learning about affordances, all on its own. We are.

10

✦ ✧ ✦ ✧ ✦

The Role of Perception
in Development beyond Infancy

The Persistence of Perceptual Learning

Perception always has a role in development, as well as in ongoing behavior, because perceiving is the way we keep in touch with the world and what is going on around us. Perception never stops; it provides the information for ongoing actions (even just sitting or standing), for planning, and for developing concepts and reasoning. It may be that the role of cognitive processes such as imagining and reasoning increases developmentally in proportion to one's getting information directly from ongoing events (we certainly make educational efforts to encourage them). Of course, what we learn verbally increases enormously as spoken, and then written, language is acquired. Does that mean that perceptual development ceases, or at least slows down, after infancy?

Our answer is *no*. Potential new affordances never stop becoming available, nor do people of any age stop learning to perceive them. We have seen that as reaching, handling, and locomotion develop, encounters with the environment broaden and potential affordances multiply. New opportunities don't stop with physical growth, they increase. The nervous system develops, as well as stature and muscles. Increasing experience provides a backlog of knowledge that breeds new opportunities. Environments change from home to school to scenes outside both, imposing new demands that lead to learning about new affordances. What doesn't change is human nature itself, the properties we have described as "hallmarks of human behavior." Control, prospectivity, seeking and using order, and flexibility in finding and using new means to ends all point to continuing development, whatever aspect of behavior we may consider.

Cognition is a trendy word in psychology today. Often it appears to be used to refer only to "representations" of the world and to "mental capacities," without reference to the environment and the way we obtain and use information about it. It seems to us, in contrast to this position, that to be useful (indeed, to have evolved at all), cognition must be grounded on knowledge about the world that is obtained in encounters with that world. Knowledge for good or ill, of people, or things, or places, is meaningful and is obtained in the first place from learning what people, things, and events may afford for us. Perception thus has a role in all cognition, as the primary process that makes it possible.

There is a change, however, in what is learned via perceptual learning after infancy. Babies' earliest encounters with the world are much the same everywhere, and the human species has evolved a species-typical program of development in infancy, beginning with the other people on whom that development depends. The earliest information about external events comes via an infant's mother's voice. Babies are prepared to be responsive to human voices and faces, quickly learning a great deal about their characteristics and the consequences and meaning of encounters with the people to whom the voices and faces belong. Learning about objects and how they can be used comes next, and late in the first year, most babies are engaged in learning about locomotion. These are great accomplishments, as well as ubiquitous. But following infancy, things become more specialized. Each child's life gradually becomes unique, and perceptual learning is engaged in adjusting to more and more specialized tasks: acquiring language, using many kinds of implements (spoons and crayons to name just two), and extending body actions to athletic and recreational skills. All these more specialized tasks have their beginnings in the basic ones, starting with one's native language. Almost all human infants learn to speak, but their speech fairly rapidly becomes specialized, marked by familial, cultural, and class distinctions. Consider now a few examples of perceptual learning as humans develop through infancy and beyond it.

Perceptual Learning in Specialized Tasks

Speech

As we have noted, learning one's native language begins very early in infancy, in fact during the gestational period. That this is indeed perceptual learning, and as such specifies some particular environmental event, is evident. The specificity is documented in fetal learning that can be measured reliably before birth. A.J. DeCasper, Lecanuet, Busnel, Granier-Deferre, and Maugeais (1994) asked pregnant women to recite one of two short nursery rhymes aloud three times in succession every day for 4 weeks, beginning when their fetuses' gestational age was 33 weeks. Then, in a testing phase, both rhymes (spoken by a different person) were played over a speaker placed 20 cm above the mother's abdomen. Heart rate measures showed a decrease in fetal heart rate for the rhyme that had been read, but not for the control rhyme. Evidently, intonation contours, meter, pattern of syllable beats, or all of these that characterized the rhyme they heard were perceived and attuned to by the fetuses. As we discussed in chapter 5, this ability to perceive intonation patterns heard during gestation is further borne out in experiments with newborns.

We also discussed (chap. 5) research attesting to infants' increasing attunement to sounds and patterns of their native language during their first year of life. During this period, infants lose sensitivity to sound patterns not used in their native language as they become more and more attuned to their own. Not only do they become attuned perceptually to prosodic features and pronunciation of the language, but toward the end of the first year they begin to differentiate the morphological pattern, learning to segment the words from phrases. Breaking up utterances by identifying word boundaries is an excellent example of perceptual differentiation, providing smaller units that serve to predict and differentiate meanings. Infants begin to show recognition of certain words around 8 to 10 months, perhaps for their own names even earlier (Mandel, Jusczyk, & Pisoni, 1995).

Receptive language knowledge based on perceptual learning has developed remarkably by the end of the first year, and during the second year, as active utterances begin, the participation of perceptual learning becomes even more obvious in the young child's attempts to speak, when it is essential to listen to and evaluate one's own utterances. This story is so manifold and so complex that it requires a volume to itself (see, e.g., L. Bloom, 1993, 1997; Jucszyk, 1997). We have tried here to show only how firmly language, the most human and elaborate of cognitive achievements, is grounded in perception from its very beginning. Differentiating words and phrases spoken by others, and eventually developing capability for producing them, involves great feats of perceptual skill. The story continues, with further elaboration of perceptual skills, some years later, as a young child learns to differentiate printed symbols representing speech, and so to read.

Manual Skills and Tool Use

We have seen how infants, beginning at around 4 months, reach for things, pick them up, catch them, and eventually finger and handle them. Perceptual skill in manipulating objects becomes even more flexible and also potentially more specialized as infants learn to extend this skill to using objects as tools. As we pointed out in chapter 6, tool use is a means-end task, in which control may be extended beyond the bounds of the child's own limbs. Of course a tool may be designed to increase natural human potential in other ways too, as a lever is used to increase power of lifting something or a turntable pushed to change an object's location. Learning the affordance of a tool is an example of perceptual learning that occurs at all stages of life beyond infancy. Exploratory activity plays a major role in this learning, as it does earlier, but so does another factor, imitation through observation, a kind of social perceptual learning that we discussed in chapter 5.

Use of an object to extend one's reach requires knowledge of bodily dynamics and dimensions as part of perceiving the affordance of using the object in a particular situation. Research by McKenzie and colleaguess (1993), discussed in chapter 6, provides some insight into the learning problem involved in wielding a wooden spoon to extend the reach in order to make contact with an object. In one experiment, 10- and 12-month-old infants were observed when a toy was placed at varying distances from where they were seated. On some trials, the infants were provided with wooden spoons to extend their ability to come into contact with the object. There was a significant age difference in successfully using the spoon to touch the toy. Maintaining postural control while leaning and also manipulating an implement were apparently beyond the 10-month-olds' capability. Perceiving that the reach could be extended with the implement and then reaching with it was only emerging by 12 months.

This experiment tells us that use of a tool depends on the child's ability to control the object while maintaining postural stability and maneuvering both self and object. However, learning how to use a tool as a means of achieving a goal also requires learning the limits of one's own dynamic ability in relation to what the tool itself affords. The affordance of the tool can be discovered in two ways, by *exploratory activities* and by *imitation*, and both are likely to play a role in most tasks. Imitation plays a communicative role in perceptual learning for young infants (see chap. 5). Whereas in very young infants, imitation serves mainly to promote and maintain communication, toward the end of the first year imitation begins to facilitate learning the affordance of a novel object or action as a tool or means to an end. Adults commonly use demonstration to tutor an older infant. In the experiment just cited, the authors demonstrated the use of the tool for prodding a toy placed out of reach. The demonstration may have aided the older infants in perceiving what the tool afforded as a means of reaching the toy.

It seems obvious that discovering the affordance of a tool is most easily learned from a demonstration by another person, permitting the potential user to imitate the action. But how early can a child profit from observational learning of this kind? What is learned from observation is not how to manipulate the tool, but what the tool might afford, for example, pulling in food with a rake when the food is beyond arm's length, or leaving marks on a surface with a crayon. Clearly, the age at which observational learning can be profitable depends on the task and the nature of the tool. We illustrate with an experiment on 2-year-old children (Nagell, Olquin, & Tomasello, 1993). The researchers wished to compare human children with chimpanzees on use of imitation in a raking-in task. The chimps varied in age from 4 to 8 years. How does one select a comparable age for human children for this task? In a preliminary experiment, children of 18 months, 2 years, and 3 years were given the rake task. They were to rake in a toy, placed out of reach, to within reaching access so as to grasp the toy. The prongs of the rake were placed widely enough apart for the small toy to slip through. If the rake were flipped over, the toy could be pulled in. The task demanded motor skill too difficult for the 18-month-old children, who played with the tool rather than trying to rake in the toy. It proved too easy, however, for the 3-year-olds, who needed no model. The 2-year-olds were selected. Of three groups of them, one group was given no demonstration, one a partial demonstration, and one a full demonstration before every trial. The authors concluded that the children, given a chance, imitated the model. Children in the no-model group achieved only 1 success out of 10 trials, but the other groups averaged 2.5 successes. A model may be useful for demonstrating a potential affordance, but learning efficient use of a tool requires, in addition, exploratory action and practice with varying consequences. It is interesting that the chimpanzees were thought to engage less in imitative learning and to rely more on their own strategies, although those given a demonstration performed better than those given none. They engaged in what Tomasello (in press) terms "emulation behavior" rather than "imitative behavior." Perhaps they learned something about an object's affordances that they did not know beforehand and then used this information to devise their own behavioral strategy. Surely this happens frequently in human infants as well.

For many years, following the lead of Wolfgang Köhler, a founder of Gestalt psychology, psychologists thought of novel tool use as signaling the emergence of "insight." During World War I, Köhler was stranded on the island of Teneriffe, where he had at his disposal a group of chimpanzees. He experimented with the chimpanzees, giving them many problems that could only be solved by use of a tool. For example, a banana was hung overhead and could only be reached by knocking it down with a stick, or climbing on a box, or even piling one box on another. These interesting examples and Köhler's lucid description (Köhler, 1925) convinced many psychologists that a special sort of intuition or insight was responsible for success in such problems. In recent years, however, as we gain more and better descriptions of development of perception of affordances in human infants and the kind of exploratory activity and perceptual learning that goes on, we see how much preparatory learning has gone on before use of some tool is discovered and mastered. We present an illustration of early learning that foreshadows learning how to grip a writing tool.

One of the prime examples of learning during the first year of life is how to pick up a small object. This learning was studied in great detail many years ago as the development of prehension (Halverson, 1931) and again recently by Butterworth and colleagues (1997; discussed in chap. 6). Butterworth et al. observed infants between 24 and 83 weeks as they acquired skill in grasping a small object. The exploratory repertoire of the youngest infants contained a great variety of exploratory grips. But with development, there was a trend toward the more efficient precision grips, so that the oldest group showed greatly decreased variability as well as selection from earlier exploratory acts of the most efficient method.

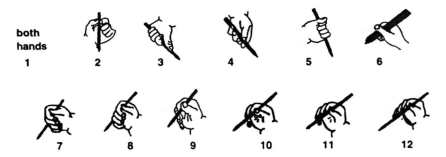

both
hands
1

2

3

4

5

6

7

8

9

10

11

12

FIGURE 10.1. Distribution of pen grips used by 3-year-olds in investigations. From "Using Writing Instruments: Invariances in Young Children and Adults," by T. Greer and J.J. Lockman, 1998, *Child Development, 69,* p. 894. Copyright © 1998 by the Society for Research in Child Development, Inc. Reprinted with permission.

It is instructive to compare this transition with an analogous one for older children learning to grip a writing tool. Greer and Lockman (1998) asked 3- and 5-year-olds and adults to draw horizontal and vertical lines under routine writing conditions, and he compared their grip patterns for holding a thick pen and a thin pen. Across trials, the 3-year-olds changed grip patterns very often, but almost all the 5-year-olds used the same grip pattern. The younger children exhibited many patterns (see fig. 10.1), sometimes displaying the typical adult grip. Greer and Lockman suggest that they were exploring methods and, over time, settled down to a stable efficient form, showing a developmental process of exploration and discovery. Connolly and Dalgleish (1989) found a similar trend for infants learning to manipulate a spoon. They observed two groups of infants longitudinally for 6 months, one group beginning at 11 months of age, and one group beginning at 17 months. Over the course of the 6 months, there was a decrease in the variety of grips for all of the infants, but even the oldest children, who were nearly 2 years old at the end of the study, still were not exclusively using an efficient adult grip.

The trend toward selection of an invariant, efficient method of gripping a spoon is remarkably similar to the younger infants' trend in development of prehension, even though the problem becomes how to wield a tool in a controlled way, not simply pick up something. The writing tool and the spoon are means toward accomplishing a further goal involving a relation between two objects, not only a relation between the actor and an object.

This relation between actor, objects, and an object's affordance for acting on another object is a kind of nested event. The nested event can be relatively simple or much more difficult for both perceiving and accomplishing. The relation of the tool to a goal object may be presented so as to make perceiving it as a *means* relatively easy or more difficult. This point is stressed in experiments in which children were given a crooked stick (like a cane) to rake in a cookie or small toy placed out of reach on a table surface (van Leeuwen, Smitsman, & van

FIGURE 10.2. Goal objects, presented in various positions, to be obtained with a raking tool. From "Affordances, Perceptual Complexity, and the Development of Tool Use," by L. van Leeuwen, A.W. Smitsman, and C. van Leeuwen, 1994, *Journal of Experimental Psychology: Human Perception and Performance, 20*, p. 178. Copyright © 1994 by the American Psychological Association, Inc. Reprinted with Permission.

Leeuwen, 1994). The tool was presented in various positions in relation to the goal object, for instance, with the crook in an appropriate position for raking the object or with the object farther away on the wrong side of the crook (see fig. 10.2). The easy configuration promoted success, as would be expected. Children who succeeded with a more difficult arrangement always performed successfully with the others. The youngest group observed in this experiment (mean of 10.6 months) were unsuccessful, however, even with the easiest configuration and after seeing a demonstration. They did not yet perceive the nested relation—that is, the role of the tool as an agent—no matter how it was presented. A means-end, nested affordance relation is not detected before major first-order affordance relations, but the eventual learning process does not appear to be very different.

We conclude that infants during the first year are engaged principally in perfecting perception-action affordance skills of the first order, that is, learning about the direct relations of their own actions and the affordances offered by the surrounding environment. Serious learning about second-order relations, such as affordances of tools and actions that are intermediate means to a goal, is prominent during the second year. Perceiving an object-object relation may be "insightful," but whether discovered on one's own or discovered through observing a model, it is a matter of perceptual learning. What is learned are not individual movements, but means-end strategies, which can vary in suitability with new and changing situations. Functions remain constant, but conditions can change, demanding flexibility as part of successful learning about affordances. There is a trend toward specificity in the learning, but other strategies that have been tried are potentially available when conditions change.

In a study of spoon handling in 2- to 4-year-old children (mean age 36.2 months), Steenbergen, van der Kamp, Smitsman, and Carson (1997) found considerable flexibility in using spoons for pickup and transport of rice from one container to another, despite changes in the design of spoons, which were created for the experiment. The experimental spoons varied in their geometrical relation of bowl to stem. The children were already aware of the function of a spoon, as determined in pretests. But they accommodated their grip to features of the experimental spoons, varying the grip pattern to preserve the affordance of the spoon as a scooping device. The children all could handle a normal spoon with an adult grip, but they were nevertheless flexible in their attempts with the aberrant spoons, and they attempted to control the essential functional relation under changed conditions.

Adaptive tool use not only requires flexibility, it also exhibits prospectivity in a marked degree. Learning the affordance of a tool for securing a goal is, as we have noted, a means-end task. Several steps or actions are required before a goal is secured, one being manipulation of the tool itself. The steps preceding securing the goal may be more or less efficient. Recent research by McCarty, Clifton, and Collard (1999) took advantage of this property to study the development of "planning" in 9-, 14-, and 19-month old children as they reached for and wielded a loaded spoon to get food into their mouth. The spoon was presented, already loaded, on props so that it could be picked up from underneath, but all of these children seized it with an overhand grip, four fingers simultaneously clutching the spoon firmly, with the thumb bent under the spoon. When the spoon was presented with its loaded bowl at the same end as the thumb, the food could be transported effectively to the mouth (and was). The younger children all seized the spoon with the preferred hand, so that when the spoon was presented with the bowl already at the thumb end of that hand the children were successful. When the bowl was at the "wrong" end (the end opposite the thumb), the children either brought the handle of the spoon to the mouth or corrected the spoon-hand relation, for example, by rotating the spoon and then transporting it to the mouth. The correction could be made either early in the sequence, indicating "planning ahead," or after an unsuccessful transport. Many 19-month-old children solved the problem by reaching with their nonpreferred hand, indicating still earlier planning, since no correction was needed. The results reflected a general developmental trend toward earlier planning for an efficient transport, that is, increasing prospectivity of the whole perception-action cycle.

This experiment also reminds us of the important interaction of the emergence of an action system with the development of more efficient affordance learning. An adult reaching for the spoon would not shift to the nonpreferred hand but would rotate the spoon before transporting it to the mouth (as did the 14-month-olds). But the adult would use independent finger manipulation and an underhand grasp to make the grasp and transport efficient. Thus, when a child achieves independent finger manipulation and an underhand grasp becomes available, the child can again use the preferred hand and rotate the spoon before transport, a nice example of increasing efficiency and prospectivity prompted by the availability of a more sophisticated action system.

Locomotor Skills

Nearly all human children learn to walk, usually beginning toward the end of the first year, gaining ease and economy of gait and adaptability of pace and manner of stride with practice and encounters with changing surfaces, obstacles, and needs. After that, they may graduate to more specialized and demanding locomotor tasks. One of the most interesting stories of such learning is told by McGraw (1935) in a classic report of her study of identical twin boys, Johnny and Jimmy, from birth. Johnny was selected for training and exercise daily in every motor skill as it developed (lifting the head, rolling over, sitting, reaching, creeping, walking, etc.), while Jimmy received no special exercise. Despite the vast difference in exercise, the ubiquitous skills (termed by McGraw "phylogenetic activities") such as sitting and walking emerged at about the same time, although Johnny's performance was said to be a little more confident and smooth. But during the second year, Johnny was trained on climbing up slopes, getting off high stools, and roller skating, among other more specialized pursuits. His accomplishments were astonishing and the learning process interesting.

Johnny was first placed on roller skates at 350 days. He was walking, but not maturely. He could stand erect briefly on the skates, but he attempted to take a walking step, lifting a foot, and fell down. The experimenter pushed Johnny's feet to demonstrate rolling, but Johnny persisted in various other inept attempts, such as spreading his legs as if to secure balance, for some time, with isolated and slow movements. He extended his arms for balance. As small changes were presented in surface slope, and so on, he varied his methods of progression and eventually engaged his upper body in a skater's posture; he attained a rhythmical sequence by 694 days. McGraw then complicated Johnny's task by putting him on two-wheel roller skates. He again had difficulty maintaining balance and broadened his base. He never became as skillful on these skates as on the four-wheel skates, but on those he attained great skill, succeeding in stooping to pick up toys from the floor and in rising from a sitting position. What is striking here is the child's increasing control of his own performance and his gradual achievement of a graceful, efficient style of locomotion. He spontaneously learned to steer, stop, and avoid obstacles. Indeed, he even taught himself to steer and turn while rolling backwards. Many maneuvers were tried and dropped again as he progressed. McGraw comments (p. 167), "One cannot avoid noting the difference in the way a deliberate experimental act on the part of the child is eliminated in contrast to the way excess activities associated with developmental stages of a behavior-pattern are gradually reduced to the minimum."

McGraw here is stressing the difference between development of what she calls "phylogenetic activity" and the learning that goes on in a more specialized activity. The difference appears to be principally in the degree of control exercised; however, we see the same pronounced variability in earlier stages of the developing activity and eventual selection on the basis of perceived consequences of the actions. Acquisition of athletic skills by older children is still more deliberate and controlled and generally makes use of models, but perceptual learning remains an essential part of the process.

It is interesting to consider what affordances Johnny was learning as he skated. The skates, in fact, are a kind of tool. They afford rolling over the ground. Johnny, a novice walker, had just learned to locomote by standing erect on the ground and picking up his feet, one after the other. He tried this on skates and fell with a crash. The experimenter helped by giving Johnny's ankles a gentle push that sent him rolling, demonstrating the function of roller skates. After only a couple of demonstrations, Johnny perceived what the skates afforded and thereafter made many and varied attempts to send them rolling (such as pushing with one foot), eventually achieving a skater's posture and an efficient method of progression. We do routinely demonstrate the affordances of locomotor tools such as skates, skis, and tricycles to children, but eventual skilled performance is attained through perceptual-motor learning of the kind we have already discussed, better controlled by a highly motivated, more experienced learner.

As vehicles are used, such as skates and tricycles, the task combines tool use with activities characteristic of locomotion, such as steering. The child must learn the function of the new means of achieving a goal, as well as adaptive performance by this means in encounters with the environment. Johnny's mastery of a tricycle, for example, was long and arduous as he learned the nonobvious function of the pedals and how to operate them. Demonstration was less helpful, and the sequence of maneuvers more complex. But the initial variability of action patterns and gradual achievement of an economical pattern was repeated, along with observational learning of what the vehicle afforded

The Role of Perceptual Learning in Conceptual Development

Categorizing

That's all very well for *perceptual* development in early life, a cognitivist may protest, but where do you go from there? Don't children have concepts? Don't they think? Don't they talk? Of course they do all these things, some sooner, some later. It is not the purpose of a book on perceptual development to deal with them all, but it is essential to point out how very fundamentally perceptual development underlies them. We have already made a case for the importance of perceptual learning for language in the development of preverbal infants. Now we turn our attention to concepts and their origin in preverbal infants. How the more general concept is formed on the basis of perceptually accessed information is the subject of several theories, which typically refer to the information as "representations" (e.g., Karmiloff-Smith, 1992; Mandler, 1992). We find the theories unsatisfactory, on several counts. First, the term "representation" sounds too static and leads inevitably to speculation about what sort of format the representation takes. Is it linguistic? Is the concept represented in the form of an image? Mandler (1997) suggests that it begins as a spatial "image-schema." Second and more important, neither Mandler nor Karmiloff-Smith suggests that the burgeoning concept includes the relation between the event or object and the perceiver—in other words, the affordance relation. But in our view, that relation is how the first meanings develop, and concepts are surely about meaning.

Some authors claim that meaning only develops with symbolic representations of some kind, following early perception of "mere appearances." Mandler (1997) suggests that "because perceptual categories (perceptual schemas) tell us what things look like, we use them to recognize the objects and events around us. Conceptual categories, or concepts, on the other hand, represent the meaning of the objects and events that we see" (p. 291). How is the meaning attained and on what basis? According to Mandler, analysis, simplification, and summary of experiences are the processes involved, but these operations do not seem themselves to provide meaning.

Meaning begins, we suggest, with the discovery of what is afforded by some object or event for oneself. What is discovered is intrinsically functional and abstract, as is any relation. Repeated experiences of an event with a comparable functional relation to oneself and a comparable outcome, over varying details of context, would serve to enhance the abstractness of the meaning. For example, babies frequently experience the pouring of liquid into a container, consequent splashing, a feeling of wetness as it is tasted and swallowed or felt with a finger; on another occasion, babies experience the pouring of bath water from a cup as the baby is allowed to play in the bath, scooping up water, hearing it splash, feeling the wetness. These events provide a basis for forming concepts of liquidity, of pouring, of containers, and more. From early beginnings, such events go on daily for many months before a baby begins to talk. The multimodal perceptual experiences, with interesting consequences for the baby, provide a rich basis for developing meaningful knowledge.

Developing a concept begins with experiencing a number of encounters involving the same affordance; whatever is *invariant* in these encounters (each one meaningful if some affordance was achieved) is abstracted by the system. Certainly not as a verbal representation; we do not need to speculate about "format" except to require that it be relational. Generalizability is a major criterion of conceptual knowledge, even in infancy. We have noted that the newborn's recognition of the cadences of the native language (as spoken by the mother) generalizes to other voices. Perceptual learning picks up on generalizable temporal invariants, in this case at least, very early indeed.

A number of experiments have shown that young infants generalize categories of geometrical forms (Bomba & Siqueland, 1983) and of simple objects, usually presented as pictures. Eimas and Quinn (1994) presented 3- to 4-month-old infants pairs of pictures of either cats or horses. After visual familiarization

trials during which the infants saw 12 pictures in all, the infants were presented with test trials in which new pictures of cats or horses were paired with pictures of animals in a different category (e.g., zebras, giraffes). The infants discriminated between the novel and familiar category members by looking longer
at the pictures of the novel category.

While infants may be trained to categorize on the basis of pictorial simili-
tude, it seems to us unlikely that babies normally begin the formation of everyday categories on the basis of static visual resemblance, as research based on
pictorially presented exemplars suggests. Babies encounter the world in the
course of events and learn about what things and situations afford by observing
and especially by exploring them spontaneously. Pick and her colleagues un-
dertook a program of research on the role of children's exploratory activity in
their categorizing of objects (A.D. Pick, 1997). It was Pick's contention that perceiving and categorizing are continuous learning processes and that this continuity can best be shown when children learn to categorize on the basis of exploratory activities that permit discovery of affordances and functions, rather
than on the basis of static pictorial features.

In one set of studies, comparisons were made of the way preschoolers categorized sets of objects after they were allowed either to explore them actively
or to observe pictorial representations (photographs or colored line drawings)
of them (Melendez, Bales, & Pick, 1993; Melendez, Bales, Ruffing, & Pick, 1995).
Sets of toys were constructed so that they could be categorized with a "target"
toy either according to function or according to a static attribute such as color
or size. For example, one collection of toys included four red musical instruments (a piano, a tambourine, a trumpet, and a flute), a silver saxophone, two
silver "look-through" toys (a kalaidoscope, binoculars), and a red Viewmaster.
The "target" toys: silver saxophone and red Viewmaster, were similar in function to the toys in one group, but similar in color to the toys in the other group.

Children participated in either a real-object condition or in one of the pictorial conditions. The children in the real-object condition were invited to play
with the toys (presented in an unsystematic heap), which permitted multimodal
exploration, whereas the children in the pictorial conditions were given the representations (also presented in an unorganized order) and could freely look
them over. Then the experimenter picked up the target items and placed each
on a separate table. The children were asked to place the remaining toys (or representations of them) with the target items with which they belonged. The question was whether the children would sort the toys (or pictures of toys) systematically, either according to their function or according to a static attribute. Over
a number of sets, the children who had played with the toys overwhelmingly
sorted them by function. The children who had looked over pictures more often sorted the sets by the matching static attribute, although a few children
sorted by function. Mode of presentation evidently influences the way children
categorize in experimental situations. Exploratory activity, especially, serves as

a means for learning about affordances and for consequent categorization by a functional relational property.

In a second set of studies, preschoolers' flexibility in using different criteria for categorizing objects was investigated (Deak, Flom, & Pick, 1995). The general procedure was to invite children to explore each of a set of three objects and then to categorize the "target" object with one of the remaining two. The target object of a set had the same function as one object and the same shape as the other. For example, one object set included an egg-shaped kitchen timer, a tea infuser with a handle, and an egg-shaped tea infuser (target). Another set included a small football, a telephone, and a telephone in the shape of a football (target). Groups of children were instructed, by means of demonstration, to categorize objects by function or by shape; control groups were uninstructed. The children were highly consistent in how they categorized the objects: the children in the function-training group categorized by function, and those in the shape-training group categorized by shape. More children in the control group categorized the sets by shape than by function. However, for children in a second control group, the target objects were presented for categorizing when their functional attributes were clearly apparent (e.g., the tea infuser was swished in water; the receiver of the football-shaped telephone was separated from it, revealing the dial and cord). These children showed no predisposition to categorize the objects by shape; about half sorted consistently by shape, and half by function.

In a separate, final phase of the procedure, the children were asked to name all of the objects, and their labels or descriptions for the target objects were coded as to whether they referred in some way to the same-shape objects or to the same-function objects. Most of the children's names for these target objects referred to the object functions, and this was true for the children in all three experimental conditions. Thus, although the children categorized the objects as they had been asked, by demonstration, to do, their names or descriptions of the objects were unaffected by their prior categorization activity but reflected, instead, the objects' important attributes for their own behavior, namely the affordances. These experiments all demonstrate that young children are both flexible and systematic in how they categorize objects they have explored. They are not bound by specific static attributes but can consider different object properties in different contexts and tasks.

Haith and Benson (1997), in a recent handbook chapter, emphasized function of objects in an event as a basis for early categorizing of objects. Research supporting this view includes that of Smitsman, Loosbroek, and Pick (1987), who found that an affordance, "cuddliness," was a foundation of young children's categorization of toy animals, and not the species (duck, dog, etc.) represented. Greco, Hayne, and Rovee-Collier (1990) also demonstrated the role of function for categorizing with 3-month-old infants in the mobile-kicking learning paradigm. They conclude, "Infants of 3 months, like adults, categorize a physically dissimilar object on the basis of their prior knowledge of its function" (p. 630). We turn now from categorizing to the forming of abstract concepts.

Abstract Concepts

Abstraction is not a new cognitive process that appears suddenly at about 2 or 3 years of age. Abstraction occurs as soon as a baby begins to discover relational properties in the world and recognize them as invariant over certain events. That is just what is happening when infants learn about affordances of events and things and places in their worlds. This knowledge is relational and meaningful. Smiles directed at another mean that comfort and companionship is available. The looming bottle means something suckable that will swiftly appease hunger. As experience is gained, deeper abstraction becomes possible. Some kinds of things smile, and these are differentiated from things that never do. Mother (who also speaks to me) and some other beings smile, for example; but the bottle, the washcloth, and the blanket, all suckable, never smile or talk. Relational and meaningful abstract properties, like animacy, are discovered by means of perceiving; their discovery depends on detecting temporally extended information that is invariant over transformations. We now consider some examples of abstract concepts, grounded in perceiving, that have been studied from infancy onward.

ANIMACY

Animate and inanimate objects can be differentiated perceptually in the course of events. Properties marking the distinction are displayed in contrasting types of movement, and it has been demonstrated that infants are sensitive to the differences between animate and inanimate movement from an early age. Common sense supports such a notion, since the first events of importance to infants are their mothers smiling, speaking, and holding them, providing multimodal dynamic information in animate action. An extended concept of animacy, applicable to all living things, has a long way to go from such canonical and warm interactions, but a fundamental difference in the way animals and rigid objects move provides information for the beginning of a generalizable concept.

Johansson (1973) pioneered in now classical studies of biological motions and the information for perceiving them (see chaps. 5 and 8). A few light-points placed on joints suffice, he showed, to specify the biomechanical motions of a person walking. The pattern of motions suggested by the light-points, without any other pictorial information, is sufficient to specify the animate motions of a person walking, dancing, or engaging in other varied activities. The human frame contains rigid parts (the bones and skeleton), but the joints move flexibly, as do the muscles—for example, in the face, as one changes expression or speaks.

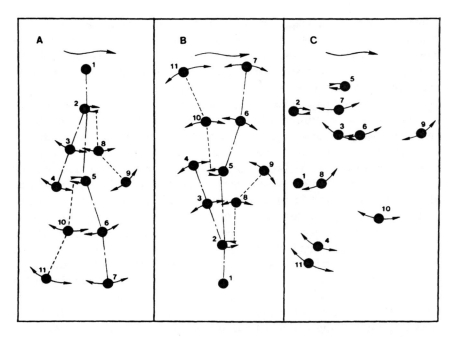

FIGURE 10.3. Point-light displays of a "walker" used by Bertenthal, Profitt, and Cutting (1984) to investigate detection of animate motion by 3-to-5-month-old infants. From "Infant Sensitivity to Figural Coherence in Biomechanical Motions," by B.I. Bertenthal, D.R. Profitt, and J.E. Cutting, 1984, *Journal of Experimental Child Psychology, 37*, p. 215. Copyright © 1984 by the Academic Press, Inc. Reprinted with permission.

An experiment by Bertenthal and colleagues (1984) with 5-month-old infants demonstrated that these infants could discriminate between a moving-light display of a person walking and the inverted image of the same display. Infants did not discriminate between static displays of the light-points in the two examples (fig. 10.3). While one cannot conclude that these infants identified a walking person, they did differentiate configural information specifying human motion from a dynamic display that did not specify a unitary figure in motion.

In further experiments Bertenthal, Profitt, Spetner, and Thomas (1985) again showed point-light displays of walkers to infants (20 to 36 weeks of age), but in these experiments appropriate occlusion of lights when a leg or an arm was momentarily covered by another limb was included in some displays. If infants detected the three-dimensional structure of the human body in these displays in the upright orientation, it might be inferred that they perceived a human body (as do adults, who can tell us so). The case would be especially convincing if infants behaved differently when watching displays with inappropriate occlusion. The oldest infants (36 weeks) were sensitive to the appropriate occlusion information, when upright figures were presented, but the younger groups were not. The authors concluded that the older infants, at 9 months, had been learning to recognize a familiar invariant dynamic relation that had increased in meaningfulness since the earlier age, when only "connectivity" was detected, as it seemed to be in the younger infants, who appeared to detect a coherent unit, at least, when lights were placed so as to permit it.

Infants have opportunities to experience deforming human facial movements very early. An experiment by Stucki, Kaufmann-Hayoz, and Kaufmann (1987) presented 3-month-old infants with motion patterns in a real human face and in a mask-pattern moved artificially by a concealed hand. The woman's face and a rubber mask of the face were both covered with black make-up and an identical pattern of white triangles painted on them. The woman's face was then videotaped as she pretended an interaction with a baby. The mask was videotaped while being moved and deformed by a human hand. Using a visual habituation procedure, infants were familiarized with either upright or inverted positions of the tapes, half of them seeing the face, half the mask. Following habituation, infants were shown the alternative (upright or upside-down) position of the tape to which they had been habituated. Infants habituated to the upright position showed significantly greater dishabituation. More importantly, the infants discriminated the motion patterns produced by the real face from those artificially produced with the mask. Discrimination of face and mask was greater when both were presented in an upright position. The authors argue that the face was easily recognized as such in the upright position and thus easily discriminated from the inverted face (as it is by adults). It is indeed reasonable that a face changing expression should be recognizable from the motion pattern alone, at an earlier age even than a walking person.

Young infants' differentiation of animate motion gives them a firm basis for developing a general concept of animacy. Another feature of animate motion, *spontaneity,* as opposed to inanimate movement that depends on outside force, is also differentiated relatively early. (This feature underlies the conception of agency and causality as well, so we shall return to it.) *Responsiveness* of things in the environment is another feature of animacy that is noticed early, as we saw in chapter 5 in the discussion of communication. Perhaps more than any other feature, this social feature from the beginning provides information for perceiving the affordance of animate things and gives the growing concept meaning. Babies quickly learn to expect a parent facing them to respond to their own vocalizations. K. Bloom (1977) found that infants' vocal patterns shifted depending on the responsiveness of a potentially interacting adult. A responsive adult (smiling and vocalizing) caused an increase in pauses between an infant's vocalizations, timed to coincide with adult vocalizing. The contingent withdrawal of responsive behavior noticeably affected the infant's behavior, eliciting a pause after a time-out when a response might be expected. At 3 months, infants recognized the difference between contingent and noncontingent stimulation, thus showing awareness of responsiveness of an adult in an interactive situation. The responsiveness to children of the people around them plays an important role not only as a foundation for their developing concept of animacy but also in their healthy social development.

The concept of animacy has a wealth of knowledge, acquired by perceiving, to build on. Our next example, agency, is another concept based in knowledge that is abstract and meaningful and acquired by perceiving.

AGENCY AND CAUSALITY

We discussed in chapter 9 agency and its discovery by infants. Babies begin to learn about control as part of their earliest learning of affordances, and opportunities increase to generalize across situations where consequences are self-controlled and actions are perceived to be effective. We bring it up again here because agency is sometimes said to be the origin of the notion of causality. Piaget (1954) thought that understanding of causality began with infants' discovery of their own ability to make something happen. Perhaps these two concepts are related and have a common origin, but there is research on early perception of causal relations, apart from agency. We discussed in chapter 8 infants' learning about causal relations in events and suggested there that what is being learned is to differentiate events into episodes, or subevents, in which objects have different functions. For example, in launching events, one object is agent and another is recipient. We also argued that the learning that is reflected in infants' perception of causal relations in events may provide the foundation for later conceptual development about causality.

A way of viewing learning about physical causality, for example, in the launching experiment, is by analogy with learning about tool use. One toy moves off and strikes another, and the second toy moves off simultaneously with the impact. Children learn that a tool is a means to an end, achieving an affordance that the child puts in motion—for example, reaching with a rake or prodding with a stick. The tool analogously exerts a force on the recipient object, producing an observable consequence. The whole relation—mover imparting force, which yields a consequent change—is a perceived relation. But from the child's view, it is a means-end relationship that is not as immediate as the child's own action on an object, in which the force is felt in muscle and joint as the action is produced, and the consequence follows directly. Good control of objects with one's own limbs and hands is learned earliest, before a tool is used as intermediary for achieving an affordance. Observing an impact and its consequence when the mover object (the tool) is not controlled by oneself demands generalization about an affordance at an even more abstract level and probably occurs later.

There is evidence that preschoolers can make generalizations about affordances of objects and events as causal agents. Goswami and Brown (1990) presented 3- and 4-year-old children with a task in which they were asked to complete a sequence of pictures. The first three pictures represented the outcome of an object transformation, for example, pictures of Playdoh, an apple, and bread, each cut into pieces. To complete the sequence correctly, the children would select a picture of the appropriate causal agent, for example, a knife, from among a group of foils. The transformations tested included cutting, breaking, getting wet by being rained on, burning, opening, melting, getting muddy, and switching on an appliance—all events the children had witnessed and participated in countless times during their lives. Most of the 4-year-olds and 30% of the 3-year-olds performed the task at significantly above chance. Furthermore, the children who could successfully represent causal agency with the pictures could generalize causality by completing picture sequences representing analogies. For example, when presented with pictures of a wad of Playdoh, cut-up Playdoh, and an apple, they could select the picture of the cut-up apple to complete the sequence. Certainly the perception of causality develops over time, beginning in the first year and continuing long after.

In our view, causality is a rather sophisticated concept, founded originally on learning about *control*. Control is first discovered in oneself—in controlling hand movements, for example, that have the consequence of moving some object. Observing control in a totally external event may very likely occur first as infants observe another person control a simple situation, perhaps by hand movements that resemble their own. Infants frequently witness the hand of an adult contacting and moving an object. In fact, we know from experiments by Leslie (1984a) that infants do detect something like a causal relation when they are shown a hand reaching out and moving a doll. Infants of 7 months were habituated to looking at a film of a hand reaching out, grasping a doll, and carrying it off. Following habituation, the infants were shown either a mirror image of the film, or a film in which the hand reached out but stopped short of the doll so there was no contact, and the doll moved off the screen following the hand. Looking time rose sharply when the films differed in the contact event, but not in the control mirror-image film, in which only the direction of action was changed. A further experiment contrasted a hand picking up the doll with a white oblong-shaped object maneuvered in a similar performance (each with suitable controls). Infants recovered interest and looked longer at the no-contact test event when the hand pickup was involved. Contact, hand, and pickup all were important in the event that engaged the infants' attention. Infants have the opportunity at a very early age to observe events in which other persons' hands perform as agents of change. Witnessing such animate events, external to themselves, may be one step in the development of a concept of causality. Perceiving agency (intentional action) in another person has been noted in recent studies with infants (e.g., Tomasello, 1995).

Generalization of the notion of control needed to effect an environmental change in object-object relations, such as the launching experiment, may come much later, after many observations of different events involving animate exchange of force and interaction with other persons. An understanding of agency may underlie a true understanding of causality, even though expectations of the results of particular familiarized collisions could be formed earlier in a more superficial manner.

We noted in chapter 6 that infants very early perceive objects as segregated from background and as units, certainly by 4 months. Presumably, an array of objects is detectable as well under conditions of adequate contrast, separation in space, and so on. But how large an array is perceived as an aggregation of units? And can arrays of different numbers of items be discriminated from one another? When can an infant detect how many, or that one array has more or less than another?

In chapter 6 we discussed evidence that infants can discriminate size of sets of items in moving arrays by 5 or 6 months (van Loosbroek & Smitsman, 1990) and in static arrays a few months later (Strauss & Curtis, 1981), provided the sets are of small size. But can they detect addition or subtraction of an item from a previously observed set? An experiment by Wynn (1992) with 5-month-old infants suggests that this is possible. In a looking-preference study, babies were shown a single doll, which was then occluded by a curtain. A hand appeared holding a second doll, which disappeared behind the curtain. The curtain was then withdrawn, disclosing either one or two dolls. Infants looked longer when the display contained only one doll, as if they were expecting to see two dolls. Consistent results were obtained when one doll was subtracted from a display of two. Positive results were again obtained when three items were revealed after infants saw only two placed. Wynn's study was replicated by Simon, Hespos, and Rochat (1995), who changed the identity of one of the objects during the period of occlusion, at the same time repeating Wynn's arithmetical operations of addition or subtraction. The outcome was still consistent with Wynn's results, suggesting that the infants were differentiating purely mathematical invariants regardless of individual identities.

In later experiments, Wynn (1996) showed 6-month-old infants a sequential dynamic display. The infants watched a puppet on a small stage. When a curtain rose, the puppet could be seen to jump either two or three times; then it remained motionless on the stage for a short interval, after which the curtain descended. Infants were habituated either to two jumps or to three jumps, and then they were presented with both old number and novel number sequences. The infants successfully discriminated sequences of two jumps from three jumps by looking longer at the stationary puppet following the novel number of jumps versus the old number of jumps. Wynn hypothesized that the babies enumerated specific entities. However, individuating entities within a sequential, dynamic display may present special difficulties. In a second experiment, Wynn (1996) showed the puppet jumping twice or thrice, as before, but now, instead of remaining motionless between jumps, its head wagged from side to side between jumps and following the final jump. The babies still detected a difference between the habituated and the novel number of jumps, but the looking-time difference, though significant, was not as great as in the first experiment. The head wagging made the differentiation and enumeration of entities more difficult.

Evidence for sequential enumeration in 5-month-old infants was found by Canfield and Smith (1996) using a different method, the "visual expectation paradigm." The infants' eye movements were recorded and reaction time monitored as they viewed a sequence of pictures in which placement of one picture (to the right of a preceding one) was either numerically predictable or unpredictable. A sequence of two or three, followed by one displaced to the right, was successfully predicted, as indicated by the infants' anticipatory eye movements. The authors concluded that these infants used the number of pictures that appeared on the left to anticipate the appearance of a succeeding one to the right, thus enumerating up to three sequentially presented events. The babies apparently treated the appearance of a picture as a unitary event, a separate member of a sequence, and learned to expect a change of location depending on the number of events witnessed. Since the infants were surely unaware of their eye movements, their performance was not comparable to counting behavior. Nevertheless, anticipatory perception of an ordered event in a sequence is important for underlying future development of numerical ability, and for perceptual search for order in any sequence of events. Units were segregated and an invariant succession pattern was detected, an important achievement for perceptual economy.

We have previously discussed numerous examples of infants' perception of invariant properties of events. These properties are not pictorial or representative in the sense of being similar to static objects. Perceiving is functional and ongoing. Learning to expect that something interesting will happen is a simple affordance relation, not unlike other examples of early perceptual learning. We recall that very young infants distinguish their mother's voice on the basis of intonation patterns, as well as some features of their native language. However, they do not segment single words from a spoken sequence until past the second half of the first year. The differentiation process is apparently more difficult than perceiving a less deeply embedded invariant characterizing the event sequence as a whole.

It seems likely that true understanding of number begins when infants become able to pick up objects, hold them, transfer an object from one hand to another, and transfer too many objects to be held to a container. This is an exercise that infants enjoy, and it provides a very objective foundation, based on perceiving, for abstracting a concept such as number of things that is not tied to a particular kind of object or event. The very abstract concept, number, plausibly has its beginning in self-initiated events in infancy, well before an adult says "That's too many" or "Give one (two, some) to your brother." The foundation is laid in a simple perception-action encounter for a concept that becomes increasingly abstract as its invariant aspect takes on usefulness in later exchanges of a social nature.

Learning about "more" and "less" in a meaningful sense also involves perceptual learning of an affordance, perhaps in social situations when parents discourage "more," or when competition with another child occurs. Counting systems with a base of 10 have always been assumed to be based on a bodily dimension, but even so, counting as an abstract process is achieved well after the end of the first year and may involve participation and action in situations where objects that afford something useful or enjoyable to a child can be collected or consumed.

We conclude that infants very early perceive things and events as separate, collections of things as aggregations, order within the aggregation, and addition or withdrawal of an item from a small aggregation, but learning about numbers and what counting affords goes on for many years. Starkey, Spelke, and Gelman (1990) presented evidence that infants recognize numerical equivalence of visual and auditory displays with sets of two and three items. They argued that their results reflect infants' ability to establish abstract one-one correspondence across different sets of discrete items. However, attempts to replicate their findings met with difficulty (Mix, Levine, & Huttenlocher, 1997), and research with young children suggests that ability to establish one-one correspondences across sets of items emerges during the preschool years and may be linked to mastery of counting. Mix, Huttenlocher, and Levine (1996) asked 3- and 4-year-olds to perform tasks of matching sets of sounds, hand claps, to numerically equivalent visible displays of small black circles on white cards. The children saw and heard the experimenter clap her hands two, three, or four times and selected from a pair of cards the one matching the hand claps. On one card of the pair, the display of circles was equivalent to the hand claps. On the other card, the display was either one more or one less than the number of hand claps. The 4-year-olds, but not the 3-year-olds, performed this task significantly above chance. However, both groups of children successfully performed a control task in which they were asked to match visible arrays of small objects to numerically equivalent visible displays of circles. Success on this task may depend on accurate pattern matching, but not necessarily on being able to detect numerical correspondences across the visible arrays. In contrast, success on the experimental task, matching a series of sounds to numerically equivalent visible arrays, seems to require detecting numerical correspondences. Thus all the children were capable of performing the simpler match-to-sample task, but only the older children could perform the task requiring abstraction of numerical equivalences.

Whether knowledge about numerical operations such as addition and subtraction and other mathematical principles has innate underpinnings is the subject of considerable recent speculation (e.g.. Wynn, 1995; Gelman & Williams, 1997). Our argument here is that such knowledge is grounded perceptually in early encounters with an environment that offers meaningful affordance relations to be acted upon and learned from. Conceptual knowledge about number begins with perceptual differentiation of units, discovery of order in an array, and detection of invariance of small numbers of things in aggregates; only later does it develop toward enumeration of individual members of temporally sequenced arrays. As a child discovers that using members of these arrays in multiples may have consequences of value, further discoveries about number can be made and generalized to new situations.

The Hallmarks Revisited: A Last Word

We consider, finally, how conceptualization and generalization are reflected in the hallmarks of human behavior. In chapter 9, we discussed development of these hallmarks, noting that they become more pronounced and recognizable as children learn and mature. While they are detectable very early in life, they are enhanced as cognitive activities progress to include language and conceptualization at higher levels.

Agency and the Self

Agency is itself conceptualized as infants *generalize* control over more and more varied situations. Perceptual learning, during infancy and beyond, also functions extensively in *differentiating* an infant's domain of control. As action systems develop, control extends more broadly over behaviors such as using objects and moving from place to place to explore new spaces. But the domain of control is also influenced by social factors, as parents, caretakers, and siblings communicate by gestures and simple commands such as "No no," "Here" (meaning take this or come here), "Don't touch," or "That's mine, not yours." The world gradually becomes divided up into what an infant rightfully controls and what is prohibited. Things begin to "belong" to the baby, especially the baby's own name.

These events promote a feeling of self, which becomes accentuated and at the same time more abstract as more aspects of experience, such as one's appearance and voice (Legerstee et al., 1998), are assimilated to it. Parents encourage this development by showing infants their image in a mirror, engaging them in vocal interactions, and addressing them by name. The core of the self concept, however, is founded earlier on control of things and other people by perceiving, kinesthetically and otherwise, one's own actions and the environmental changes that ensue. There are many aspects of the "self," as Neisser (1993) tells us. Agency is not only a hallmark of our behavior as human beings; it is richly extended conceptually over time, continuing to develop into old age.

Prospectivity

Prospectivity, the forward-looking aspect of behavior, is evident in an infant's earliest head turnings and reaches, as we have shown. It is extended as infants learn about the affordances of means to ends, like strategies for acting and using tools; and of course it is extended further as concepts and language become available. Language, indeed, provides obvious examples of prospectivity; verbs in many languages have tenses for referring to the future. Prospectivity is extended temporally with development, and plans can be formulated as knowledge of what the world affords increases. The development of prospectivity, indeed, seems to be a vast ramification of what affordance means: the relation between behavior and what the world offers, in any prospective encounter, for an individual's use.

Seeking and Using Order

The propensity for seeking order, and for discovering it, has been illustrated now in many experiments with young infants. Order in spatial relations, for example, is detected as early as 3 to 4 months. Behl-Chadda and Eimas (1995) presented infants with pairs of pictures of a horse and a zebra. Across a series of pictures, the horses and zebras varied in size and location on a card, but the left-right relation of the two animals remained invariant. After a familiarization phase, the infants were tested with two new pictures. Both pictures portrayed an identical novel horse-zebra pair in a novel location on the cards; in one picture the familiar left-right relation of the animals was maintained, and in the second picture it was reversed. The infants looked longer at the picture of the animals in the new left-right relation, evidence that they discriminated the new order from the old.

Invariance over changes, a more abstract kind of order, has been shown to be noted by infants again and again. The orderly information in spatial relations, the arrangement and invariance of features of objects, of vocal rhythms and patterns, and especially of events is sought for and detected, as we have seen, from neonatal life on. The development of this propensity beyond infancy will be obvious to any reader, considering almost any domain—numerical, linguistic, and activity of all kinds, even dancing and sports. We point out, once more, the economy in use of information that is accomplished by detection of order and invariance, and we repeat that economy is an important selective mechanism for perceptual learning.

Specificity and Flexibility

We have emphasized many times that perceptual learning shows a trend toward specificity; we learn to detect information that best and most economically specifies some affordance. Does this mean that perception and, consequently, actions become more fixed and stereotyped as development goes on? The answer is no. What is learned is a relation that is invariant over time, not over fixed muscles or neurons. The learning process is one of selection, not of association or addition. As we have seen, there is variability early in the developmental process, with selection eventually of the most efficient information-action pattern for an animal-environment fit. This pattern is, above all, functional. In a situation where an activity such as locomotion is involved, the style of locomotion will adapt to new environmental conditions, such as changes in surface properties. If the surface becomes slippery from ice or rain, it no longer affords moving along at a brisk walk. The style of locomotion will shift to one suitable to a slippery surface. One of the earlier patterns of locomotion, such as wider separation of the legs with feet pointing outward, may be selected and adapted anew. The point is that what is learned is a functional relation. A relation is itself an abstraction, fostering continuity in development as a child progresses toward conceptualization.

Ability to generalize and categorize increases with development, as more and more experience of things and people and events is amassed. The progression toward categorizing these experiences is itself a prime example of moving toward cognitive economy, as perceptual development does. But generalization also promotes flexibility, because it enables transfer between tasks and within tasks, as situations change. Generalization that promotes flexibility is possible primarily because categorization can occur on the basis of function, of what is afforded, as A.D. Pick's (1997) research shows. Let us consider further how generalization and what generalizes might enhance flexibility as development progresses.

Static, descriptive features of objects and contexts of an event may be generalized in a category, as we saw. There is some evidence that learning in a young infant is rather specific as regards such features, but that the specificity decreases and generalizability increases with age (Hayne et al., 1997). Early specificity has been demonstrated in a number of experiments with 3-month-old infants learning to kick to turn a mobile, a now familiar experimental task. Specificity of learning is tested in experiments with so-called "delayed recognition," and recognition signaled by responsive kicking is referred to as "memory retrieval." Changes in the features of a mobile, such as its color or the shape of the articles dangling from the frame, or changes in the context of the surround, such as the crib lining, prevent "retrieval" of the kicking performance, although use of different mobiles and contextual features during training promotes later retrieval. However, Hayne and colleagues (1997) found in another test paradigm (a simple imitation task) that generalization to changed features of objects used in the tasks increased significantly in the course of infants' second year. These authors concluded that there is a "developmental increase in the flexibility of memory processing per se, irrespective of the paradigm used to assess it" (p. 241).

Flexibility of perceptual learning, however, is much broader than the recognition of features of objects or context. As A.D. Pick (1997) showed, it tends to be based on functions or on what objects afford, rather than on "cues," when exploratory activities have taken place during learning. True flexibility refers to adaptive behavior in a changed situation, so that the organism-environment fit is maintained. This fit can be disrupted by changes in either the organism or the environment. An organism itself changes with age or with accident. A changed environment, even within a similar task, may require a change in an individual's activity; as we noted, a surface that afforded walking briskly or even running no longer does so if it becomes wet or icy. Behavior is always adjusting. Fixed, inflexible actions, as opposed to flexibility in changed circumstances, whatever the source of change, do not promote survival. A trend from specificity of learning to greater generalizability and flexibility may characterize development, although we have seen very little research on this question. The view of perceptual learning that we take—one based on spontaneous search, exploratory activity, and observation of consequences, with selection based on an affordance-fit—predicts that behavior tends toward flexibility and that learning is geared to maintaining an adaptive relation with the environment. That learning is also geared to economy and efficiency of action means that a balance must be achieved; it is possible, even likely, that this balance improves with development, with increasing overall flexibility following achievement of efficiency in a task. It has been suggested by Stephen Jay Gould (1998) that the human species' very long period of ontogenetic development promotes flexibility.

As humans, we must be flexible and adaptable to change, but we also strive for economy and efficiency in perceiving the world, in action, and in thinking. Keeping the balance seems to be hardest with regard to our concepts. As our knowledge of ourselves, our ability to guide behavior, and our use of order in the world progresses, we strive (one hopes) to avoid rigid thinking and to maintain the power of flexibility. This is a goal as well as a birthright.

References

Abernethy, B. (1993). Searching for the minimal essential information for skilled perception and action. *Psychological Research, 55,* 131–138.

Adams, R., & Courage, M. (1998). Human newborn color vision: Measurement with chromatic stimuli varying in excitation purity. *Journal of Experimental Child Psychology, 68,* 22–34.

Adams, R., Courage, M., & Mercer. (1994). Systematic measurement of human neonatal color vision. *Vision Research, 34,* 1691–1701.

Adams, R., Maurer, D., & Davis, M. (1986). Newborns' discrimination of chromatic from achromatic stimuli. *Journal of Experimental Child Psychology, 41,* 267–281.

Adolph, K.E. (1995). Psychophysical assessment of toddlers' ability to cope with slopes. *Journal of Experimental Psychology: Human Perception and Performance, 21,* 734–750.

Adolph, K.E. (1997). Learning in the development of infant locomotion. *Monographs of the Society for Research in Child Development, 62* (3, Serial No. 251).

Adolph, K.E., Eppler, M.A., & Gibson, E.J. (1993a). Crawling versus walking infants' perception of affordances for locomotion over sloping surfaces. *Child Development, 64,* 1158–1174.

Adolph, K.E., Eppler, M.A., & Gibson, E.J. (1993b). Development of perception of affordances. Pp. 51–98 in C. Rovee-Collier & L.P. Lipsitt (Eds.), *Advances in infancy research,* Vol. 8. Norwood, NJ: Ablex.

Adolph, K.E., Vereijken, B., Byrne, K., & Ilustre, I. (1996, April). Footprint method of gait analysis: New insights into infant walking. Paper presented at International Conference for Infant Studies, Providence, RI.

Ahmed, A., & Ruffman, T. (1996). Do infants know when they are searching incorrectly? Looking times in a non-search A not B task. *Infant Behavior and Development, 19,* 297. (Abstract).

Ahrens, R. (1954). Beiträge zur Entwicklung des Physiognomie-und Mimikerkennes. *Zeitschrift für Experimentelle und angewandte Psychologie, 2,* 412–454, 599–633.

Alegria, J., & Noirot, E. (1978). Neonate orientation behavior towards the human voice. *International Journal of Behavioral Development, 1,* 291–313.

Alessandri, S.M., Sullivan, M.W., & Lewis, M. (1990). Violation of expectancy and frustration in early infancy. *Developmental Psychology, 26,* 738–744.

Amiel-Tison, C., & Grenier, A. (1986). *Neurological assessment during the first year of life.* New York: Oxford University Press.

Antell, S.E., & Keating, D.P. (1983). Perception of numerical invariance in neonates. *Child Development, 54,* 695–701.

Ashmead, D.H., Davis, D.L., Whalen, T., & Odom, R.D. (1991). Sound localization and sensitivity to interaural time differences in human infants. *Child Development, 62,* 1111–1126.

Aslin, R.N. (1988). Anatomical constraints on oculomotor development: Implications for infant perception. Pp. 67–104 in A. Yonas (Ed.), *Perceptual development in infancy: The Minnesota symposia on child psychology,* Vol. 20. Hillsdale, NJ: Erlbaum.

Aslin, R.N., Jusczyk, P.W., & Pisoni, D.B. (1997). Speech and auditory processing during infancy: Constraints on and precursors to language. Pp. 147–198 in *Handbook of child psychology:* Vol. 2, *Cognition, perception, and language.* New York: Wiley.

Aslin, R.N., Pisoni, D.B., & Jusczyk, P.W. (1983). Auditory development and speech perception in infancy. Pp. 573–687 in P.H. Mussen (Ed.), *Handbook of child psychology,* Vol. 2. New York: Wiley.

Bahrick, L.E. (1987). Infants' intermodal perception of two levels of temporal structure in natural events. *Infant Behavior and Development, 10,* 387–416.

Bahrick, L.E., Netto, D., & Hernandez-Reif, M. (1998). Intermodal perception of adult and child faces and voices by infants. *Child Development, 69,* 1263–1275.

Bahrick, L.E. (1988). Intermodal learning in infancy: Learning on the basis of two kinds of invariant relations in audible and visible events. *Child Development, 59,* 197–209.

Bahrick, L.E. (1992). Infants' perceptual differentiation of amodal and modality-specific audio-visual relations. *Journal of Experimental Child Psychology, 53,* 180–199.

Bahrick, L.E., Walker, A.S., & Neisser, U. (1981). Selective looking by infants. *Cognitive Psychology, 13,* 377–390.

Bahrick, L.E., & Watson, J.S. (1985). Detection of intermodal proprioceptive visual contingency as a potential basis of self-perception in infancy. *Developmental Psychology, 21,* 963–973.

Bai, D.L., & Bertenthal, B.I. (1992). Locomotor status and the development of spatial search skills. *Child Development, 63,* 215–226.

Baillargeon, R. (1993). The object concept revisited: New directions in the investigation of infants' physical knowledge. Pp. 265–315 in C.E. Granrud (Ed.), *Visual perception and cognition in infancy.* Hillsdale, NJ: Erlbaum.

Baillargeon, R. (1994). How do infants learn about the physical world? *Current Directions in Psychological Science, 3,* 133–140.

Baillargeon, R. (1995). A model of physical reasoning in infancy. Pp. 305–371 in C. Rovee-Collier & L.P. Lipsitt (Eds.), *Advances in infancy research,* Vol. 9. Norwood, NJ: Ablex.

Baillargeon, R., Needham, A., & DeVos, J. (1992). The development of young infants' intuition about support. *Early Development and Parenting, 1,* 69–78.

Bakeman, R., & Adamson, L. (1984). Coordinating attention to people and objects in mother-infant and peer-infant interaction. *Child Development, 55,* 1278–1289.

Baldwin, D. (1991). Infants' contribution to the achievement of joint reference. *Child Development, 62*, 875–890.

Ball, W.A., & Tronick, E. (1971). Infant responses to impending collision: Optical and real. *Science, 171*, 818–820.

Banks, M.S. (1988). Visual recalibration and the development of contrast and optical flow perception. Pp. 145–196 in A. Yonas (Ed.), *Perceptual development in infancy: The Minnesota Symposia on Child Psychology*, Vol. 20. Hillsdale, NJ: Erlbaum.

Banks, M.S., & Salapatek, P. (1983). Infant visual perception. Pp. 435–572 in P.H. Mussen (Ed.), *Handbook of child psychology*, Vol. 2. New York: Wiley.

Banks, M.S., & Shannon, E. (1993). Spatial and chromatic visual efficiency in human neonates. Pp. 1–46 in C. Granrud (Ed.), *Visual perception and cognition in infancy.* Hillsdale, NJ: Erlbaum.

Barnard, K.E., & Bee, H.E. (1983). The impact of temporally patterned stimulation on the development of preterm infants. *Child Development, 54*, 1156–1167.

Bauer, P. (1996). What do infants recall of their lives? Memory for specific events by one- to two-year-olds. *American Psychologist, 51*, 29–41.

Behl-Chadda, G., & Eimas, P.D. (1995). Infant categorization of left-right spatial relations. *British Journal of Developmental Psychology, 13*, 69–79.

Benson, J.B. (1993). Season of birth and onset of locomotion. *Infant Behavior and Development, 16*, 69–81.

Benson, J.B., & Uzgiris, I.C. (1985). Effect of self-initiated locomotion on infant search activity. *Developmental Psychology, 21*, 923–931.

Bernstein, N.A. (1967). *The coordination and regulation of movements.* Oxford: Pergamon.

Bertenthal, B., & Bai, D. (1989). Infants' sensitivity to optical flow for controlling posture. *Developmental Psychology, 25*, 936–945.

Bertenthal, B.I. (1993). Infants' perception of biomechanical motions: Intrinsic image and knowledge-based constraints. Pp. 175–214 in C.E. Granrud (Ed.), *Visual perception and cognition in infancy.* Hillsdale, NJ: Erlbaum.

Bertenthal, B.I., & Campos, J.J. (1990). A systems approach to the organizing effects of self-produced locomotion during infancy. Pp. 1–60 in C. Rovee-Collier (Ed.), *Advances in infancy research*, Vol. 6. Norwood, NJ: Ablex.

Bertenthal, B.I., Campos, J.J., & Barrett, K.C. (1984). Self-produced locomotion: An organizer of emotional, cognitive, and social development in infancy. Pp. 195–210 in R. Emde & R. Harmon (Eds.), *Continuities and discontinuities in development.* New York: Plenum.

Bertenthal, B.I., Profitt, D.R., & Cutting, J.E. (1984). Infant sensitivity to figural coherence in biomechanical motion. *Journal of Experimental Child Psychology, 37*, 171–178.

Bertenthal, B.I., Profitt, D.R., Spetner, N.B., & Thomas, M.A. (1985). The development of infants' sensitivity to biomechanical displays. *Child Development, 56*, 531–543.

Bigelow, A. (1998). Infants' sensitivity to familiar imperfect contingencies in social interaction. *Infant Behavior and Development, 21*, 149–162.

Bigelow, A.E. (1992). Locomotion and search behavior in blind infants. *Infant Behavior and Development, 15*, 179–189.

Blake, R. (1993). Cats perceive biological motion. *Psychological Science, 4*, 54–57.

Bloom, K. (1977). Patterning of infant vocal behavior. *Journal of Experimental Child Psychology, 23*, 367–377.

Bloom, L. (1993). *The transition from infancy to language: Acquiring the power of expression.* Cambridge: Cambridge University Press.

Bloom, L. (1997). Language acquisition in its developmental context. Pp. 309–370 in *Handbook of child psychology: Vol. 2, Cognition, perception, and language.* New York: Wiley.

Bomba, P.C., & Siqueland, E.R. (1983). The nature and structure of infant form categories. *Journal of Experimental Child Psychology, 35,* 294–328.

Bornstein, M.H. (1976). Infants are trichromats. *Journal of Experimental Child Psychology, 21,* 425–445.

Bornstein, M.H., Krinsky, S.J., & Benasich, A.A. (1986). Fine orientation discrimination and shape constancy in young infants. *Journal of Experimental Child Psychology, 41,* 49–60.

Bower, T.G.R. (1966). Slant perception and shape constancy in infants. *Science, 151,* 832–834.

Bower, T.G.R. (1967). The development of object permanence: Some studies of existence constancy. *Perception and Psychophysics, 2,* 411–418.

Bower, T.G.R. (1972). Object perception in infants. *Perception, 1,* 15–30.

Bower, T.G.R. (1989). *The rational infant.* New York: Freeman.

Bower, T.G.R., Broughton, J.M., & Moore, M.K. (1970). Demonstration of intention in the reaching behavior of neonate humans. *Nature, 228,* 677–681.

Bower, T.G.R., Broughton, J.M., & Moore, M.K. (1971). Infant responses to approaching objects: An indication of response to distal variables. *Perception and Psychophysics, 9,* 193–196.

Bremner, J.G. (1978). Egocentric vs. allocentric spatial coding in nine-month-old infants: Factors influencing the choice of code. *Developmental Psychology, 14,* 346–355.

Bremner, J.G., & Bryant, P.E. (1977). Place vs. response as the basis of spatial errors made by young infants. *Journal of Experimental Child Psychology, 23,* 162–171.

Broadbent, D.E. (1958). *Perception and communication.* New York: Pergamon.

Broen, P. (1972). *The verbal environment of the language learning child* (American Speech and Hearing Association Monograph 17).

Burnham, D. (1993). Visual recognition of mother by young infants: Facilitation by speech. *Perception, 22,* 1133–1153.

Bushnell, E.W., & Boudreau, J.P. (1993). Motor development and the mind: The potential role of motor abilities as a determinant of perceptual development. *Child Development, 64,* 1005–1021.

Bushnell, E.W., McKenzie, B.E., Lawrence, D.A., & Connell, S. (1995). The spatial coding strategies of one-year-old infants in a locomotor search task. *Child Development, 66,* 937–958.

Bushnell, E.W., Shaw, L., & Strauss, D. (1985). Relationship between visual and tactual exploration by 6-month-olds. *Developmental Psychology, 21,* 591–600.

Bushnell, I., Sai, F., & Mullin, J. (1989). Neonatal recognition of the mother's face. *British Journal of Developmental Psychology, 7,* 3–15.

Bushnell, I.W.R. (1979). Modification of the externality effect in young infants. *Journal of Experimental Child Psychology, 28,* 211–229.

Butterworth, G. (1991). The ontogeny and phylogeny of joint visual attention. Pp. 223–232 in A. Whiten (Ed.), *Natural theories of mind.* Cambridge, MA: Basil Blackwell.

Butterworth, G., & Cochran, E. (1980). Towards a mechanism of joint visual attention in human infancy. *International Journal of Behavioral Development, 3,* 253–272.

Butterworth, G., & Grover, L. (1990). Joint visual attention, manual pointing, and preverbal communication in human infancy. Pp. 605–624 in M. Jeannerod (Ed.), *Attention and Performance: Vol. XIII, Motor representation and control*. Hillsdale, NJ: LEA Associates.

Butterworth, G., & Hicks, L. (1977). Visual proprioception and postural stability in infancy: A developmental study. *Perception, 6*, 255–262.

Butterworth, G., & Hopkins, B. (1988). Hand-mouth coordination in the new-born baby. *British Journal of Developmental Psychology, 6*, 303–314.

Butterworth, G., & Jarrett, N. (1991). What minds have in common is space: Spatial mechanisms serving joint visual attention in infancy. *British Journal of Developmental Psychology, 9*, 55–72.

Butterworth, G., Verweij, E., & Hopkins, B. (1997). The development of prehension in infants: Halverson revisited. *British Journal of Developmental Psychology, 15*, 223–236.

Campos, J.J., Hiatt, S., Ramsay, D., Henderson, C., & Svedja, M. (1978). The emergence of fear on the visual cliff. Pp. 149–182 in M. Lewis & L.A. Rosenblum (Eds.), *The development of affect*. New York: Plenum.

Campos, J. & Langer, A. (1971). The visual cliff: Discriminative cardiac orienting responses with retinal size held constant. *Psychophysiology, 8*, 264–265.

Campos, J., Langer, A., & Krowitz, A. (1970). Cardiac responses on the visual cliff in prelocomotor infants. *Science, 170*, 196–197.

Canfield, R.L., & Haith, M.M. (1991). Young infants' visual expectations for symmetric and asymmetric stimulus sequences. *Developmental Psychology, 27*, 198–208.

Canfield, R.L., & Smith, E.G. (1996). Number-based expectations and sequential enumeration by 5-month-old infants. *Developmental Psychology, 32*, 269–279.

Caron, A., Caron, R., & McLean, R. (1988). Infant discrimination of naturalistic emotional expressions: The role of face and voice. *Child Development, 59*, 604–616.

Caron, A.J., Caron, R.F., & Carlson, V.R. (1979). Infant perception of the invariant shape of objects varying in slant. *Child Development, 50*, 716–721.

Carroll, J.J., & Gibson, E.J. (1981, April). *Differentiation of an aperture from an obstacle under conditions of motion by three-month-old infants*. Paper presented at the meeting of the Society for Research in Child Development, Boston, MA.

Caruso, D.A. (1993). Dimensions of quality in infants' exploratory behavior: Relationships to problem-solving activity. *Infant Behavior and Development, 16*, 441–454.

Cernoch, J., & Porter, R. (1985). Recognition of maternal axillary odors by infants. *Child Development, 56*, 1593–1598.

Chomsky, N. (1965). *Aspects of the theory of syntax*. Cambridge, MA: MIT Press.

Cichetti, D., & Sroufe, L.A. (1978). An organizational view of affect: Illustration from the study of Down's Syndrome infants. Pp. 309–350 in M. Lewis & L.A. Rosenblum (Eds.), *The development of affect*. New York: Plenum.

Clifton, R. (1998). Representation expressed by action on unseen objects. *Infant Behavior and Development, 21*, 149.

Clifton, R., Perris, E., & Bullinger, A. (1991). Infants' perception of auditory space. *Developmental Psychology, 27*, 187–197.

Clifton, R.K., Muir, D.W., Ashmead, D.H., & Clarkson, M.G. (1993). Is visually guided reaching in early infancy a myth? *Child Development, 64*, 1099–1110.

Clifton, R.K., Rochat, P., Litovsky, R.Y., & Perris, E.E. (1991). Object representation guides infants' reaching in the dark. *Journal of Experimental Psychology: Human Perception and Performance, 17*, 322–329.

Cohen, L., & Oakes, L.M. (1993). How infants perceive a simple causal event. *Developmental Psychology, 29*, 421–433.

Cohn, J., & Tronick, E. (1987). Mother-infant face-to-face interaction: The sequencing of dyadic states at 3, 6, and 9 months. *Developmental Psychology, 23*, 68–77.

Cohn, J., & Tronick, E. (1988). Mother-infant face-to-face interaction: Influence is bidirectional and unrelated to periodic cycles in either partner's behavior. *Developmental Psychology, 24*, 386–392.

Collis, G. (1977). Visual co-orientation and maternal speech. Pp. 335–375 in H. Schaffer (Ed.), *Studies in mother-infant interaction*. London: Academic.

Collis, G., & Schaffer, H. (1975). Synchronization of visual attention in mother-infant pairs. *Journal of Child Psychology and Psychiatry, 16*, 315–320.

Condon, W., & Sander, L. (1974). Synchrony demonstrated between movements of the neonate and adult speech. *Child Development, 45*, 456–462.

Connolly, K., & Dalgleish, M. (1989). The emergence of a tool-using skill in infancy. *Developmental Psychology, 25*, 894–912.

Cooper, R., Abraham, J., Berman, S., & Staska, M. (1997). The development of infants' preference for motherese. *Infant Behavior and Development, 20*, 477–488.

Cooper, R., & Aslin, R. (1990). Preference for infant-directed speech in the first month after birth. *Child Development, 61*, 1584–1595.

Cooper, R., & Aslin, R. (1994). Developmental differences in infant attention to the spectral properties of infant-directed speech. *Child Development, 65*, 1663–1677.

Corkum, V., & Moore, C. (1998). The origins of joint visual attention in infants. *Developmental Psychology, 34*, 28–38.

Craton, L.G. (1996). The development of perceptual completion abilities: Infants' perception of stationary partially occluded objects. *Child Development, 67*, 890–904.

Cruikshank, R.M. (1941). The development of visual size constancy in early infancy. *Journal of Genetic Psychology, 58*, 327–351.

Daniel, B.M., & Lee, D.N. (1990). Development of looking with head and eyes. *Journal of Experimental Child Psychology, 50*, 200–216.

Darwin, C. (Ed.). (1974). *The descent of man, and selection in relation to sex*. Quoted, pp. 81–82, in S. Diamond (Ed.), *The roots of psychology*. New York: Basic Books. (Original work published in 1874.)

Day, R.H. (1987). Visual size constancy in infancy. Pp. 67–91 in B.E. McKenzie & R.H. Day (Eds.), *Perceptual development in early infancy: Problems and issues*. Hillsdale, NJ: Erlbaum.

Deak, G., Flom, R., & Pick, A. (in press). Effects of gesture and target on 12- and 18-month-olds' visual attention to objects in front of or behind them. *Developmental Psychology*.

Deak, G., & Pick, A.D. (1994). *What is a penlight? Preschoolers' systematic and flexible use of abstract categorization criteria*. Paper presented at the American Psychological Society, Washington, DC.

DeCasper, A., & Fifer, W. (1980). Of human bonding: Newborns prefer their mothers' voices. *Science, 208*, 1174–1176.

DeCasper, A., & Prescott, P. (1984). Human newborns' perception of male voices: Preference, discrimination and reinforcing value. *Developmental Psychobiology, 17*, 481–491.

DeCasper, A., & Spence, J. (1986). Prenatal maternal speech influences newborns' perception of speech sounds. *Infant Behavior and Development, 9*, 133–150.

DeCasper, A.J., Lecanuet, J.-P., Busnel, M.-C., Granier-Deferre, C., & Maugeais, R. (1994). Fetal reactions to recurrent maternal speech. *Infant Behavior and Development, 17,* 159–164.

Eddington, A.S. (1928). *The nature of the physical world.* The Gifford Lectures. Cambridge: Cambridge University Press.

Eimas, P.D., & Quinn, P.C. (1994). Studies on the formation of perceptually based basic-level categories in young infants. *Child Development, 65,* 908–917.

Eimas, P.D., Siqueland, E.R., Jusczyk, P.W., & Vigorito, J. (1971). Speech perception in infants. *Science, 171,* 303–306.

Emmorey, K., & Reilly, J.S. (Eds.). (1995). *Language, gesture, & space.* Mahwah, NJ: Erlbaum.

Eppler, M.A. (1995). Development of manipulatory skills and the deployment of attention. *Infant Behavior and Development, 18,* 391–405.

Eppler, M.A., Adolph, K.E., Gibson, E.J., Lax, A., & Shahinfar, A. (1992). Differential exploration of sloping surfaces in relation to development of crawling skill. *Infant Behavior and Development, 15,* 397.

Fagan, J.F. (1974). Infant recognition memory: The effects of length of familiarization and type of discrimination task. *Child Development, 45,* 351–356.

Fagen, J.W., Morrongiello, B.A., Rovee-Collier, C., & Gekoski, M.J. (1984). Expectancies and memory retrieval in 3-month-olds. *Child Development, 55,* 936–943.

Fantz, R.L. (1961). The origin of form perception. *Scientific American, 204,* 66–72.

Fantz, R.L. (1963). Pattern vision in newborn infants. *Science, 140,* 296–297.

Fantz, R.L. (1965). Ontogeny of perception. Pp 365–403 in A.M. Schrier, H.F. Harlow, & F. Stollnitz (Eds.), *Behavior of non-human primates.* New York: Academic.

Fantz, R.L., Fagan, J.F., III, & Miranda, S.B. (1975). Early visual selectivity as a function of pattern variables; previous exposure, age from birth and conception, and expected cognitive deficit. Pp. 249–345 in L.B. Cohen & P. Salapatek (Eds.), *Infant perception: From sensation to cognition,* Vol. 1. New York: Academic.

Fantz, R.L., Ordy, J.M., & Udelph, M.S. (1962). Maturation of pattern vision during the first six months. *Journal of Comparative and Physiological Psychology, 55,* 907–917.

Fernald, A. (1984). The perceptual and affective salience of mothers' speech to infants. Pp. 5–29 in L. Feagans, C. Garvey, & R. Golinkoff (Eds.), *The origins and growth of communication.* Norwood, NJ: Ablex.

Fernald, A. (1985). Four-month-old infants prefer to listen to motherese. *Infant Behavior and Development, 8,* 181–185.

Fernald, A. (1989). Intonation and communication intent in mothers' speech to infants: Is the melody the message? *Child Development, 60,* 1497–1510.

Fernald, A. (1993). Approval and disapproval: Infant responsiveness to vocal affect in familiar and unfamiliar languages. *Child Development, 64,* 657–674.

Fernald, A., & Kuhl, P. (1987). Acoustic determinants of infant preference for motherese speech. *Infant Behavior and Development, 10,* 279–293.

Fernald, A., & Simon, T. (1984). Expanded intonation contours in mothers' speech to newborns. *Developmental Psychology, 20,* 104–113.

Fernald, A., Taeschner, T., Dunn, J., Papousek, M., Boysson-Bardies, B., & Fukui, I. (1989). A cross-language study of prosodic modifications in mothers' and fathers' speech to preverbal infants. *Journal of Child Language, 16,* 477–501.

Field, J. (1976). The adjustment of reaching behavior to object distance in early infancy. *Child Development, 47,* 304–308.

Field, T., Cohen, D., Garcia, R., & Greenberg, R. (1984). Mother-stranger face discrimination by the newborn. *Infant Behavior and Development, 7,* 19–25.

Fifer, W.P. (1981). *Early attachment: Maternal-voice preference in one- and three-day old infants.* Unpublished doctoral dissertation, University of North Carolina at Greensboro.

Fodor, J.A. (1983). *The modularity of mind.* Cambridge, MA: MIT Press.

Fogel, A. (1988). Cyclicity and stability in mother-infant face-to-face interaction: A comment on Cohn and Tronick (1988). *Developmental Psychology, 24,* 393–395.

Fogel, A., Dedo, J., & McEwen, I. (1992). Effect of postural position and reaching on gaze during mother-infant face-to-face interaction. *Infant Behavior and Development, 15,* 231–244.

Fogel, A., & Hannan, T. (1985). Manual actions of nine-to-fifteen-week-old human infants during face-to-face interaction with their mothers. *Child Development, 56,* 1271–1279.

Fogel, A., & Thelen, E. (1987). Development of early expressive and communicative action: Reinterpreting the evidence from a dynamic systems perspective. *Developmental Psychology, 23,* 747–761.

Fraiberg, S. (1977). *Insights from the blind: Comparative studies of blind and sighted infants.* New York: Basic Books.

Freedland, R.L., & Bertenthal, B.I. (1994). Developmental changes in interlimb coordination: Transition to hands-and-knees crawling. *Psychological Science, 5,* 26–32.

Frye, D., Rawling, P., Moore, C., & Myers, I. (1983). Object-person discrimination and communication at 3 and 10 months. *Developmental Psychology, 19,* 303–309.

Gable, S., & Isabella, R. (1992). Maternal contributions to infant regulation of arousal. *Infant Behavior and Development, 15,* 95–107.

Gallistel, C.R. (1990). *The organization of learning.* Cambridge, MA: MIT Press.

Garner, W.R. (1962). *Uncertainty and structure as psychological concepts.* New York: Wiley.

Gelman, R., & Williams, E.M. (1997). Enabling constraints for cognitive development and learning: Domain specificity and epigenesis. Pp. 575–630 in *Handbook of child psychology: Vol. 2, Cognition, perception, and language.* New York: Wiley.

Gesell, A. (1946). The ontogenesis of infant behavior. Pp. 295–331 in L. Carmichael (Eds.), *Manual of child psychology.* New York: Wiley.

Gesell, A.I., Ilg, F.L., & Bullis, G.E. (1949). *Vision: Its development in infant and child.* New York: Hoeber (Harper & Bro).

Gibson, E.J. (1952). The role of shock in reinforcement. *Journal of Comparative and Physiological Psychology, 45,* 18–30.

Gibson, E.J. (1969). *Principles of perceptual learning and development.* New York: Appleton-Century-Crofts.

Gibson, E.J., & Spelke, E.S. (1983). The development of perception. Pp. 1–76 in J.H. Flavell & E.M Markman (Eds.), *Handbook of Child Psychology, Vol. 3, Cognitive Development.* New York: John Wiley & Sons.

Gibson, E.J. (1991). The concept of affordances in development: The renascence of functionalism. Pp. 557–570 in E.J. Gibson, *An odyssey in learning and perception.* Cambridge, MA: MIT Press. (Reprinted from *The concept of development: The Minnesota Symposium on Child Psychology,* Vol. 15, pp. 55–81, W.A. Collins, Ed., 1982.)

Gibson, E.J. (1984). Reflections on awareness of causality: What develops? Pp. 136–144 in L.P. Lippsitt & C. Rovee-Collier (Eds.), *Advances in infancy research*, Vol. 3. Norwood, NJ: Ablex.

Gibson, E.J. (1991). Perception as a foundation for knowledge: Thoughts inspired by papers of Fraiberg and Bellugi. Pp. 552–526 in E.J. Gibson, *An odyssey in learning and perception.* Cambridge, MA: MIT Press.

Gibson, E.J. (1993). Ontogenesis of the perceived self. Pp. 25–42 in U. Neisser (Ed.), *The perceived self.* New York: Cambridge University Press.

Gibson, E.J. (1994). Has psychology a future? *Psychological Science, 5,* 69–76.

Gibson, E.J. (1995). Are we automata? Pp. 3–15 in P. Rochat (Ed.), *The self in infancy: Theory and research.* Amsterdam: Elsevier Science B.V.

Gibson, E.J., & Bergman, R. (1954). The effect of training on absolute estimation of distance over the ground. *Journal of Experimental Psychology, 48,* 473–482.

Gibson, E.J., Owsley, C.J., & Johnston, J. (1978). Perception of invariants by five-month-old infants: Differentiation of two types of motion. *Developmental Psychology, 14,* 407–415.

Gibson, E.J., Owsley, C.J., Walker, A.S., & Megaw-Nyce, J.S. (1979). Development of the perception of invariants: Substance and shape. *Perception, 8,* 609–619.

Gibson, E.J., Riccio, G., Schmuckler, M.A., Stoffregen, T.A., Rosenberg, D., & Taormina, J. (1987). Detection of the traversability of surfaces by crawling and walking infants. *Journal of Experimental Psychology: Human Perception and Performance, 13,* 533–544.

Gibson, E.J., & Schmuckler, M.A. (1989). Going somewhere: An ecological and experimental approach to development of mobility. *Ecological Psychology, 1,* 3–25.

Gibson, E.J., & Walk, R.D. (1960). The "visual cliff". *Scientific American, 202,* 64–71.

Gibson, E.J., & Walker, A.S. (1984). Development of knowledge of visual-tactual affordances of substance. *Child Development, 55,* 453–460.

Gibson, J.J. (1958). Visually controlled locomotion and visual orientation in animals. *British Journal of Psychology, 49,* 182–194.

Gibson, J.J. (1962). On Information. Manuscript in the James J. Gibson Archives, Olin Library Manuscript Room, Cornell University.

Gibson, J.J. (1966). *The senses considered as perceptual systems.* Boston: Houghton-Mifflin.

Gibson, J.J. (1979). *The ecological approach to visual perception.* Boston: Houghton-Mifflin; reprinted, (1986). Hillsdale, NJ: Erlbaum.

Gibson, J.J., & Gibson, E.J. (1955). Perceptual learning: Differentiation or enrichment? *Psychological Review, 62,* 32–41.

Gibson, J.J., Jack, E.G., & Raffel, G. (1932). Bilateral transfer of the conditioned response in the human subject. *Journal of Experimental Psychology, 15,* 416–421.

Gleitman, L.R., Gleitman, H., Landau, B., & Wanner, E. (1988). Where learning begins: Initial representations for language learning. Pp.150–193 in F. Newmayer (Ed.), *The Cambridge linguistic survey.* New York: Cambridge University Press.

Goldfield, E.C. (1995). *Emergent forms: Origins and early development of human action and perception.* New York: Oxford University Press.

Goldfield, E.C., & Dickerson, D.J. (1981). Keeping track of locations during movement in 8- to 10-month-old infants. *Journal of Experimental Child Psychology, 32,* 48–64.

Goldfield, E.C., Kay, B.A., & Warren, W.H. (1993). Infant bouncing: The assembly and tuning of action systems. *Child Development, 64,* 1128–1142.

Golinkoff, R.M. (1975). Semantic development in infants: The concepts of agent and recipient. *Merrill-Palmer Quarterly, 21*, 181–193.

Goodwin, B. (1990). The causes of biological form. Pp. 49–63 in G. Butterworth & P. Bryant (Eds.), *Causes of development: Interdisciplinary perspectives*. Hillsdale, NJ: Erlbaum.

Goren, C., Sarty, M., & Wu, P.Y.K. (1975). Visual following and pattern discrimination of facelike stimuli by newborn infants. *Pediatrics, 56*, 544–549.

Goswami, U., & Brown, A. (1990). Melting chocolate and melting snowmen: Analogical reasoning and causal relations. *Cognition, 35*, 69–95.

Gould, S.J. (1998). *Ontogeny and phylogeny revisited, or why the child is not the evolutionary father to the man*. Keynote address, 11th Biennial International Conference on Infant Studies, Atlanta, GA.

Granrud, C.E. (1987). Size constancy in newborn human infants. *Investigative Ophthalmology and Visual Science, 28* (Supplement), 5.

Granrud, C.E., Yonas, A., Smith, I.M., Arterberry, M.E., Glickman, J.L., & Sorknes, A.C. (1984). Infants' sensitivity to accretion and deletion of texture as information for depth at an edge. *Child Development, 55*, 1630–1636.

Greco, C., Hayne, H., & Rovee-Collier, C. (1990). Roles of function, reminding, and variability in categorization by 3-month-old infants. *Journal of Experimental Psychology: Learning, Memory, and Cognition, 16*, 617–633.

Greenough, W.T., Black, J.E., & Wallace, C.S. (1987). Experience and brain development. *Child Development, 58*, 539–559.

Greer, T., & Lockman, J.J. (1998). Using writing instruments: Invariances in young children and adults. *Child Development, 69*, 888–902.

Gregory, R. (1991). Seeing as thinking: An active theory of perception. Pp. 511–519 in E.J. Gibson (Ed.), *An odyssey in learning and perception*. Cambridge, MA: MIT Press. (Reprinted from *London Times Literary Supplement*, June 23, 1972.)

Grieser, D., & Kuhl, P. (1988). Maternal speech to infants in a tonal language: Support for universal prosodic features in motherese. *Developmental Psychology, 24*, 14–20.

Gustafson, G.E. (1984). Effects of the ability to locomote on infants' social and exploratory behaviors: An experimental study. *Developmental Psychology, 20*, 397–405.

Haith, M.M. (1993). Future-oriented processes in infancy: The case of visual expectations. Pp. 235–264 in C.E. Granrud (Ed.), *Visual perception and cognition in infancy*. Hillsdale, NJ: Erlbaum.

Haith, M.M., & Benson, J.B. (1997). Infant cognition. Pp. 199–254 in W. Damon (Ed.), *Child psychology: Vol. 2, Cognition, perception, and language*. New York: Wiley.

Haith, M.M., Hazen, C., & Goodman, G.S. (1988). Expectation and anticipation of dynamic visual events by 3.5-month-old babies. *Child Development, 59*, 467–479.

Haith, M.M., Wentworth, N., & Canfield, R.L. (1993). The formation of expectations in early infancy. Pp. 251–297 in C. Rovee-Collier & L.P. Lipsitt (Eds.), *Advances in infancy research*, Vol. 8. Norwood, NJ: Ablex.

Hall, G. (1991). *Perceptual and associative learning*. Oxford: Clarendon.

Halverson, H.M. (1931). An experimental study of prehension in infants by means of systematic cinema records. *Genetic Psychology Monographs, 10*, 107–285.

Harlow, H.F. (1959). Learning set and error factor theory. In Koch, S. (Ed.), *Psychology: A study of science*, Vol. 2. New York: McGraw-Hill.

Haviland, J., & Lelwica, M. (1987). The induced affect response: 10-week-old infants' responses to three emotion expressions. *Developmental Psychology, 23*, 97–104.

Hay, J.C., & Pick, H.L. Jr. (1966). Visual and proprioceptive adaptation to optical displacement of the visual stimulus. *Journal of Experimental Psychology, 71*, 150–158.

Hayne, H., MacDonald, S., & Barr, R.C. (1997). Developmental changes in the specificity of memory over the second year of life. *Infant Behavior and Development, 20*, 233–245.

Hayne, H., & Rovee-Collier, C. (1995). The organization of reactivated memory in infancy. *Child Development, 66*, 893–906

Hebb, D.A. (1974). What psychology is about. *American Psychologist, 29*, 71–79.

Held, R., Birch, E., & Gwiazda, J. (1980). Stereoacuity in human infants. *Proceedings of the National Academy of Sciences, USA, 77*, 5572–5574.

Held, R., & Hein, A. (1963). Movement-produced stimulation in the development of visually guided behavior. *Journal of Comparative and Physiological Psychology, 56*, 872–876.

Hermer, L., & Spelke, E. (1996). Modularity and development: The case of spatial reorientation. *Cognition, 61*, 195–232.

Higgins, C., Campos, J., & Kermoian, R. (1993). *The influence of creeping on infant postural compensation to optical flow.* Paper presented at the meeting of the Society for Research in Child Development, New Orleans, LA.

Hirsh-Pasek, K., Nelson, D., Jusczyk, P., Cassidy, K., Druss, B., & Kennedy, L. (1987). Clauses are perceptual units for younger infants. *Cognition, 26*, 269–286.

Hofstader, M.T., & Reznick, J.S. (1996). Response modality affects human infant delayed-response performance. *Child Development, 67*, 646–658.

Horobin, K., & Acredolo, L. (1986). The role of attentiveness, mobility history, and separation of hiding sites on Stage IV search behavior. *Journal of Experimental Child Psychology, 41*, 114–127.

Horowitz, F.D., Paden, L., Bhana, K., & Self, P. (1972). An infant-control procedure for studying fixations. *Developmental Psychology, 7*, 90.

House, B.J. (1964). Oddity performance in retardates. I. Size-discrimination functions from oddity and verbal methods. *Child Development, 35*, 645–651.

House, B.J., & Zeaman, D. (1963). Learning sets from minimum stimuli in retardates. *Journal of Comparative and Physiological Psychology, 56*, 735–739.

Hull, C.L. (1934a). The concept of the habit-family hierarchy and maze learning I. *Psychological Review, 41*, 33–52.

Hull, C.L. (1934b). The concept of the habit-family hierarchy and maze learning II. *Psychological Review, 41*, 134–152.

Hull, C.L. (1943). *Principles of behavior.* New York: Appleton-Century.

James, W. (1879). Are we automata? *Mind, 4*, 1–22.

James, W. (1890). *Principles of psychology.* New York: Holt.

Johansson, G. (1950). *Configurations in event perception.* Uppsala: Almqvist & Wiksel.

Johansson, G. (1973). Visual perception of biological motion and a model for its analysis. *Perception and Psychophysics, 14*, 210–211.

Johnson, M.H., Dziurawiec, S., Ellis, H., & Morton, J. (1991). Newborns' preferential tracking of face-like stimuli and its subsequent decline. *Cognition, 40*, 1–19.

Johnson, S.P., & Aslin, R.N. (1995). Perception of object unity in 2-month-old infants. *Developmental Psychology, 31*, 739–745.

Johnson, S.P., & Nañez, J.E., Sr. (1995). Young infants' perception of object unity in two-dimensional displays. *Infant Behavior and Development, 18*, 133–143.

Johnston, T.D. (1985). Introduction: Conceptual issues in the ecological study of learning.

Pp. 1–24 in T.D. Johnston & A.T. Pietrewicz (Eds.), *Issues in the ecological study of learning.* Hillsdale, NJ: Erlbaum.

Johnston, T.D. (1987). The persistence of dichotomies in the study of behavioral development. *Developmental Review, 7,* 149–182.

Jones, H.E., & Yoshioka, J.G. (1938). Differential errors in childrens' learning on a stylus maze. *Journal of Comparative Psychology, 25,* 463–480.

Jones, S. (1996). Imitation or exploration? Young infants' matching of adults' oral gestures. *Child Development, 67,* 1952–1969.

Jouen, F., & Lepecq, J. (1989). La sensibilité au flux optique chez le nouveau-né. *Psychologic Francais, 34,* 13–18.

Jusczyk, P.C. (1997). *The discovery of spoken language.* Cambridge, MA: MIT Press

Kaiser, M.K., & Profitt, D.R. (1984). The development of sensitivity to causally relevant dynamic information. *Child Development, 55,* 1614–1624.

Karmiloff-Smith, A. (1992). Beyond modularity: A developmental perspective on cognitive science. Cambridge, MA: MIT Press.

Kellman, P.J. (1984). Perception of three-dimensional form by human infants. *Perception and Psychophysics, 36,* 353–358.

Kellman, P.J. (1993). Kinematic foundations of infant visual perception. Pp. 121–173 in C.E. Granrud (Ed.), *Visual perception in infancy.* Hillsdale, NJ: Erlbaum.

Kellman, P.J., Gleitman, H., & Spelke, E. (1987). Object and observer motion in the perception of objects by infants. *Journal of Experimental Psychology: Human Perception and Performance, 13,* 586–593.

Kellman, P.J., & Short, K.R. (1987a). Development of three-dimensional form perception. *Journal of Experimental Psychology: Human Perception and Performance, 13,* 545–557.

Kellman, P.J., & Short, K.R. (1987b). *Infant perception of partly occluded objects: The problem of rotation.* Paper presented at the Third International Conference on Event Perception and Action, Uppsala, Sweden.

Kellman, P.J., & Spelke, E. (1983). Perception of partly occluded objects in infancy. *Cognitive Psychology, 15,* 483–524.

Kellman, P.J., & von Hofsten, C. (1992). The world of the moving infant: Perception of motion, stability, and space. Pp. 147–184 in C. Rovee-Collier & L.P. Lipsitt (Eds.), *Advances in infancy research,* Vol. 7. Norwood, NJ: Ablex.

Kendal-Reed, M. (1992). How do babies smell? Accounting for olfactory competence in human infancy. *British Psychological Society, 1992 Abstracts,* p. 18.

Kermoian, R., & Campos, J.J. (1988). Locomotor experience: A facilitator of spatial cognitive development. *Child Development, 59,* 908–917.

Kessen, W., Levine, J., & Wendrich, K.A. (1979). The initiation of pitch in infants. *Infant Behavior and Development, 2,* 93–100.

Kimmerle, M., Mick, L.A., & Michel, G.F. (1995). Bimanual role-differentiated toy play during infancy. *Infant Behavior and Development, 18,* 299–307.

Kisilevsky, B.S., Stack, D.M., & Muir, D.W. (1991). Fetal and infant response to tactile stimulation. Pp. 63–98 in J.J.S. Weiss & P.R. Zelasso (Eds.), *Newborn attention.* Norwood, NJ: Ablex.

Koch, J. (1962). Die Veränderung des Exitations Prozesses mach der Nahrungseinnahme und nach dem Schlafe bei Säuglingen in Alter von 5 Monaten. *Zeitschrift für ärtlich Fortbildung, 55,* 219–223.

Koffka, K.K. (1931). *Growth of the mind.* New York: Harcourt.

Köhler, W. (1925). *The mentality of apes*. E. Winter, trans. New York: Harcourt Brace. (Originally published 1917)

Koslowski, B., & Bruner, J.S. (1972). Learning to use a lever. *Child Development, 43*, 790–799.

Kuhl, P.K. (1991). Perception, cognition, and the ontogenetic and phylogenetic emergence of human speech. Pp. 73–106 in S.E. Brauth, W.S. Hall, & R.J. Dooling (Eds.), *Plasticity of Development*. Cambridge, MA: MIT Press.

Kuhl, P.K., & Meltzoff, A. (1984). The intermodal representation of speech in infants. *Infant Behavior and Development, 7*, 361–384.

Kuhl, P.K., & Meltzoff, A. (1988). Speech as an intermodal object of perception. In A. Yonas (Ed.), *Perceptual development in infancy. The Minnesota symposia on child psychology* (Vol. 20, pp. 235–266). Hillsdale, NJ: Erlbaum.

Kuhl, P.K., Williams, K., Lacerda, F., Stevens, K., & Lindblom, B. (1992). Linguistic experience alters phonetic perception in infants by 6 months of age. *Science, 255*, 606–608.

Kuhl, P.K., Williams, K., & Meltzoff, A. (1991). Cross-modal speech perception in adults and infants using nonspeech auditory stimuli. *Journal of Experimental Psychology: Human Perception and Performance, 17*, 829–840.

Lashley, K.S. (1942). The problem of cerebral organization in vision. Pp. 301–322 in H. Kluever (Ed.), *Biological symposia: Vol. 7, Visual mechanisms*. Lancaster, PA: Cattell.

Lecanuet, J.P., Granier-Deferre, C., Jaquet, A.Y., Capponi, I., & Ledru, L. (1993). Prenatal discrimination of a male and a female voice uttering the same sentence. *Early Development and Parenting, 2*, 217–228.

Lee, D.N. (1974). Visual information during locomotion. Pp. 250–267 in R.B. MacLeod & H.L. Pick, Jr. (Eds.), *Perception: Essays in honor of J. Gibson*. Ithaca: Cornell University Press.

Lee, D.N. (1976). A theory of visual control of braking based on information about time-to-collision. *Perception, 5*, 437–459.

Lee, D.N. (1980). The optic flow field: The foundation of vision. *Philosophical Transactions of the Royal Society, B290*, 169–179.

Lee, D.N., & Aronson, E. (1974). Visual proprioceptive control of standing in human infants. *Perception and Psychophysics, 15*, 529–532.

Lee, D.N., & Reddish, P.E. (1981). Plummeting gannets: a paradigm of ecological optics. *Nature, 293*, 293–294.

Legerstee, M. (1990). Infants use multimodal information to imitate speech sounds. *Infant Behavior and Development, 13*, 343–354.

Legerstee, M. (1991). The role of person and object in eliciting early imitation. *Journal of Experimental Child Psychology, 51*, 423–433.

Legerstee, M., Anderson, D., & Schaffer, A. (1998). Five- and-eight-month-old infants recognize their faces and voices as familiar and social stimuli. *Child Development, 69*, 37–50.

Legerstee, M., Corter, C., & Kienapple, K. (1990). Hand, arm, and facial actions of young infants to a social and nonsocial stimulus. *Child Development, 61*, 774–784.

Leslie, A.M. (1984a). Infant perception of a manual pick-up event. *British Journal of Developmental Psychology, 2*, 19–32.

Leslie, A.M. (1984b). Spatiotemporal contiguity and the perception of causality in infants. *Perception, 13*, 287–305.

Leslie, A.M., & Keeble, S. (1987). Do six-month-old infants perceive causality? *Cognition, 25*, 265–288.

Leung, E., & Rheingold, H. (1981). Development of pointing as a social gesture. *Developmental Psychology, 17*, 215–220.

Lewin, K. (1946). Behavior and development as a function of the total situation. Pp. 791–844 in L. Carmichael (Ed.), *Manual of child psychology.* New York: Wiley.

Lewis, M., Alessandri, S.M., & Sullivan, M.W. (1990). Violation of expectancy, loss of control, and anger expressions in young infants. *Developmental Psychology, 26*, 745–751.

Lewis, M., Sullivan, M.W., & Brooks-Gunn, J. (1985). Emotional behavior during the learning of a contingency in early infancy. *British Journal of Developmental Psychology, 3*, 307–316.

Ling, B.C. (1944). Form discrimination as a learning cue in infants. *Comparative Psychology Monographs, 17* (*2*, whole No. 86).

Litovsky, R.Y., & Clifton, R. (1992). Use of sound pressure level in auditory distance perception by six-month-old infants and adults. *Journal of the Acoustical Society of America, 92*, 794–802.

Lockman, J.J. (1984). The development of detour behavior in infancy. *Child Development, 55*, 482–491.

Lockman, J.J., & McHale, J.P. (1989). Object manipulation in infancy: Developmental and contextual determinants. Pp. 129–167 in J.J. Lockman & N.L. Hazen (Eds.), *Action in social context: Perspectives on early development.* New York: Plenum.

Loveland, K. (1984). Learning about points of view: Spatial perspective and the acquisition of "I/you." *Journal of Child Language, 11*, 535–556.

Mandel, D.R., Jusczyk, P.W., & Pisoni, D.B. (1995). Infants' recognition of the sound pattern of their own names. *Psychological Science, 6*, 314–317.

Mandler, J.M. (1992). How to build a baby. 2. Conceptual primitives. *Psychological Review, 99*, 587–604.

Mandler, J.M. (1997). Representation. Pp. 255–308 in *Handbook of child psychology:* Vol. 2, *Cognition, perception, and language.* New York: Wiley.

Marr, D. (1982). *Vision.* San Francisco: Freeman.

Maurer, D., & Young, R.E. (1983). The scanning of compound figures by young infants. *Journal of Experimental Child Psychology, 35*, 437–448.

McCarty, M.E., Clifton, R.K., & Collard, R.R. (1999). Problem solving in infancy: The emergence of an action plan. *Developmental Psychology, 35*, 1091–1101.

McGraw, M.B. (1935). *Growth: A study of Johnny and Jimmy.* New York: Appleton-Century.

McGraw, M.B. (1945). *The neuromuscular maturation of the human infant.* New York: Columbia University Press.

McKenzie, B.E. (1987). The development of spatial orientation in human infancy: What changes? Pp. 125–141 in B.E. McKenzie & R.H. Day (Eds.), *Perceptual development in early infancy: Problems and issues.* Hillsdale, NJ: Erlbaum.

McKenzie, B.E., & Bigelow, F. (1986). Detour behavior in young human infants. *British Journal of Developmental Psychology, 4*, 139–148.

McKenzie, B.E., Skouteris, H., Day, R.H., Hartman, B., & Yonas, A. (1993). Effective action by infants to contact objects by reaching and leaning. *Child Development, 64*, 415–429.

Mehler, J., Bertoncini, J., Barriere, M., & Jassik-Gerschenfeld, D. (1978). Infant perception of mother's voice. *Perception, 7*, 491–497.

Mehler, J., Jusczyk, P., Lambertz, G., Halsted, N., Bertoncini, J., & Amiel-Tison, C. (1988). A precursor of language acquisition in young infants. *Cognition, 29*, 143–178.

Melendez, P., Bales, D., & Pick, A.D. (1993). *Direct and indirect perception: Four-year-olds' grouping of toys.* Poster presented at the Society for Research in Child Development, New Orleans, LA.

Melendez, P., Bales, D., Ruffing, M., & Pick, A.D. (1995). *Preschoolers' categorization of objects and representations.* Poster presented at the Society for Research in Child Development, Indianapolis, IN.

Meltzoff, A. (1985). Immediate and deferred imitation in fourteen- and twenty-four-month-old infants. *Child Development, 56,* 62–72.

Meltzoff, A. (1988a). Imitation of televised models by infants. *Child Development, 59,* 1221–1229.

Meltzoff, A. (1988b). Infant imitation after a 1-week delay: Long-term memory for novel acts and multiple stimuli. *Developmental Psychology, 24,* 470–476.

Meltzoff, A. (1988c). Infant imitation and memory: Nine-month-olds in immediate and deferred tests. *Child Development, 59,* 217–225.

Meltzoff, A., & Moore, M. (1977). Imitation of facial and manual gestures by human neonates. *Science, 198,* 75–78.

Meltzoff, A., & Moore, M. (1983). Newborn infants imitate adult facial gestures. *Child Development, 54,* 702–709.

Meltzoff, A., & Moore, M. (1989). Imitation in newborn infants: Exploring the range of gestures imitated and the underlying mechanisms. *Developmental Psychology, 25,* 954–962.

Meltzoff, A., & Moore, M. (1992). Early imitation within a functional framework: The importance of person identity, movement, and development. *Infant Behavior and Development, 15,* 479–505.

Menzel, E. (1973). Chimpanzee spatial memory organization. *Science, 182,* 943–945.

Michotte, A. (1954). *La perception de la causalité.* Louvain: Publications Universitaires de Louvain.

Michotte, A. (1963). *The perception of causality.* New York: Basic Books.

Miller, G.A. (1956). The magical number seven, plus or minus two: Some limits on our capacity for processing information. *Psychological Review, 63,* 81–97.

Miller, N.E., & Dollard, J. (1941). *Social learning and imitation.* New Haven: Yale University Press.

Mix, K. , Huttenlocher, J., & Levine, S.C. (1996). Do preschool children recognize auditory-visual numerical correspondences? *Child Development, 67,* 1592–1608.

Mix, K.S., Levine, S.C., & Huttenlocher, J. (1997). Numerical abstraction in infants: Another look. *Developmental Psychology, 33,* 423–428.

Montgomery, K.C. (1952). A test of two explanations of spontaneous alternation. *Journal of Comparative and Physiological Psychology, 45,* 287–293.

Moon, C., Cooper, R., & Fifer, W. (1993). Two-day-olds prefer their native language. *Infant Behavior and Development, 16,* 495–500.

Moore, D., Spence, M., & Katz, G. (1997). Six-month-olds' categorization of natural infant-directed utterances. *Developmental Psychology, 33,* 980–989.

Morgan, R., & Rochat, P. (1995). The perception of self-produced leg movement in self- versus object-oriented contexts by 3.5-month-old infants. Pp. 243–246 in B.G. Bardy, R.J. Bootsma, & Y. Guiard (Eds.), *Studies in perception and action III.* Hillsdale, NJ: Erlbaum.

Morton, J., & Johnson, M. (1991). CONSPEC and CONLERN: A two-process theory of infant face recognition. *Psychological Review, 98,* 164–181.

Mosier, C., & Rogoff, B. (1994). Infants' instrumental use of their mothers to achieve their goals. *Child Development, 65,* 70–79.

Munn, N.L. (1946). Learning in children. Pp.370–449 in L. Carmichael (Ed.), *Manual of child psychology.* New York: Wiley.

Murray, L., & Trevarthen, C. (1985). Emotional regulation of interactions between two-month-olds and their mothers. Pp. 177–197 in T.M. Field & N. Fox (Eds.), *Social perception in infants.* Norwood, NJ: Ablex.

Nagell, K., Olquin, R.S., & Tomasello, M. (1993). Processes of social learning in the tool use of chimpanzees (Pan troglodytes) and human children (Homo sapiens). *Journal of Comparative Psychology, 107,* 174–186.

Nanez, J.E. (1988). Perception of impending collision in 3- to 6-week-old human infants. *Infant Behavior and Development, 11,* 447–463.

Nazzi, T., Bertoncini, J., & Mehler, J. (1998). Language discrimination by newborns: Toward an understanding of the role of rhythm. *Journal of Experimental Psychology: Human Perception and Performance, 24,* 756–766.

Needham, A. (1998). Infants' use of featural information in the segregation of stationary objects. *Infant Behavior and Development, 21,* 47–75.

Needham, A., & Baillargeon, R. (1997). Object segregation in infancy. Pp. 1–44 in C. Rovee-Collier & L.P. Lipsitt (Eds.), *Advances in infancy research,* Vol. 11. Greenwich, Conn.: Ablex.

Needham, A., & Baillargeon, R. (1998). Effects of prior experience on 4.5-month-old infants' object segregation. *Infant Behavior and Development, 21,* 1–24.

Neisser, U. (1988). Five kinds of self-knowledge. *Philosophical Psychology, 1,* 35–39.

Neisser, U. (1993). *The perceived self.* New York: Cambridge University Press.

Oakes, L.M. (1994). Development of infants' use of continuity cues in their perception of causality. *Developmental Psychology, 30,* 869–879.

Oakes, L.M., & Cohen, L.B. (1990). Infant perception of a causal event. *Cognitive Development, 5,* 193–207.

Oakes, L.M., & Cohen, L.B. (1995). Infant causal perception. Pp. 1–54 in C. Rovee-Collier & L.P. Lipsitt (Eds.), *Advances in infancy research,* Vol. 9. Norwood, NJ: Ablex.

Oyama, S. (1985). *The ontogeny of information.* Cambridge: Cambridge University Press.

Palmer, C. (1989). The discriminating nature of infants' exploratory actions. *Developmental Psychology, 25,* 885–893.

Papousek, H. (1967). Experimental studies of appetitional behavior in human newborns and infants. Pp. 249–277 in H.W. Stevenson, E.H. Hess, & H.L. Rheingold (Eds.), *Early behavior: Comparative and developmental approaches.* New York: Wiley.

Papousek, J., Papousek, H., & Symmes, D. (1991). The meaning of melodies in motherese in tone and stress languages. *Infant Behavior and Development, 14,* 415–440.

Pascalis, O., de Schonen, S., Morton, J., Dernelle, C., & Fabre-Grenet, M. (1995). Mother's face recognition by neonates: A replication and an extension. *Infant Behavior and Development, 18,* 79–85.

Perris, E.E., & Clifton, R.K. (1988). Reaching in the dark toward a sound as a measure of auditory localization in infants. *Infant Behavior and Development, 11,* 473–491.

Petterson, L., Yonas, A., & Fisch, R.O. (1980). The development of blinking in response to impending collision in pre-term, full-term, and post-term infants. *Infant Behavior and Development, 3,* 155–165.

Piaget, J. (1952). *The origins of intelligence in children.* New York: International Universities Press; Norton Library, 1963.

Piaget, J. (1954). *The construction of reality in the child.* New York: Basic Books.

Piaget, J., & Inhelder, B. (1956). *The child's conception of space.* London: Routledge & Kegan Paul.

Pick, A., Gross, D., Heinrichs, M., Love, M., & Palmer, C. (1994). Development of perception of the unity of musical events. *Cognitive Development, 9,* 355–375.

Pick, A.D. (1965). Improvement of visual and tactual form discrimination. *Journal of Experimental Psychology, 69,* 331–339.

Pick, A.D. (1997). Perceptual learning, categorizing, and cognitive development. Pp. 335–370 in C. Dent-Reed & P. Zukow-Goldring (Eds.), *Changing ecological approaches to organism-environment mutualities.* Washington, DC: American Psychological Association.

Pick, H.L. (1993). Organization of spatial knowledge in children. Pp. 31–42 in N. Eilan, R. McCarthy, & B. Brewer (Eds.), *Spatial representation.* Oxford: Blackwell.

Polka, L., & Werker, J. (1994). Developmental changes in perception of nonnative vowel contrasts. *Journal of Experimental Psychology: Human Perception and Performance, 20,* 421–435.

Porter, R., Cernoch, J., & McLaughlin, F. (1983). Maternal recognition of neonates through olfactory cues. *Physiology and Behavior, 16,* 151–154.

Postman, L. (1955). Association theory and perceptual learning. *Psychological Review, 62,* 438–446.

Postman, L., & Tolman, E.C. (1959). Brunswik's probabilistic functionalism. Pp. 502–564 in S. Koch (Ed.), *Psychology: A study of a science.* New York: McGraw-Hill.

Preyer, W. (1888, 1889). *The mind of the child: Part 1. The senses and the will; Part 2. The development of the intellect.* Trans. by H.W. Brown. New York: Appleton.

Profitt, D.R., & Kaiser, M.K. (1995). Perceiving events. Pp. 227–261 in W. Epstein and S. Rogers (Eds.), *Perception of space and motion.* New York: Academic.

Querleu, D., Renard, X., Boutteville, C., & Crepin, G. (1989). Hearing by the human fetus? *Seminars in Perinatology, 13,* 409–420.

Querleu, D., Renard, X., Versyp, F., Paris-Delrue, L. & Crepin, G. (1988). Fetal hearing. *European Journal of Obstetrics and Gynaecology and Reproductive Biology, 29,* 191–212.

Rader, N., Bausano, M., & Richards, J.E. (1980). On the nature of the visual-cliff-avoidance response in human infants. *Child Development, 51,* 61–68.

Rader, N.D. (1997). Change and variation in response to perceptual information. In C. Dent-Reed & P. Zukow-Goldring (Eds.), *Changing ecological approaches To organism-environment mutualities.* Washington, DC: American Psychological Association.

Razran, G.H.S. (1933). Conditioned responses in animals other than dogs. *Psychological Bulletin, 30,* 261–324.

Rheingold, H., & Adams, J. (1980). The significance of speech to newborns. *Developmental Psychology, 16,* 397–403.

Richards, J.E. (1997). Effects of attention in infants' preference for briefly exposed visual stimuli in the paired-comparison recognition memory paradigm. *Developmental Psychology, 33,* 22–31.

Rieser, J.J. (1979). Spatial orientation of six-month-old infants. *Child Development, 50,* 1078–1087.

Robin, D.J., Berthier, N.E., & Clifton, R.K. (1996). Infants' predictive reaching for moving objects in the dark. *Developmental Psychology, 32,* 824–835.

Rochat, P. (1983). Oral touch in young infants: Response to variations of nipple characteristics in the first month of life. *International Journal of Behavior Development, 6,* 123–133.

Rochat, P. (1987). Mouthing and grasping in neonates: Evidence for the early detection of what hard or soft substances afford for action. *Infant Behavior and Development, 10,* 435–449.

Rochat, P. (1989). Object manipulation and exploration in 2- to 5-month-old infants. *Developmental Psychology, 25,* 871–884.

Rochat, P. (1995). Perceived reachability for self and for others by 3- to 5-year old children. *Journal of Experimental Child Psychology, 59,* 317–333.

Rochat, P., Blass, E.M., & Hoffmeyer, L.B. (1988). Oropharyngeal control of hand-mouth coordination in newborn infants. *Developmental Psychology, 24,* 459–463.

Rochat, P., & Bullinger, A. (1994). Posture and functional action in infancy. Pp. 15–34 in A. Vyt, H. Bloch, & M. Bornstein (Eds.), *Early child development in the French tradition.* Hillsdale, NJ: Erlbaum.

Rochat, P., & Goubet, N. (1993). *Determinants of infants' perceived reachability.* Poster session presented at the 60th meeting of the Society for Research in Child Development, New Orleans, LA.

Rochat, P., & Goubet, N. (1995). Development of sitting and reaching in 5- to 6-month-old infants. *Infant Behavior and Development, 18,* 53–68.

Rochat, P., & Morgan, R. (1995). Spatial determinants in the perception of self-produced leg movements by 3- to-5-month-old infants. *Developmental Psychology, 31,* 626–636.

Rochat, P., & Morgan, R. (1998). Two functional orientations of self-exploration in infancy. *British Journal of Developmental Psychology, 16,* 139–154.

Rochat, P., & Senders, S.J. (1991). Active touch in infancy: Action systems in development. Pp. 412–442 in M.J.S. Weiss & P.R. Zelazzo (Eds.), *Newborn attention.* Norwood, NJ: Ablex.

Rose, S.A., Gottfried, A.W., & Bridger, W.H. (1981). Crossmodal transfer in 6-month-old infants. *Developmental Psychology, 17,* 661–669.

Ross, H., & Lollis, S. (1987). Communication within infant social games. *Developmental Psychology, 23,* 241–248.

Rovee, C.K., & Rovee, D.T. (1969). Conjugate reinforcement of infant exploratory behavior. *Journal of Experimental Child Psychology, 8,* 33–39.

Rovee-Collier, C.K. (1986). The rise and fall of infant classical conditioning research: Its promise for the study of infant development. Pp. 139–159 in L.P. Lipsitt & C.K. Rovee-Collier (Eds.), *Advances in infancy research,* Vol. 4. Norwood, NJ: Ablex.

Rovee-Collier, C.K., Greco-Vigorito, C., & Hayne, H. (1993). The time window hypothesis: Implications for categorization and memory modification. *Infant Behavior and Development, 16,* 149–176.

Rovee-Collier, C.K., & Sullivan, N.W. (1980). Organization of infant memory. *Journal of Experimental Psychology: Human Learning and Memory, 6,* 798–807.

Rovee-Collier, C.K., & Capatides, J.B. (1979). Positive behavioral contrast in 3-month-old infants on multiple conjugate reinforcement schedules. *Journal of the Experimental Analysis of Behavior, 32,* 15–27.

Rovee-Collier, C.K., & Fagan, J.W. (1976). Extended conditioning and 24-hour retention in infants. *Journal of Experimental Child Psychology, 21,* 1–11.

Rovee-Collier, C.K., & Gekoski, M. (1979). The economics of infancy: A review of conjugate reinforcement. Pp. 195–255 in H.W. Reese & L.P. Lipsitt (Eds.), *Advances in child development and behavior,* Vol. 13. New York: Academic.

Rovee-Collier, C.K., & Hayne, H. (1987). Reactivation of infant memory: Implications for cognitive development. In H.W. Reese (Ed.), *Advances in child development and behavior,* Vol. 20. New York: Academic.

Rovee-Collier, C.K., Morongiello, B.A., Aron, M., & Kuperschmidt, J. (1978). Topographical response differentiation and reversal in 3-month-old infants. *Infant Behavior and Development, 1,* 323–333.

Ruff, H.A., & Kohler, C.J. (1978). Tactual-visual transfer in six-month-old infants. *Infant Behavior and Development, 1,* 259–264.

Ruff, H.A., Saltarelli, L., Capozzoli, M., & Dubiner, K. (1992). The differentiation of activity in infants' exploration of objects. *Developmental Psychology, 28,* 851–861.

Sai, F., & Bushnell, I.W.R. (1988). The perception of faces in different poses by 1-month-olds. *British Journal of Developmental Psychology, 6,* 35–41.

Sameroff, A.J. (1971). Can conditioned responses be established in the newborn infant? *Developmental Psychology, 5,* 1–12.

Scaife, J., & Bruner, J. (1975). The capacity for joint visual attention in the infant. *Nature, 253,* 265–266.

Schiff, W. (1965). The perception of impending collision: A study of visually directed avoidant behavior. *Psychological Monographs, 79* (Whole No. 604).

Schmuckler, M.A. (1997). Development of visually guided locomotion: Barrier crossing by toddlers. *Ecological Psychology, 8,* 209–236.

Schmuckler, M.A., & Li, N.S. (1998). Looming responses to obstacles and apertures: The role of accretion and deletion of background texture. *Psychological Science, 9,* 49–52.

Schwartz, M., & Day, R.H. (1979). Visual shape perception in early infancy. *Monographs of the Society for Research in Child Development, 44* (7, Serial No. 182).

Shannon, C.E., & Weaver, W. (1949). *The mathematical theory of communication.* Urbana: University of Illinois Press.

Siddiqui, A. (1991). *Determinants of tool-use in infancy.* Paper presented at the biennial meeting of the International Society for the Study of Behavioural Development, Minneapolis, MN.

Simon, T.J., Hespos, S.J., & Rochat, P. (1995). Do infants understand simple arithmetic? A replication of Wynn (1992). *Cognitive Development, 10,* 253–269.

Siqueland, E.R., & DeLucia, C.A. (1969). Visual reinforcement of nonnutritive sucking in human infants. *Science, 165,* 1144–1146.

Slater, A. (1995). Visual perception and memory at birth. Pp. 107–162 in C.K. Rovee-Collier & L.P. Lispsett (Eds.), *Advances in infancy research,* Vol. 9. Norwood, NJ: Ablex.

Slater, A., Johnson, S.P., Brown, E., & Badenoch, M. (1996). Newborn infants' perception of partly occluded objects. *Infant Behavior and Development, 19,* 145–148.

Slater, A., Mattock, A., & Brown, E. (1990). Size constancy at birth: Newborn infants' responses to retinal and real size. *Journal of Experimental Child Psychology, 49,* 314–322.

Slater, A., Morrison, V., Somers, M., Mattock, A., Brown, E., & Taylor, D. (1990). Newborn and older infants' perception of partly occluded objects. *Infant Behavior and Development, 13,* 33–49.

Slater, A.M., & Morrison, V. (1985). Shape constancy and slant perception at birth. *Perception, 14,* 337–344.

Smitsman, A. (1997). The development of tool use: Changing boundaries between organism and environment. Pp. 301–329 in C. Dent-Reed & P. Zukow-Goldring (Eds.), *Evolving explanations of development*. Washington, DC: American Psychological Association.

Smitsman, A., Loosbroek, E. v., & Pick, A.D. (1987). The primacy of affordances in categorization by children. *British Journal of Developmental Psychology, 5*, 265–273.

Smotherman, W.P., & Robinson, S.R. (1996). The development of behavior before birth. *Developmental Psychology, 33*, 425–434.

Soken, N., & Pick, A. (1992). Intermodal perception of happy and angry expressive behaviors by seven-month-old infants. *Child Development, 63*, 787–795.

Soken, N., & Pick, A. (1999). Infants' perception of dynamic affective expressions: Do infants distinguish specific expressions? *Child Development, 70*, 1275–1282.

Sorce, J., Emde, R., Campos, J., & Klinnert, M. (1985). Maternal emotional-signaling: Its effect on the visual cliff behavior of 1-year-olds. *Developmental Psychology, 21*, 195–200.

Spelke, E. (1976). Infants' intermodal perception of events. *Cognitive Psychology, 8*, 553–560.

Spelke, E. (1979). Perceiving bimodally specified events in infancy. *Developmental Psychology, 15*, 626–636.

Spelke, E. (1981). The infant's acquisition of knowledge of bimodally specified events. *Journal of Experimental Child Psychology, 31*, 279–299.

Spelke, E. (1988). Where perceiving ends and thinking begins: The apprehension of objects in infancy. Pp. 197–234 in A. Yonas (Ed.), *Perceptual development in infancy: Minnesota Symposium on Child Psychology*, Vol. 20. Hillsdale, NJ: Erlbaum.

Spelke, E. (1991). Physical knowledge in infancy. Reflections on Piaget's theory. Pp. 133–169 in S. Carey & R. Gelman (Eds.), *The epigenesis of mind*. Hillsdale, NJ: Erlbaum.

Spelke, E., Born, W., & Chu, F. (1983). Perception of moving, sounding objects by four-month-old infants. *Perception, 12*, 719–732.

Spelke, E., & Owsley, C. (1979). Intermodal exploration and knowledge in infancy. *Infant Behavior and Development, 2*, 13–27.

Spelke, E.S. (1979). Perceiving bimodally specified events in infancy. *Developmental Psychology, 15*, 626–636.

Spelke, E.S. (1990). Principles of object perception. *Cognitive Science, 14*, 29–56.

Starkey, P., & Cooper, R. (1980). Perception of numbers by human infants. *Science, 210*, 1033–1034.

Starkey, P., Spelke, E.S., & Gelman, R. (1983). Detection of intermodal correspondences by human infants. *Science, 222*, 179–181.

Starkey, P., Spelke, E.S., & Gelman, R. (1990). Numerical abstraction by human infants. *Cognition, 36*, 97–128.

Steenbergen, B., van der Kamp, J., Smitsman, A.W., & Carson, R.G. (1997). Spoon handling in two- to four-year-old children. *Ecological Psychology, 9*, 113–129.

Stern, D., Spieker, S., Barnett, R., & MacKain, K. (1983). The prosody of maternal speech. Infant age and context-related changes. *Journal of Child Language, 10*, 1–15.

Strauss, M.S., & Curtis, L.E. (1981). Infant perception of numerosity. *Child Development, 52*, 1146–1152.

Streri, A. (1987). Tactile discrimination of shape and intermodal transfer in 2- to 3-month-old infants. *British Journal of Developmental Psychology, 5*, 213–220.

Streri, A., & Pécheux, M.G. (1986). Vision to touch and touch to vision transfer of form in 5-month-old infants. *British Journal of Developmental Psychology, 4*, 161–167.

Streri, A., & Spelke, E. (1988). Haptic perception of objects in infancy. *Cognitive Psychology, 20*, 1–28.

Streri, A., Spelke, E., & Ramix, E. (1993). Modality-specific and amodal aspects of object perception in infancy: The case of active touch. *Cognition, 47*, 251–279.

Stucki, M., Kaufmann-Hayoz, R., & Kaufmann, F. (1987). Infants' recognition of a face revealed through motion: Contribution of internal facial movement and head movement. *Journal of Experimental Child Psychology, 44*, 80–91.

Teller, D.Y. (1979). The forced-choice preferential looking procedure: A psychophysical technique for use with human infants. *Infant Behavior and Development, 2*, 135–153.

Teller, D.Y., & Bornstein, M.H. (1987). Infant color vision and color perception. Pp. 185–236 in P. Salapatek & L.B. Cohen (Eds.), *Handbook of infant perception: From sensation to perception.* New York: Academic.

Thelen, E. (1984). Learning to walk: Ecological demands and phylogenetic constraints. Pp. 213–250 in L.P. Lipsitt (Ed.), *Advances in infancy research*, Vol. 3. Norwood, NJ: Ablex.

Thelen, E. (1994). Three-month-old infants can learn task-specific patterns of interlimb coordination. *Psychological Science, 5*, 280–285.

Thelen, E., & Fisher, D.M. (1982). Newborn stepping: An explanation for a "disappearing" reflex. *Developmental Psychology, 18*, 760–775.

Thelen, E., & Fisher, D.M. (1983). The organization of spontaneous leg movements in newborn infants. *Journal of Motor Behavior, 15*, 353–377.

Thelen, E., & Smith, L. (1994). *A dynamic systems approach to the development of cognition and action.* Cambridge, MA: MIT Press.

Thoman, E.B., & Ingersoll, E.W. (1993). Learning in premature infants. *Developmental Psychology, 29*, 692–700.

Tighe, T.J., & Leaton, R.N., Eds. (1976). *Habituation: Perspectives from child development, animal behavior, and neurophysiology.* Hillsdale, NJ: Erlbaum.

Titchener, E.B. (1929). *Systematic psychology: Prolegomena.* New York: Macmillan.

Tolman, E.C. (1932). *Purposive behavior in animals and men.* New York: Century.

Tolman, E.C. (1948). Cognitive maps in rats and men. *Psychological Review, 55*, 189–208.

Tolman, E.C., Ritchie, B.F., & Kalish, D. (1946). Studies in spatial learning II: Place learning versus response learning. *Journal of Experimental Psychology, 36*, 221–229.

Tomasello, M. (1995). Joint attention as social cognition. Pp. 103–130 in C. Moore and P. Dunham (Eds.), *Joint attention: Its origins and development.* Hillsdale, NJ : Erlbaum.

Tomasello, M. (in press). The cultural ecology of young children's interactions with objects and artifacts. In E. Winograd, R. Fivush, & W. Hirst (Eds.), *Ecological approaches to cognition: Essays in honor of Uric Neisser.* Hillsdale, NJ: Erlbaum.

Tomasello, M., & Farrar, J. (1986). Joint attention and early language. *Child Development, 57*, 1454–1463.

Tyler, D., & McKenzie, B.E. (1990). Spatial updating and training effects in the first year of human infancy. *Journal of Experimental Child Psychology, 50*, 445–461.

Van der Meer, A., van der Weel, F., & Lee, D. (1994). Prospective control in catching by infants. *Perception, 23*, 287–302.

Van der Meer, A.L.H., van der Weel, F.R., & Lee, D.N. (1995). The functional significance of arm movements in neonates. *Science, 267*, 693–695.

Van der Meer, A.L. H., van der Weel, F.R., & Lee, D.N. (1996). Lifting weights in neonates: Developing visual control of reaching. *Scandinavian Journal of Psychology, 37,* 424–436.

Van Leeuwen, L. (1992). *The emergence of tool use in young children.* Thesis, Katholieke Universiteit, Nijmegen.

Van Leeuwen, L., Smitsman, A.W., & Van Leeuwen, C. (1994). Affordances, perceptual complexity, and the development of tool use. *Journal of Experimental Psychology: Human Perception and Performance, 20,* 174–191.

Van Loosbroek, E., & Smitsman, A.W. (1990). Visual perception of numerosity in infancy. *Developmental Psychology, 26,* 916–922.

Vernon, M.D. (1954). *A further study of visual perception.* Cambridge: Cambridge University Press.

Vintner, A. (1986). The role of movement in eliciting early imitations. *Child Development, 57,* 66–71.

Von Hofsten, C. (1980). Predictive reaching for moving objects by human infants. *Journal of Experimental Child Psychology, 30,* 369–382.

Von Hofsten, C. (1982). Eye-hand coordination in the newborn. *Developmental Psychology, 18,* 450–461.

Von Hofsten, C. (1983). Catching skills in infancy. *Journal of Experimental Psychology: Human Perception and Performance, 9,* 75–85.

Von Hofsten, C. (1984). Developmental changes in the organization of pre-reaching movements. *Developmental Psychology, 20,* 378–388.

Von Hofsten, C. (1991). Structuring of early reaching movements: A longitudinal study. *Journal of Motor Behavior, 23,* 280–292.

Von Hofsten, C. (1993). Prospective control: A basic aspect of action development. *Human Development, 36,* 253–270.

Von Hofsten, C., & Lindhagen, K. (1979). Observations on the development of reaching for moving objects. *Journal of Experimental Child Psychology, 28,* 158–173.

Von Hofsten, C., & Ronnqvist, L. (1988). Preparation for grasping an object: A developmental study. *Journal of Experimental Psychology: Human Perception and Performance, 14,* 610–621.

Von Hofsten, C., & Rosander, K. (1996). The development of gaze control and predictive tracking in young infants. *Vision Research, 36,* 81–96.

Von Hofsten, C., & Spelke, E. (1985). Object perception and object-directed reaching in infancy. *Journal of Experimental Psychology: General, 114,* 198–212.

Walk, R.D. (1966). The development of depth perception in animals and human infants. *Child Development Monographs, 31* (107).

Walk, R.D., & Gibson, E.J. (1961). A comparative and analytical study of visual depth perception. *Psychological Monographs, 75* (15, Whole No. 519).

Walk, R.D., Gibson, E.J., & Tighe, T.J. (1957). Behavior of light- and dark-reared rats on a visual cliff. *Science, 126,* 80–81.

Walker, A.S. (1982). Intermodal perception of expressive behaviors by human infants. *Journal of Experimental Child Psychology, 33,* 514–535.

Walker, A.S., & Gibson, E.J. (1986). What develops in bimodal perception? Pp. 171–181 in L.P. Lipsitt & C. Rovee-Collier (Eds.), *Advances in infancy research,* Vol. 4. Norwood, NJ: Ablex.

Walker, A.S., Owsley, C.J., Megaw-Nyce, J.S., Gibson, E.J., & Bahrick, L.E. (1980). Detection of elasticity as an invariant property of objects by young infants. *Perception, 9*, 713–718.

Walker-Andrews, A.S. (1986). Intermodal perception of expressive behaviors: Relation of eye and voice? *Developmental Psychology, 22*, 373–377.

Walker-Andrews, A.S. (1988). Infants' perception of affordances of expressive behaviors. Vol. 5, pp. 173–221 in C.K. Rovee-Collier (Ed.), *Advances in Infancy Research*. Norwood, NJ: Ablex.

Walker-Andrews, A.S. (1997). Infants' perception of expressive behaviors: Differentiation of multi-modal information. *Psychological Bulletin, 121*, 437–456.

Walker-Andrews, A.S., Bahrick, L., Raglioni, S., & Diaz, I. (1991). Infants' bimodal perception of gender. *Ecological Psychology, 3*, 55–75.

Walker-Andrews, A.S., & Grolnick, W. (1983). Discrimination of vocal expressions by young infants. *Infant Behavior and Development, 6*, 491–498.

Walker-Andrews, A.S., & Lennon, E.M. (1985). Auditory-visual perception of changing distance by human infants. *Child Development, 56*, 544–548.

Walker-Andrews, A.S., & Lennon, E. (1991). Infants' discrimination of vocal expressions: Contributions of auditory and visual information. *Infant Behavior and Development, 14*, 131–142.

Walton, G.E., Bower, N.J.A., & Bower, T.G.R. (1992). Recognition of familiar faces by newborns. *Infant Behavior and Development, 15*, 265–269.

Watson, J. (1972). Smiling, cooing, and the "game." *Merritt-Palmer Quarterly, 18*, 323–339.

Weinberg, M., & Tronick, E. (1994). Beyond the face: An empirical study of infant affective configurations of facial, vocal, gestural, and regulatory behaviors. *Child Development, 65*, 1503–1515.

Weinberg, M., & Tronick, E. (1996). Infant affective reactions to the resumption of maternal interaction after the still-face. *Child Development, 67*, 905–914.

Wenger, M.A. (1936). An investigation of conditioned responses in human infants. *University of Iowa Studies in Child Welfare, 12*, No. 1, 7–90.

Werker, J. (1989). Becoming a native listener. *American Scientist, 77*, 54–59.

Werker, J., Gilbert, J., Humphrey, K., & Tees, R. (1981). Developmental aspects of cross-language speech perception. *Child Development, 52*, 349–353.

Werker, J., & Tees, R. (1984). Cross-language speech perception: Evidence for perceptual reorganization during the first year of life. *Infant Behavior and Development, 7*, 49–63.

Werner, H. (1961). *Comparative psychology of mental development*. New York: Science Editions.

Wertheimer, M. (1961). Psychomotor coordination of auditory and visual space at birth. *Science, 134*, 1692.

Whyte, V.A., McDonald, P.V., Baillargeon, R., & Newell, K.M. (1994). Mouthing and grasping of objects by young infants. *Ecological Psychology, 6*, 205–218.

Wickens, D.D., & Wickens, C. (1940). A study of conditioning in the neonate. *Journal of Experimental Psychology, 25*, 94–102.

Willats, P. (1989). Development of problem-solving in infancy. Pp. 143–182 in A. Slater & G. Bremner (Eds.), *Infant development*. Hillsdale, NJ: Erlbaum.

Willats, P., & Rosie, K. (1988). *Planning by 12-month-old infants*. Paper presented at The British Psychological Society Developmental Section Conference, Harlech.

Wolff, P.A. (1963). Observations on the early development of smiling. Pp. 113–134 in B.M. Foss (Ed.), *Determinants of infant behavior II*. New York: Wiley.

Wynn, K. (1992). Addition and subtraction by human infants. *Nature, 358,* 749–750.

Wynn, K. (1995). Infants possess a system of numerical knowledge. *Current Directions in Psychological Science, 4,* 172–177.

Wynn, K. (1996). Infants' individuation and enumeration of actions. *Psychological Science, 7,* 164–169.

Yonas, A., Arterberry, M., & Granrud, C. (1987). Four-month-old infants' sensitivity to binocular and kinetic information for three-dimensional object shape. *Child Development, 58,* 910–917.

Yonas, A., & Hartman, B. (1993). Perceiving the affordance of contact in four- and five-month-old infants. *Child Development, 64,* 298–308.

Zaporozhets, A.V. (1960). On the reflectory origin of visual perception of objects. Symposium 30, *Proceedings of the 16th International Congress of Psychology, Bonn,* 326–330.

Author Index

Michotte, A., 147, 149
Mick, L.A., 151
Miller, G.A., 17
Miller, N.E., 8
Mills, J., 5
Mills, J. S., 5
Miranda, S.B., 33
Mix, K.S., 197
Moon, C., 53
Moore, C., 61–62, 64, 66
Moore, D., 74
Moore, M.K., 87, 118
Morgan, R., 156, 163–164
Morongiello, B.A., 40, 146, 171
Morrison, V., 85
Morton, J., 143
Mosier, C., 69, 162
Muir, D.W., 48
Mullin, J., 54
Munn, N.L., 5, 32
Murray, L., 63, 140
Myers, I., 64

Nagell, K., 180
Nanez, J.E., 118
Nazzi, T., 54
Needham, A., 78–79, 109
Neisser, U., 141, 160, 198
Nelson, D., 72–73
Netto, D., 60
Newell, K.M., 91–92
Noirot, E., 38

Oakes, L.M., 147–149
Odom, R.D., 141
Olquin, R.S., 180
Ordy, J.M., 33
Owsley, C., 37, 84, 87
Oyama, S., 23

Paden, L., 37
Palmer, C., 91, 93–94, 98, 150
Papousek, H., 32–33, 58
Papousek, J., 58
Papousek, M., 56
Paris-Delrue, L., 53
Pascalis, O., 143

Pavlov, I.P., 139
Pécheux, M.G., 89–90
Perris, E., 92
Petterson, L., 118
Piaget, J., 5, 6, 7, 8, 9, 12, 27, 39–40, 87,
    99, 101, 124–125, 127–128, 144, 145,
    170, 193
Pick, A., 60, 67, 91, 144, 151, 188, 189,
    200–201
Pick, H.L., Jr., 50, 174
Pisoni, D.B., 39, 179
Polka, L., 72
Porter, R., 54
Postman, L., 8, 9
Prescott, P., 53
Preyer, W., 32
Profitt, D.R., 147, 157, 191

Querleu, D., 53
Quinn, P.C., 187–188

Rader, N.D., 167
Raglioni, S., 60
Ramsay, D., 113
Rawling, P., 64
Razran, G.H.S., 5
Reddish, P.E., 166
Reilly, J.S., 128
Renard, X., 53
Reznick, J.S., 121
Rheingold, H., 55, 67
Riccio, G., 110, 111
Richards, J.E., 153
Rieser, J.J., 130
Robin, D.J., 165
Robinson, S.R., 135
Rochat, P., 30, 46, 83, 91, 92, 95, 96, 97–
    98, 156, 163–164, 195
Rogoff, B., 69, 162
Rönnqvist, L., 96–97, 165
Rosander, K., 165
Rose, S.A., 90
Rosenberg, D., 110, 111
Rosie, K., 145
Ross, H., 69
Rovee, C.K., 137, 146
Rovee, D.T., 137, 146

Subject Index

Lightning Source UK Ltd.
Milton Keynes UK
UKOW04f1127180314

228333UK00004B/64/P